Methods of Teaching Botany

Methods of Teaching Botany

Vinayak Malhotra

CRESCENT
PUBLISHING CORPORATION

Methods of Teaching Botany

Edition 2026

ISBN 81-8342-028-1

Published by
CRESCENT PUBLISHING CORPORATION
4806/24, Mathur Lane,
Ansari Road, Darya Ganj,
New Delhi - 110 002
Ph.: 011 - 23244131
Mob.: + 91 - 9711991838, 9999021668
E-mail: crescentbook@gmail.com
Website: www.crescentpublishingcorp.weebly.com

Printed at:
Balaji Digital
Delhi

Preface

Botany is the scientific study of plants. Plants, to most people, means a wide range of living organisms from the smallest bacteria to the largest living things — the giant sequoia trees. By this definition plants include: algae, fungi, lichens, mosses, ferns, conifers and flowering plants. Today scientists believe bacteria, algae and fungi are in their own distinct kingdoms, but most general botany courses, and most botany departments at colleges and universities, still teach about these groups.

Nowadays, the plant science field is developing rapidly, and new offshoot disciplines and research fields come forth continually. The web has become a foundation that students use to learn the professional courses further and thus will be useful in training botany-based professionals of the highest calibre. While, the teaching literature contains hundreds of errors or misconceptions about plants, but this problem has not received enough attention to prevent its negative impacts. Teachers often cannot detect even glaring errors because new teachers coming out of our universities and colleges are very poorly trained in basic botany. Once learned, misinformation may be difficult to correct.

A major goal of botany teaching is enhancing students' learning. Teachers often pay attention to more knowledge than skills, and students gain very detailed knowledge.

However, with rapid developments in biology, knowledge is exploding so that teachers cannot give students all the knowledge they need in university. Students need to achieve self-directed and lifelong learning skills, and integration of relevant knowledge, they are active learners.

This book is designed as an introductory text in teaching botany. It provides highly useful information on diverse core issues of botany with special emphasis on teaching aspect of the subject. The teaching strategies and approaches described will guide to teachers to prepare for better performance in the classroom. Besides teachers and student-teachers, researchers, educationists, policy planners and students will be find this work of utmost use.

Vinayak Malhotra

Contents

1

Introduction to Botany

Botany is the scientific study of plants. "Plants," to most people, means a wide range of living organisms from the smallest bacteria to the largest living things - the giant sequoia trees. By this definition plants include: algae, fungi, lichens, mosses, ferns, conifers and flowering plants. Today scientists believe bacteria, algae and fungi are in their own distinct kingdoms, but most general botany courses, and most Botany Departments at colleges and universities, still teach about these groups.

Because the field is so broad, there are many kinds of plant biologists and many different opportunities available. Botanists interested in ecology study interactions of plants with other organisms and the environment. Other field botanists search to find new species or do experiments to discover how plants grow under different conditions. Some botanists study the structure of plants. They may work in the field, concentrating on the pattern of the whole plant. Others use microscopes to study the most detailed fine structure of individual cells.

Many botanists do experiments to determine how plants convert simple chemical compounds into more complex chemicals. They may even study how genetic information in DNA controls plant development. Botanists study processes that occur on a time scale ranging from fractions of a second in individual cells to those that unfold over eons of evolutionary time.

The results of botanical research increase and improve our supply of medicines, foods, fibers, building materials, and other plant products. Conservationists use botanical knowledge to help manage parks, forests, range lands, and wilderness areas. Public health and environmental protection professionals depend on their understanding of plant science to help solve pollution problems.

Plants have intrigued people for thousands of years. They provide aesthetic beauty as well as materials for our basic needs. Today our world presents new and complex problems that were never dreamed of a century ago. For instance, increasing human population is linked to environmental problems of gigantic proportion. Coupled to the need for more food is increasingly greater environmental impact.

Air and water pollution increase while biological diversity is reduced. Recent progress in technology and molecular biology provide powerful new tools that can help us solve these and other challenging problems. Some of the tools you might learn to use include: electron microscopes, radioisotopes, digital imaging analysis, polymerase chain reaction, cell and tissue culture, satellite imaging and telemetry.

One of the best things about plant science is the number of different specialties and career opportunities from which you can choose. This diversity allows people with different backgrounds, aptitudes, and interests to find satisfying careers in plant biology. More than many other scientific fields, botany continues to provide opportunities for women as well as men. There are few things more fulfilling than to work in a job that is both fun to do and a benefit to others.

Among the careers available to a person who enjoys the outdoors are positions as an ecologist, taxonomist, conservationist, forester, or plant explorer. Your work may take you to foreign and exotic lands. It may allow you to live and work in the great outdoors. A person with a mathematical background might find biophysics, developmental botany, genetics, modeling, or systems ecology to be exciting fields. Someone with an interest in chemistry might become a plant physiologist, plant biochemist, molecular biologist, or chemotaxonomist. Many people do not realize that most of the basic biological processes are the same in both plants and animals. Plants, however, are easier to grow and manipulate.

Plant structure may appeal to a person who enjoys microscopy and the beauty of intricate form and design. Persons fascinated with microscopic organisms often choose microbiology, phycology or mycology. On a larger scale, ornamental horticulture and landscape design requires artistic use of plant form and color. A person concerned about the world food supply might study plant pathology (diseases) or plant breeding. At larger universities there are frequently separate departments specializing in different applied subdisciplines of botany. Some examples are: Agronomy (field crops), Horticulture (ornamentals, fruits and vegetables), Microbiology (microbes such as bacteria and fungi) and Plant Pathology (diseases of plants). Plant biologists who enjoy working with people have a wide range of opportunities in teaching and public service.

Botany and Society

The explosive growth of human population is changing the earth dramatically. Only by understanding how human activities affect our environment can we predict global climatic changes. Scientific studies of these changes and their effect on natural ecosystems and crop production are crucial to the future of our society.

Other environmental issues, such as pollution, also interest botanists. Many plant species are especially sensitive to certain pollutants. Botanists study the effects of different types of pollution on plants. They use their results to advise lawmakers on legislation for environmental protection and on ways to save priceless natural areas.

By using plant tissue culture, botanists can grow entire plants from single cells. This has exciting potential in biotechnology, horticulture, forestry, and plant pathology. For example, the stately American chestnut was once a widespread tree in our Eastern forests. Today it has virtually disappeared because of a disease-producing fungus that causes chestnut blight. The American chestnut recently has been grown in plant tissue culture. If we can develop a blight-resistant strain of American chestnut, we will be able to propagate disease-resistant trees very quickly. These trees could then be planted in our forests and the American chestnut would once again be one of our most important hardwood species.

Plants are chemical factories. Many of the chemicals that they produce are useful to humans. Besides food, plants provide raw materials for paper, building materials, solvents and adhesives, fabrics, medicines, and many other products. Botanists study the chemicals produced by different plants to find new uses for them. For example, we use some plant chemicals to treat certain types of cancer.

The earth's biological diversity, or the kinds of organisms that populate the earth, is decreasing. As humans change the environment for their own purposes, plants and animals living in these areas become increasingly endangered. Plant taxonomists and plant ecologists work to identify and understand new plant species, especially in such biologically rich areas as tropical rain forests. Plants of the rain forests are important in their own right, but they could be major new resources for people as well. Perhaps a plant as yet undiscovered will become an important food crop. There are probably many undiscovered plants that produce useful drugs to cure or treat human diseases. Biological diversity also provides an important source of new genes to improve the plants we now use. As techniques of genetic engineering improve, so will our ability to improve our domestic plants.

Current Issues

One of the most exciting fields in botany today is biotechnology. Because of very recent advances in genetics, plant scientists have tools to splice genes from one plant into another. The potential usefulness of this is staggering. For example, several amino acids required in the human diet are not produced very well by plants - It may be possible to make major food crops more nutritious by adding genes to produce these deficient amino acids. More research is required, however, before this type of gene transfer becomes useful and practical.

Another challenging area of basic biological research involves cell membranes. All forms of life have cells and all cells have membranes. Plant scientists are trying to understand the important cell activities that involve membranes. For example, living things need energy to survive, but they need cell membranes to use this energy. Membranes also help move materials into and Out of cells. Plant biologists want to understand how membranes work since living things could not exist without cell membranes.

We are learning more and more about plant genes and what they do. Now botanists are turning their attention to how genes work, or express" themselves. Plants are complex living organisms. How a plant develops from a single cell into a complex organism with billions of cells is a problem that will occupy many botanists for years to come. The ease with which we can manipulate plant cells, compared to animal cells, makes plants an ideal model system for such studies.

Teaching botany is a challenging and rewarding career. A teaching botanist must understand a variety of subdisciplines of the field and be able to explain them to students. This provides an opportunity to inspire new generations with an understanding of, and appreciation for, plants.

Many other careers for botanists do not involve teaching or research. Some botanists work in marketing or administration of plant-related industries such as pharmaceutical companies, seed companies, biotechnology firms, scientific publishers and biological supply houses. Other plant biologists work in museums, herbaria, and botanical gardens. Some, with additional training, become scientific writers, computer programmers, botanical illustrators, or even lawyers or physicians. Service in public affairs, at the community and national levels, is an increasingly important role for plant biologists.

Specialization areas in Botany

Anatomy- microscopic plant structure (cells and tissues).

Biochemistry- chemical aspects of plant life processes. Includes the chemical products of plants (Phytochmeistry).

Biophysics- application of physics to plant life processes.

Cytology- structure, function, and life history of plant cells.

Ecology- relationships between plants and the world in which they live, both individually and in communities.

Genetics- plant heredity and variation. Plant geneticists study genes and gene function in plants.

Molecular Biology- structure and function of biological macromolecules, including biochemical and molecular aspects of genetics.

Morphology- macroscopic plant form. Morphologists also study the evolution and development of leaves, roots and stems.

Paleobotony- biology and evolution of fossil plants.

Physiology- functions and vital processes of plants. Photosynthesis and mineral nutrition are two examples of subjects studied by plant physiologists.

Systematics- evolutionary history and relationships among plants.

Systems Ecology, uses mathematical models to demonstrate concepts like nutrient cycling.

Taxonomy is the subdiscipline of identifying, naming, and classifying plants.

Applied Plant Sciences

Agronomy - crop and soil sciences. Agronomists make practical use of plant and soil sciences to increase the yield of field crops.

Biotechnology - using biological organisms to produce useful products. Most people today have a narrower view of biotechnology as the genetic modification of living organisms to produce useful products. Plant biotechnology involves inserting desirable genes into plants and having those genes expressed.

Breeding-development of better types of plants. Breeding involves selecting and crossing plants with desirable traits such as disease resistance.

Economic Botony- plants with commercial importance. Economic botany includes the study of botany harmful and beneficial plants and plant products.

Food science and Technology- development of food from vanous plant products.

Forestry- forest management for the production of timber, and conservation.

Horticulture- the production of ornamental plants and fruit and vegetable crops. Landscape design is also an important subdiscipline in horticulture.

Natural Resource Management- the responsible use and protection of our natural resources for the benefit of society.

Plant Pathology-diseases of plants. Plant pathologists are concerned with both the biological aspects of disease and with disease management, or control.

Organismal Specialities

Bryology- the study of mosses and similar plants. Bryologists study all aspects of these plants, including their identification, classification, and ecology.

Lichenology- the biology of lichens, dual organisms composed of both a fungus and an alga.

Mycology- the biology,of fungi. Fungi have a tremendous impact on our world. They are crucial in the biosphere because they help recycle dead organic material. Some fungi are important producers of biological products such as vitamins and antibiotics.

Microbiology- the study of microorganisms. Microbiologists may be specialized by organism (for example, microbiologists that study bacteria) of by a branch of biology (for example, Microbial Ecology).

Pteridology - the study of ferns and similar plants. Pteridologists study all aspects of fem biology.

Phycology- the study of algae, which are the base of the food chain in the aquatic environments of the world. Phycologists that study algae in oceans are sometimes called *Marine Botanists.*

The major employers of plant biologists are educational institutions, federal and state agencies, and industries. Job opportunities usually depend upon educational training and Leading students to discover more about plants and the botanical sciences can be a rewarding and fulfilling experience.

New positions in botany are expected to increase at an above-average rate through the turn of the century. Growing world population continues to increase the need for better food supplies. Environmental concerns, such as air, water and soil pollution, will create openings for ecologists in government and industry. The search for new drugs and medicines and useful genes for improving crop plants will continue to create a need for botanical explorers.

Educational institutions, which employ most plant biologists, range from high schools and community colleges to universities. High schools and community colleges have few openings for those who wish to teach specialized courses and there is little time or equipment for research activity. Nevertheless, for botanists who primarily enjoy teaching, such positions are very satisfying.

Most positions for professional plant scientists are in colleges and universities. Almost all colleges and universities offer courses in plant science and there are faculty positions for botanists who have different specialties. In addition, educational institutions employ botanists as researchers and as administrators.

Federal and state agencies need botanists in many different fields. Plant biologists work in various branches of the U.S. Department of Agriculture, including the Medical Plant Resources Laboratory, the Germplasm Resources Laboratory, the Animal and Plant Health Inspection Service, the National Arboretum, and the U.S. Forest Service. The U.S. Department of the Interior, which includes the National Park Service, the Bureau of Land Management and the U.S. Geological Survey, also employs botanists. Plant scientists also work in several other federal agencies, including the Public Health Service, State Department, National Aeronautics and Space Administration, Smithsonian Institution, and Environmental Protection Agency. In addition, each of the 50 state governments employs plant scientists in agencies similar to those of the federal government. Environmental organizations, like the Nature Conservancy, also hire botanists.

Industry is the third major employer of plant biologists. Drug companies, the oil industry, the chemical industry, lumber and paper companies, seed and nursery companies, fruit growers, food companies, fermentation industries (including breweries), biological supply houses and biotechnology firms all hire men and women trained in botany. Recently the first genetically altered food crop, the FlavrSavr(tm) tomato, reached store shelves. This opens a new career field for botanists.

Botany offers many interesting and worthwhile career opportunities. The work is frequently varied and the surroundings pleasant. Because of the great diversity in the plant sciences, people with many different backgrounds, abilities, and interests can find a satisfying career in botany.

Salaries and Availability of Jobs

Today the range of job opportunities and potential earnings for plant biologists is wider than ever before. The American Institute for Biological Science 2003 salary survey "Compensation of Life Scientists in the United States of America"; indicates the 2003 median income (salary plus cash compensation, such as bonus, profit sharing, or both) for people with less than one year of experience was estimated at $33,000 and for those with 30 years or more $108,000. The median for all positions without supervisory responsibilities was $48,000 and for those supervising 10 or more professional and sub professional employees, the median income was $126,500.

A few of the position/salary examples are: Intermediate research technicians $33,000, Postdoctoral researchers (12 month appointment) $36,366, Secondary school teachers $44,200, Assistant professors (9 to 10 month appointment) $49,713, Intermediate researchers $50,250, Laboratory managers $53,000, Professors (9 to 10 month appointment) $85,000, Research unit supervisors $85,000, Laboratory directors $90,000, Government section heads $98,000, Research section heads $108,387, Professors (12 month appointment) $118,000, "Distinguished" researchers$126,000, College department heads $129,000, Research managers $139,000, Research vice presidents/ directors $142,000.

The sense of accomplishment and satisfaction that comes from doing interesting and worthwhile work is one of the rewards of a career in plant science. In addition, many positions in botany provide other benefits such as individual freedom, varied work, pleasant surroundings, stimulating associates, and the opportunity to travel. Besides depending on experience and education, the geographical location of the employer also makes a difference. In general, salaries vary with the cost of living in a particular region.

Job availability is generally good. Employment opportunities vary over time depending partly on the status of state and national economies. Some fields are more competitive than others. Challenging positions are usually available for well-trained plant scientists.

Requirements for a Career in Botany

Four years of college and a Bachelor's degree are the minimum requirements for most careers in botany. With these, positions are available as laboratory technicians or technical assistants in education, industry, government, museums, parks and botanical gardens. As in other fields, a wider range of positions is available with more education and experience. Many positions require a Master's or Doctor's degree. A Ph.D. is required for most teaching and research positions in colleges and universities.

High School Preparation

To prepare for a career in botany, you should take a college preparatory curriculum including: English, foreign language, mathematics, chemistry, physics, and biology. Courses in social studies and humanities are also valuable since botanists often get involved in public affairs at community and national levels.

Other valuable experiences include participation in science fairs and science clubs. It also helps to have summer jobs or internships related to biology, such as working in parks, plant nurseries, farms, experiment stations, laboratories, camps, or for florists or landscape architects. Hobbies such as camping, photography, and computers are also useful.

Get information on colleges and universities by writing to the Office of Admissions of each school you wish to consider and requesting a catalog describing school requirements, courses, and facilities. Your counselor or library may have some of these. Also ask for information about scholarships and other financial aid. Many schools do not have a separate department of botany or plant biology but instead have a department of biology that includes botanists. In any case, write, call, or better yet, visit the schools you are interested in and ask to meet with some of their botanists to discuss your career options and how they might help you to realize your goals. The Botanical Society of America office has a list of botanists' names, addresses and phone numbers from all areas of the country. Its address and telephone number are listed inside the back cover of this booklet.

College Program of Study

The courses you select will vary depending on the curriculum of the college you attend and your own interests. To be best prepared for the job market, you should get a broad general education in language, arts, humanities and the social sciences in addition to specializing in plant biology. Most curricula require math, through calculus, and/or statistics as well as chemistry and physics. You should know how to use a computer. Some schools recommend, or require, a foreign language. This is especially important if you hope to work in the tropics.

Many colleges and universities require a core program in biology before you may enroll in specialized botany courses. At other institutions you can take botany courses right away. A faculty advisor will help you decide what courses to take. Whether your advisor is a botanist or not, visit with other botany professors in the department and ask for their suggestions.

If possible, you should arrange to do an undergraduate research project under one of your professors. The project might include helping the professor with his/her research or pursuing your own independent interests. This experience will help you decide which area or areas of botany you like best. It will also give you valuable insight into how science works. Research experience will also be very helpful should you decide to pursue graduate work.

Summer jobs or internships can provide important additional experience. These positions occur in government agencies, college and university research laboratories, agricultural experiment stations, freshwater and marine biological stations, and private companies. Start investigating summer opportunities early - the previous fall or winter. The best positions are usually filled by late spring.

The best piece of advice, regardless of your interests or which school you attend, is get to know the faculty. If you have questions about a course, ask your teacher after class or during office hours. If you are interested in laboratory or field work, let the faculty know and offer your services. Faculty are "turned on" to students who show interest - and you will be "turned on" to Botany!

Science of Botany

Science as we know it is the product of developments in the 17th and 18th centuries. What was conceived as science is indicated by the names Galileo, Kepler, Newton, Descartes, and Leibniz. It was the glorious rise of the physical sciences advancing from triumph to triumph. It was physics what people meant when they talked about science, biology was never included. The science of biology was a creation of the 19th century. Of course, there were branches of medicine such as anatomy, physiology, and embryology that we now include in biology but they were concerned with healing and were not considered to be the part of a separate science of biology. At the same time there was also a flourishing pursuit of natural history under the label of Natural Theology. A genuine biology remained dormant until the 19th century.

It took more than two hundred years and the occurrence of three different sets of events before a genuine science of biology originated. One can assign these events to three different sets: (A) the refutation of certain erroneous principles, (B) the demonstration that certain basic principles of physics cannot be applied to biology, and (C) the realization of the uniqueness of certain basic principles of biology that are not found in the inanimate world.

Biology could not be recognized as a science of the same rank as physics as long as most biologists accepted certain basic explanatory principles not supported by the laws of the physical sciences and eventually found to be invalid. The two major principles here involved are vitalism and a belief in cosmic teleology. As soon as it had been demonstrated that these two principles are invalid and, more broadly, that none of the phenomena of the living world are in conflict with the natural laws of the physicalists, there was no longer any reason for not recognizing biology as a legitimate autonomous science, equivalent to physics.

Vitalism

The nature of life, the property of being living, has always been a puzzle for the philosophers. Descartes tried to solve it by simply ignoring it. An organism is really nothing but a machine, he said. And other philosophers, particularly such with a background in mathematics, logic, physics, and chemistry, tended to follow him and operated as if there was no difference between living and inanimate matter. But this did not satisfy most naturalists. They were convinced that in a living organism certain forces are active which do not exist in inanimate nature. They concluded that just as the motion of planets, suns, and stars, is controlled by an occult, invisible force called by Newton gravitation, analogously the movements and other manifestations of life in organisms is controlled by an invisible force, Lebenskraft or *vis vitalis*. Those who believed in such a force were called vitalists.

Vitalism was popular from the early 17th century to the early 20th century. It was a natural reaction to the crass mechanism of Descartes. Henri Bergson and Hans Driesch were prominent vitalists in the early 20th century. The end of vitalism came when it could no longer find any supporters. Two causes were largely responsible for this, first the failure of literally thousands of failed experiments conducted to prove the existence of a Lebenskraft, and secondly, the realization that the new biology, with the methods of genetics and molecular biology, was able to solve all the problems for which one traditionally had invoked the Lebenskraft. In other words the proposal of a Lebenskraft had simply become unnecessary.

It would be ahistorical to ridicule vitalists. When one reads the writings of one of the leading vitalists like Driesch one is forced to agree with him that many of the basic problems of biology simply cannot be solved by a philosophy as that of Descartes, in which the organism is simply considered a machine. The developmental biologists in particular asked some very challenging questions. For exarnple, how can a machine regenerate lost parts, as many kinds of organisms are able to do? How can a machine replicate itself ? How can two machines fuse into a single one like the fusion of two gametes when producing a zygote ?

The logic of the critique of the vitalists was impeccable. But all their efforts to find a scientific answer to all the so-called vitalistic phenomena were failures. Generations of vitalists labored in vain to find a scientific explanation for the Lebenskraft until it finally became quite clear that such a force simply does not exist.

Teleology

Teleology is the second invalid principle which had to be eliminated from biology before it qualified as a science equivalent to physics. Teleology deals with the explanation of natural processes which automatically seem to lead to a definite end or goal. To explain the development of the fertilized egg to the adult of a given species Aristotle invoked a fourth cause, the *causa finalis*. Eventually one invoked this cause for all phenomena in the cosmos which led to an end or goal. Kant in his *Critique of Judgment* had tried to explain the biological world in terms of Newtonian natural laws but had been completely unsuccessful in this endeavor. Frustrated he ascribed all Zweckmässigkeit as being due to teleology. This was, of course, no solution.

A widely-supported school of evolutionists, for instance the so-called orthogenesists, invoked teleology to explain all progressive evolutionary phenomena. They believed that in living nature there is an intrinsic strive toward perfection. Here belongs also Lamarck's theory of evolution and orthogenesis had many followers prior to the evolutionary synthesis. Alas, no evidence for the existence of such a teleological principle could ever be found and the discoveries of genetics and paleontology eventually totally discredited cosmic teleology.

There are numerous seemingly goal-directed processes in nature, particularly in biology, which one now no longer explains by occult teleological forces but by scientifically supported chemical-physical factors. There are four groups of such factors which formerly had been referred to as teleological. The fifth group of factors, attributed to an intrinsic potential of the cosrnos to cause goal direction, could never be substantiated. Such cosmic teleology is now considered not to exist.

Emergence of Modern Biology

Biology actually consists of two rather different fields, functional biology and historical biology. Functional biology deals with the physiology of all activities of living organisms, particularly with all cellular processes, including those of the genome. These functional processes can be explained by chemistry and physics. The other branch of biology is *historical biology*. A knowledge of history is not needed for the explanation of a purely functional process. It is however all-important for the explanation of all aspects of the living world that involve the dimension of historical time, in other words, as we now know, all aspects dealing with evolution.

The two fields of biology also differ in the nature of the most frequently asked questions. To be sure in both fields one asks what? questions, in order to get the facts needed for further analysis. The most frequently asked question in functional biology, however, is how?, while in evolutionary biology it is why? This difference is not complete because in evolutionary biology one also asks occasionally how? questions, for instance how do species multiply ? However, as we will see, evolutionary biology has developed its own methodology, that of *historical narratives*, to obtain its answers, particularly in cases where experiments are inappropriate.

In order to truly appreciate the autonomy of biology one must know the remarkable difference between these two branches of biology. Indeed some of the most decisive differences between the physical sciences and biology are true for only one of these branches, for evolutionary biology.

The two hundred year period, from ca. 1730 to 1930, witnessed a radical change in the conceptual framework of biology. It included the period from 1828 to 1866 during which both branches of modern biology, functional and evolutionary biology, were established, which resulted in the eventual refutation of vitalism and cosmic teleology. Yet biology was still largely ignored by the philosophers of science from Carnap, Hempel, Nagel, Popper, to Kuhn.

The biologists, even though they now rejected vitalism and cosmic teleology, were unhappy with a purely mechanistic philosophy of biology. But all endeavors to escape from this dilemma, such as for example the writings of Jonas, Portmann, Uexküll, and several others, invariably invoked some non-mechanical forces. It was not until almost the middle of the 20th century until it became evident that a solution could not be found by a philosopher who did not have a background in biology. At the same time it became equally clear that, however the solution would be, it had to be completely compatible with the natural laws. No solution was acceptable that would invoke any occult forces. But how could such a solution be found ?

It turned out that in order to develop an autonomous science of biology one had to do two further things. First, undertake a critical analysis of the conceptual framework of the physical sciences. This revealed that some of the basic principles of the physical sciences are simply not applicable to biology. They had to be eliminated and replaced by principles pertinent to biology. And secondly, it was necessary to investigate whether biology is based among others on certain additional principles that are inapplicable to inanimate matter. This required a restructuring of the conceptual world of science that was far more fundamental than anyone had imagined at that time. It became apparent that the publication in 1859 of Darwin's Origin of Species was really the beginning of an intellectual revolution that ultimately resulted in the establishment of the autonomy of biology.

Physicalist ideas in biology

Darwin's ideas were particularly important in the discovery that a number of basic concepts of the physical sciences, which up to the middle of the 19th century were also widely held by most biologists, are not applicable to biology. There are basic physicalist concepts for which it had to be demonstrated that they are not applicable to biology, before it was realized how different biology is from the physical sciences.

Essentialism

From the Pythagoreans and Plato on the traditional concept of the diversity of the world was that it consisted of a limited number of sharply delimited and unchanging *eide* or essences. This viewpoint was called typology or essentialism. The seemingly endless variety of phenomena, it was said, actually consisted of a limited number of natural kinds (essences or types) each forming a class. The members of each class were thought to be identical, constant, and sharply separated from the members of any other essence. Therefore, variation was nonessential and accidental. The essentialists illustrated this concept by the example of the triangle. All triangles have the same fundamental characteristics and are sharply delimited against quadrangles or any other geometric figure. An intermediate between a triangle and a quadrangle is inconceivable.

Typological thinking, therefore, is unable to accommodate variation and nas given rise to a misleading conception of human races. Caucasians, Africans, Asians, or Inuits are types for a typologist that conspicuously differ from other human ethnic groups and are sharply separated from them. This mode of thinking leads to racism. Darwin completely rejected typological thinking and used instead an entirely different concept, now called population thinking.

Determinism

One of the consequences of the acceptance of deterministic Newtonian laws was that it left no room for variation or chance events. The famous French mathematician and physicist Laplade boasted that a complete knowledge of the current world and all its processes would enable him to predict the future to infinity. Even the physicists soon discovered the occurrence of enough randomness and contingencies to refute the validity of Laplace's boast. The refutation of strict determinism and of the possibility of absolute prediction freed the way for the study of variation and of chance phenomena, so important in biology.

Reductionism

Most physicalists were reductionists. They claimed that the problem of the explanation of a system was resolved in principle as soon as the system had been reduced to its smallest components. As soon as one had completed the inventory of these components and had determined thc function of each one of them, they claimed it would be an easy task to explain also everything observed at the higher levels of organization. This claim was vigorously objected to by biologists already more than one hundred years ago. Indeed analysis is a most important and heuristic method in all branches of science, including biology. But first of all, in many cases of analysis, one does not have to go anywhere near the smallest parts (electrons, protons, etc...).

Furthermore, and this is what the reductionists usually overlooked, in order to understand a system one needs to know not only the properties of its components but also the nature of the interactions among these components.

Laws

All theories in the physical sciences are based on natural laws. Normally they have no exceptions which led Popper to the claim that any exception to a theory amounted to its falsification. Indeed, on the whole, properly articulated laws are the basis of the theory structure of the physical sciences. But is this also true for biology ? This has been seriously questioned by a number of philosophers and only few biological theories are based on laws. They are usually rather based on concepts, as we shall presently see.

The inapplicability of these four principles that are so basic in the physical sciences, has contributed a great deal to the insight that biology is not the same as physics. To get rid of these erroneous ideas was the first but perhaps hardest step in developing a sound philosophy of biology.

Autonomous characteristics of biology

The last step in the development of the autonomy of biology was the discovery of a number of biology-specific concepts or principles. One is the concept of *evolution*. To be sure even before Darwin geologists knew about changes on the Earth's surface and cosmologists were aware of the probability of changes in the universe, particularly in the solar system. However, the world was seen as something quite constant, something that had not changed since the day of Creation. This view totally changed after the middle of the 19th century when science became aware of the comprehensiveness of the evolution ofthe living world.

The adoption of the concept of the *biopopulation* is responsible for what now seems probably the most fundamental difference between the inanimate and the living world. The inanimate world consists of Platonian classes, essences, types, with the members of each class being identical, and with the seeming variation being "accidental" and therefore irrelevant. In a biopopulation, by contrast, every individual is unique, while the statistical mean value of a population is an abstraction. No two of the six billion humans are the same. Populations as a whole do not differ by their essences but only by mean statistical values.

The properties of populations change from generation to generation in a gradual manner. To think of the living world as a set of forever variable populations grading into each other from generation to generation, results in a concept of the world that is totally different from that of a typologist. The Newtonian framework of unalterable laws predisposes a physicist to be a typologist, seemingly almost as if by necessity. Darwin introduced population thinking into biology rather casually, and it took a long time before it was being realized that this is an entirely different concept from the typological thinking traditional in the physical sciences.

Population thinking and populations are not laws but concepts. It is one of the most fundamental differences between biology and the so-called exact sciences that in biology theories are usually based on concepts while in the physical sciences they are based on natural laws. Examples of concepts that became important bases of theories in various branches of biology are territory, female choice, sexual selection, resource, and geographic isolation. And even though, through appropriate rewording, some of these concepts can be phrased as laws, they are something entirely different from the Newtonian natural laws.

All biological processes differ in one respect fundamentally from all processes in the inanimate world; they are subject to *dual causation*. In contrast to purely physical processes these biological ones are controlled not only by natural laws but also by genctic programs. This duality fully provides a clear demarcation between inanimate and living processes. The dual causality, however, which is perhaps the most important characteristic of biology by which it differs indubitably from the physical sciences, is a property of both areas of biology.

The remarkable fact that all living processes obey two causalities. One of them are the natural laws which, together with chance, control completely everything that happens in the world of the exact sciences. The other causality consists of the genetic programs which characterize the living world so uniquely. There is not a single phenomenon or a single process in the living world which is not controlled by a genetic program contained in the genome. There is not a single activity of any organism that is not controlled by such a program. There is nothing comparable in the inanimate world. Dual causation, however, is not the only unique property of biology to support the thesis of the autonomy of biology.

The most novel and most important concept introduced by Darwin was perhaps that of *natural selection*. Natural selection is a process that is both so simple and so convincing, that it is almost a puzzle why after 1858 it took almost 80 years before it was universally adopted by evolutionists. To be sure, the process has been somewhat modified in the course of years. It is rather a shock for some biologists to learn that natural selection, taken strictly, is not a selection process at all, but rather a process of elimination. It is the least well adapted individuals that are eliminated in every generation, and those that are better adapted have a greater chance to survive.

The production of variation and true selection are for me inseparable parts of a single process. At the first step variation is produced by mutation and recombination, and at the second step the variants are sorted by selection. Of course, during sexual selection real selection takes place. Natural selection is the driving force of organic evolution and represents a process quite unknown in inanimate nature. This process enabled Darwin to explain the "design" so important in the arguments of the natural theologians. The fact that all organisms are seemingly so perfectly adapted to each other and to their environment was attributed by the natural theologians to God's perfect design.

Darwin however showed that it could be equally well, indeed even better, explained by natural selection. Before and even after the publication of the Origin, it was widely postulated that God had given Nature the capacity to move toward perfection. Indeed many natural processes seem to move toward a final goal such as the fertilized egg toward the adult stage. Aristotle had referred to this as the "final cause", later philosophers had called it teleology.

Evolutionary biology is a *historical science*. It is very different from the exact sciences in its conceptual framework and methodology. It deals, to a large extent, with unique phenomena, such as the extinction of the dinosaurs, the origin of man, the origin of evolutionary novelties, the explanation of evolutionary trends and rates, and the explanation of organic diversity. Evolutionary biology tries to find the answer to why questions. Experiments are usually inappropriate for obtaining answers to evolutionary questions. We cannot experiment about the extinction of the dinosaurs or the origin of mankind.

There is, however, a remarkably heuristic method available, that of *historical narratives*. Just as in much of theory formation you start with a conjecture which you thoroughly test for its validity, so in evolutionary biology you construct a scenario, a historical narrative, which you test for its explanatory value. Let us take the case of the extinction of the dinosaurs. An early conjecture was that they had been the victims of a devastating viral or bacterial epidemic.

For various reasons this narrative was not very credible. A second scenario suggested that a drastic climatic event had led to the mass extinction. Geologists however could find no evidence for a drastic, climatic change. Eventually the physicist Alvarez suggested that the Earth had been hit by an asteroid which had kicked up such a large amount of dust that for a short time it had made life on Earth very precarious. The dinosaurs became extinct but a few probably nocturnal and small mammals had been lucky to survive. The impact crater of the postulated asteroid was eventually found near the Yucatan peninsula in Mexico and all other recent findings since have confirmed the impact theory to such an extent that it is now quite generally accepted.

The methodology of historical narratives is clearly a methodology of historical science. Indeed evolutionary biology as a science, is in many respects more similar to the Geisteswissenschaften than to the exact sciences. When drawing the borderline between the exact sciences and the Geisteswissenschaften it would go right through biology and attach functional biology to the exact sciences while including evolutionary biology with the Geisteswissenschaften. This, incidentally, shows the weakness of the old classification of the sciences. That classification was made by philosophers familiar with the physical sciences and the humanities but completely ignorant of the existence of biology.

Chance

The natural laws usually effect a rather deterministic outcome in the physical sciences. Neither natural nor sexual selection guarantee such determinism. Indeed the outcome of an evolutionary process is usually the result of an interaction of numerous incidental factors. Chance is also rampant in the production of variation. It governs both crossing-over and the movement of chromosomes in the reduction division. It was curiously this chance aspect of natural selection for which this theory was most often criticized.

Some of Darwin's contemporaries, for instance the geologist Sedgwick, declared that invoking chance was unscientific. Actually, it is precisely the chanciness of variation that is so characteristic of Darwinian evolution. Even today there is much argument concerning the role of chance in the evolutionary process. Selection, of course, always has the last word.

Holistic thinking

Reductionism was the declared philosophy of the physicalists. Reduce everything to the smallest parts, determine the properties of these parts, and you have explained the whole system. However, in a biological system there are so many interactions among the parts, for instance among genes of the genotype, that a complete knowledge of the properties of the smallest parts by necessity gives only a partial explanation. Nothing is as characteristic of biological processes as interactions at all levels, among genes of the genotype, between genes and tissues, between cells and other components of the organism, between the organism and its inanimate environment, and between different organisms. It is precisely this interaction of parts that gives nature as a whole, or the ecosystem, or the social group, or the organs of a single organisms, its most pronounced characteristics. No complex system can be understood except through careful analysis. However the interactions of the components must be considered as much as the properties of the isolated components. And this is what the reductionists had neglected.

2

Teaching Botany

Botany is the science of plants. What does this mean? Is science what is worked on in laboratories or what is found out in field studies or is it something you can find in big libraries? All these are certainly aspects of science, but they do not present the whole picture. Science might be defined as an intellectual analysis of a given subject. It is the attempt to conclude from single observations to a general validity, to extrapolate from known to unknown and to have a look at different arguments.

Plant science has a long history. It has -just like all human cultural science- no straight course, nor a declared aim: phases of profound gain of knowledge alternate with periods of ignorance. Especially during the last centuries, opinions have often been expressed with utter harshness, with polemics or even with personal defamation of people having different views, peaking maybe in Galilei's inquisition.

Misinterpretation of results and corrections belong to the everyday-life of science. An accepted opion is one, that gains wide approval at a certain time. It has to be in accord with related opinions and observations and it must resist almost all attempts to prove it wrong. Differing results are often, and sometimes for very long periods, seen as "unimportant results" before they may be confirmed by a new hypothesis or by results that are gained with new methods and thus obtain a new complexion.

The history of science is the history of a continuous process of learning. The occupation with plants and the development of human culture cannot be separated. Without plants, human and animal nutrition would not be possible and thus, they are of paramount importance. Since animals avoid poisonous or bitter plants instinctively or due to experience, the knowledge of nutritious plants precedes the cultural achievements of man. But the use of plants is not limited to food alone. They can also be used as tools or as building material.

The crucial aspect seems to be the selection and cultivation of certain varieties, which generated new tasks. The developement of human settlements and new social structures were as important as the development of growing methods and the storage of the harvested goods. The understanding that higher yields could be gained by selection of suitable seed was the result of experience. It formed the basis of the cultivation of plants and resulted in cultivated varieties, that the greeks called "tame plants". Cultivated varieties began to differ more and more from the wild types.

Among the first cultivated plants were a number of graminaceous plants, the cereals, that continue to be the most important cultivated plants until today. Unprocessed, their seeds are difficult to digest and the question of how to make them edible must have been a challenge to the human mind. But cereals were not the only cultivated plants. Early artwork and documents show us, that man used a wide variety of plant species and that the experience to use them for special purposes was well developed already rather early in human history. Advice on how to prepare the soil can be found in ancient Babylonian documents, where instruction is given, too, about how to improve seeds, trees and fruits and how to protect plants from damage. Great store was set especially by the description of poisons and the exploitation of medicinal plants.

The Egyptians produced paper out of the pith of papyrus (*Cyperus papyrus*), but papyrus was not only used for the production of paper. It was needed for the wreathes of kings and gods, too. Beside this, it served as a model for the columns of the temples in Upper Egypt and was often seen to decorate their reliefs.

The Egyptians knew initially only spring wheat; winter wheat being cultivated from spring wheat only much later. They knew also olive trees, grapevines and fig trees, the latter giving tasty fruit, but only bad building timber. Plants were not only looked at from the point of view of utility. Special powers were attributed to them and some were even considered holy. Lotus (*Nelumbo nucifera*), for example, was sacred to the ancient Egyptians, to the Hindus and to other people of the east. They did nevertheless eat the lotus fruits: these were forbidden only to Egyptian priests.

In many ancient tales, plants were seen as symbols of gentle and delicate feelings and in all cultures the beauty and transitory nature of flowers was noticed and attributed emotional values. Only few depictions of plants by the Greeks or the Romans were handed down on us, but plants were very often subjects of their mythology. The creation of plants was connected to the myths of gods. The Spartan *Hyacinthos*, for example, was loved by *Appolon* and, when accidentally killed by the god, was turned into a flower with the same name. This happened to *Narcissos*, too, who committed suicide after falling in love with his own reflection. The Heliads, daughters of the sun, were transformed into electron (amber)-excreting poplars.

Homer distinguishes clearly between wild and cultivated varieties, though his knowledge of plants was confined to the useable species of Asia Minor. Among the most important cultivated plants of Greece and Asia Minor was the olive tree. It was said to have been brought to Greece from the Caucasus by Prometheus.

Medicinal plants had outstanding importance in ancient Greece. They were collected by rhizotoms, who operated with superstition and alledged witchcraft. The direction of the wind, the hour of the day or the night decided about the success of their mission. Dances and prayers, and often also obscene comments went with the search. The most skilful rhizotom according to *Theophrastus* was Thyrasyas of Mantinea. He was preoccupied with the preparation of poison out of poppy sap and hemlock and he found out that one and the same plant can be sometimes poisonous and sometimes medicinal, depending on the constitution of the treated body.

Algae and Seaweed

With algae, we leap into the realm of chlorophyll producing plants that enters into the reciprocal relationship of life with the human being. For green plants—algae being the most rudimentary form—produce the oxygen that sustains the human being and the animal kingdom. The mushrooms and fungi do not do this. The reciprocal relationship is found in the expelled carbon dioxide from the breath of human being and animals; this exhaled gas sustains the green plant.

Though algae helps to supply the air and water with oxygen, when it grows very thick on the surface of a pond, it actually serves to cut off the oxygen to the water and kill the life below. Such thick algal blooms are often stimulated by the intrusion of sewage and fertilizer run off—human pollution.

Most algae is found in water such as the ocean, ponds, lakes, and marshy areas, though one can usually find it growing on the surface of moist soil. The tiniest of algae are so small that they can be seen only with a microscope. On the other hand, kelp, which is called a brown algae, can be found in the ocean in lengths up to 200 feet. The slippery coating on rocks along streams and rivers or the slimy coating on wet soil is usually an algae. One thing that is interesting about lower plants such as algae or bacteria, is that they often reside on the borderline between plant and animal.

Some zoologists claim that one variety of the single celled algae is actually an animal. In both the animal kingdom and the plant kingdom, the simplest organisms tend to live on this borderland between the two. When we study the conifers, we will see a plant that is more intimately connected to the mineral kingdom than many of the other plants. The connection between plant and animal is remarkably evident when one explores the tidepools along the seashore. There one will find forms of animals that resemble plants, and as we have just pointed out, there one will also find microscopic plants that seem to belong to the animal kingdom. Of course, we need to keep in mind that the algae belong to the oldest living things on earth as do the rudimentary animal forms.

If we keep in mind the parts of the fully developed plant with its blossom, roots, fruit, etc. then it becomes evident, that the algae belong to the middle part of the plant. Algae are unrooted floating leaves that will never blossom. Though large pieces of kelp and oarweed appear to anchor themselves to rock, if one looks closely he will not find a true root system, but a structure that is like the leaf part of the plant mimicking a root. Botanist call this a "holdfast." The same is true of what looks like a stalk. These are usually stringy part of leaves that are stretched out and function with the support of the water's buoyancy like a stalk. If we were to take a piece of beeswax, and begin with a simple leaf shape, then mold the wax into various shapes by stretching it out or clumping it; thickening and making the form bulbous; rounding it and flattening it, we could make all of the many forms of seaweed that we find along the shores and out at sea. For every form of seaweed is nothing more than a stretched, flattened, or bulbous leaf.

The many shapes created by the transformed leaf motif tend to be rounded, limp, and yielding as they sway with the motion of the waves. On land, the light of the sun plays directly on the surface of many of the plants which helps to give definition and articulation to their forms. Think for example of the dandelion and the intricate clefts and serrations written into the shape of its leaves. Compare this to the indefinite and rounded forms found in the plants of water and we can see that the form-giving force of the sun has been mediated by the refractive and reflective qualities of water.

The deeper regions of the water let only some of the light of the upper world through. Notice the shape of the red seaweed on the following page. Doesn't it remind you of a rounded and flattened silhouette of a tree? Here we see again a kind of mirroring or mimicking of the land plants— or the shapes of land plants that have been modified by a watery existence. Along the California coast, when the tide is out, one can see exposed rocks that are covered over with a kind of seaweed called sea palms that sway with each undulation of the waves.

The overall impression is of a tropical island seen in the distance where groves of palm trees are gathered on the shore. Some varieties of red seaweed have leaves that resemble those found on deciduous trees. When we see the bladders formed on many varieties of seaweed we get the impression of a fruit. However, these bladders are not fruit, but again, are a transformed leaf that has been rounded and puffed out. When we look at the underwater plant world, we gain the impression of the meadows and forests of the upper world but they have the quality of a dreamy phantom-like existence. Our dreams tend to evaporate as we awaken in the morning light of day, so too do these watery dream-like plants dry and shrivel to something far less than their original form when taken from their dreamy watery realm and are brought into the light and warmth of the upper world.

There are beds of kelp that float like green islands upon the sea along the California coast. A tiny ecosystem is formed there, and the principle inhabitant is the sea otter. He feeds on the shellfish that adhere to the kelp and the creature often wraps itself in the kelp to make a floating bed. The kelp forest helps to hide the otter from predators like the shark. Find out more information on this topic of the creatures of the kelp forest especially the life of the otter. The student can write a short story on the day in the life of Willy Otter.

Seaweed and products made from seaweed provide some of the food used by the human being as well as other useful products. Some people use powdered kelp on their sandwiches and cooked food as a salt substitute that contains many minerals. The Japanese wrap sushi in seaweed. An important gelling agent known as algin is extracted from seaweed, and has many uses such as thickening dyes, glazing paper, waterproofing, a food stabilizer and a suspending agent for medicines, paints and cosmetics. Use part of a lesson to gather as many products together in the household that have seaweed extracts as their basis. Have sushi for dinner tonight.

As was suggested in the description on algae and seaweed, procure a large hunk of plastilina for modeling (or beeswax if you have a lot of it) and create a simple leaf shape. Set this aside and begin again making the same leaf shape only this time add more material and elongate and flatten it to make strips of seaweed. Experiment to create as many of the shapes of seaweed as you can. You will probably have to refer to pictures for the forms. Each time, begin from the basic leaf shape and then thicken or flatten it, contract or expand the form to make the many shapes of seaweed.

As an alternative to this exercise, cut out shapes of construction paper to make various forms of the seaweed and algae. The cutout shapes can be then glued in place in the main lesson book. Algae grows only in the water; it will collapse when taken into the air. It is commonly found in the sea where it is known as seaweed.

The algae takes many forms, some look like moss, yet other resemble lettuce, shrubs, and even palm trees. The algae are nearly all leaf, even their stalks are stretched out leaf forms. They make no flowers because they have no roots. The forms of the higher plants are created by the interplay of light and the earth. Algae are formed by the reflective glowing qualities of water; their undefined forms reveal that they are watery phantoms of the higher plants.

3

Teaching about Plants

One plant misconception can potentially mislead thousands of teachers and students. The teaching literature contains hundreds of errors or misconceptions about plants, but this problem has not received enough attention to prevent its negative impacts.

Teachers often cannot detect even glaring errors because "new teachers coming out of our universities and colleges are very poorly trained in basic botany." Once learned, misinformation may be difficult to correct. Many research studies have examined student misconceptions about plants.

Not surprisingly, some misconceptions about plants also appear in the teaching literature, misleading students and teachers. Student misconceptions are difficult to correct even when teachers specifically attempt to correct them. There are 50 plant misconceptions and five categories of misconceptions:

— Oversimplifications

— Overgeneralizations

— Obsolete concepts and terms

— Misidentifications

— Flawed research

Oversimplifications

Oversimplification is prevalent at the precollege level. Many misconceptions involve oversimplification of concepts, particularly at the precollege level. Such an "extreme of simplification" in plant teaching is not new. The following summary equation for plant photosynthesis is an oversimplification that contains several misconceptions:

$$6\ CO_2 + 6\ H_2O \xrightarrow{\text{sunlight, chlorophyll}} 6\ O_2 + \underset{\text{(glucose)}}{C_6H_{12}O_6}$$

— Chlorophyll alone is insufficient for plant photosynthesis. Many other enzymes and organic compounds are required. "Chloroplasts" is a better requirement.

— Glucose is not the major photosynthetic product. There is virtually no free glucose produced in photosynthesis. The most common product is starch or sucrose, and students often test leaves for starch. Starch is approximated as $(C_6H_{10}O_5)n$, where n is in the thousands. The six water molecules consumed per glucose molecule generated underestimates the water required. Much larger amounts are transpired to keep the stomata open. Without open stomata, photosynthesis is limited by lack of carbon dioxide. Submerged aquatic plants require large amounts of water for their aquatic environment.

— Drawing a single arrow wrongly implies that photosynthesis occurs in one step. Many small arrows should be used.

— Some of the energy captured in the light reactions of photosynthesis is used in the chloroplast to synthesize fatty acids and proteins. Thus, there are other types of "photosynthesis."

— The biology teaching literature contains much information on photosynthesis, yet it often has minimal discussion of mineral nutrient uptake by plants. To counter this problem, "mineral nutrients" should be added to the equation. Most essential mineral nutrients play a role in photosynthesis.

Taking these misconceptions into account gives the following summary equation for photosynthetic carbon fixation in plants:

chloroplasts, light, mineral nutrients

$$H_2O + CO_2\text{-->-->-->-->-->-->-->-->-->-->}O_2 + (C_6H_{10}O_5)_n \text{ [starch]}$$

water for transpiration or an aquatic environment

Overgeneralizations

A major theme of biology is the great biodiversity of life. Overgeneralizations inaccurately minimize biodiversity.

— Teaching publications sometimes state that all plants are photosynthetic. Although they constitute less than 1% of plant species, a few hundred parasitic species lack chlorophyll, including the world's largest flower, Rafflesia arnoldii.

— Biology textbooks often portray plants as land organisms. They rarely mention seagrasses, flowering plants that live submerged in shallow ocean waters.

— Books sometimes state that all seeds have one or two cotyledons. This is one of several examples of focusing on angiosperms or flowering plants and ignoring gymnosperms, the nonflowering seed plants. Gymnosperm seeds often have more than two cotyledons.

Obsolete Concepts and Terms

A saprophyte is defined as a plant that obtains its energy from dead organic matter. Plants once thought to be saprophytes, such as Indian pipe (Monotropa uniflora), are now known to be indirectly parasitic on trees. They are myco-heterophytes because a mycorrhizal fungus connects the nonphotosynthetic parasitic plant to the photosynthetic host plant. The mycorrhizal fungus transfers nutrients from the host to the parasite. "Saprophyte" is an obsolete term because organisms that get energy from dead organic matter, such as some fungi, are no longer in the Plant Kingdom. Such fungi can correctly be termed "saprobes" or "saprotrophs."

Knops solution was developed in the 1860s to grow terrestrial plants without soil. Its use in teaching today is misleading because it contains just 6 mineral nutrients. Today there are 14 mineral nutrients considered essential for plants.

"Geotropism" is misleading because the stimulus is gravity, not the Earth. The correct term is "gravitropism."

Misidentifications

A celery stalk is often misidentified as a stem. "Stalk" is short for "leafstalk," so a celery stalk is a leaf part. This should be obvious because stems are circular to square in cross section. A celery stalk is crescent shaped in cross section. If all the stalks are removed from a bunch of celery, a short conical stem remains.

Carrot storage root tissues are sometimes misidentified. The storage root lacks the epidermis and cortex found in young roots. Most of the storage root consists of secondary phloem.

Terms that only apply to angiosperms are frequently applied to gymnosperms, for example, pine nuts, ginkgo nuts, juniper berries, and yew berries. Nuts and berries are specific types of fruits. Gymnosperms do not produce fruits.

Flawed Research

The most difficult misconceptions for teachers to catch are those caused by flawed research.

— Many textbooks state that seeds of the tambalacoque, or calvaria, tree have to pass through the digestive system of the dodo bird before they will germinate. Supposedly, no endangered tambalacoques had germinated since the dodo became extinct in the 1680s. The only experimental data in support of this hypothesis was germination of 3 of 17 seeds in tambalacoque fruits force-fed to turkeys. However, there were no control fruits not fed to turkeys. Several authors disputed this hypothesis. Young tambalacoques exist in the wild. Widespread deforestation and introduced plant and animal species endangered the tambalacoques.

— A widespread misconception involves allelopathy, defined as a plant excreting chemicals that inhibit growth of neighboring plants. A zone of bare soil around a California shrub was assumed to be caused by the shrub's allelochemicals.16 Fencing the shrubs caused the bare zones to disappear, so the bare zone was in fact caused by rodents and birds that hid in the shrubs.

Allelopathy lab experiments are artificial because they use unrealistically high doses of allelochemicals and lack soil. In nature, allelochemicals are often inactivated by soil or soil microbes. Even in nature, it is very difficult to determine if growth inhibition of neighboring plants is caused by allelochemicals or competition among plants for light, water, and mineral nutrients.

Common Misconceptions by Topic

Pollination

Pollination is often defined as transfer of pollen from anther to stigma. That definition inaccurately excludes gymnosperms, which have pollination but lack anthers and stigmas. In gymnosperms, pollination is the transfer of pollen from a microsporangiate, or "male," cone to the micropyle of a megasporangiate, or "female," cone.

The importance of animal pollination is often overestimated for crop production. While about 90% of plant species are animal pollinated, our most important food crops are wind pollinated, including corn, wheat, and rice. Other major crops are asexually propagated and have vegetative edible parts, such as potatoes, sweet potatoes, and cassavas. Still other major crops are primarily self-pollinated, such as peanuts, soybeans, and beans.

Self-pollination is often defined as pollination with pollen from the same plant. However, self-pollination also occurs with pollen from another plant of the same clone. Plant clones are extremely important in agriculture and in many wild species.

Plants that are considered self-pollinated may depend on animal pollination. Tomatoes are self-fertilizing but pollinated by bumblebees that vibrate the flowers.19 Greenhouse tomato flowers may need to be vibrated manually to obtain pollination.

Pollination is not the same as fertilization nor does pollination ensure fertilization.

Texts sometimes say animal pollination is an advance found only in angiosperms. Cycads are gymnosperms pollinated by beetles.

Photosynthesis

A widespread misconception states that leaves reflect all green light and do not use green light in photosynthesis. Leaves often absorb more than 50% of the green light and use it efficiently in photosynthesis. The origin of this misconception is probably the chlorophyll absorption spectrum in textbooks. The chlorophyll absorption spectrum is a graph of light absorption versus light color. It shows that chlorophyll absorbs much red and blue light but little green light. However, accessory pigments absorb green light and pass that energy on to chlorophyll.

A common student misconception is that plants photosynthesize during the day and conduct cellular respiration only at night. Some teaching literature even states this. Cellular respiration occurs continuously in plants, not just at night.

The "dark reactions" of photosynthesis are a misnomer that often leads students to believe that photosynthetic carbon fixation occurs at night. It is preferable to use the term "Calvin cycle" instead of dark reactions. Bubble formation on leaves submerged in water is not always caused by photosynthesis. If the water is cold, bubbles form on leaves as the water warms and gases become less soluble.

The aquatic plant Elodea is often used to visualize gas formation in photosynthesis. The gas produced is not pure oxygen, as often claimed.6 As photosynthetic oxygen dissolves, some of the nitrogen comes out of solution.

Tropisms

Texts often state that shoots are only positively phototropic. However, shoot tips of some vines, such as English ivy, are negatively phototropic. If vine shoot tips were positively phototropic, they would grow away from walls or tree trunks, rather than climb them.

Several simple classroom activities that supposedly demonstrate hydrotropism merely show that roots require water to grow. Most hydrotropism research is artificial because it studies roots grown in air, not soil. Hydrotropism is unlikely under natural conditions because the sharp relative humidity gradients required for hydrotropism rarely occur in soils. Relative humidity in soil pores is above 98% even when the soil is so dry that plants remain permanently wilted unless more water is added.

Physiology

Texts usually state that phloem transports organic compounds. However, phloem normally contains high concentrations of potassium. It also transports phosphate, potassium, and magnesium from dying leaves and from old to young parts when those mineral nutrients are deficient.

Boron was long considered immobile in phloem. However, some species, such as celery, grape, apple, and peach, are able to transport boron in phloem.

Stomata do not open because a pair of guard cells have thicker cell walls on their adjoining side. Rather the radial arrangement of cellulose microfibrils in the cell walls cause the guard cells to bend apart when they swell.

Capillarity is not a factor in upward water movement in stems. Capillarity occurs in tubes of small diameter that are initially empty. Water spontaneously moves up such tubes. Functional xylem comprises small diameter tubes that are not empty to begin with.

Most cultivated flower, vegetable, and lawn grass seeds are not dormant because they will germinate promptly when given environmental conditions required for germination. Such seeds are quiescent. Dormant seeds will not germinate even when given environmental conditions needed for germination.

Reproduction

The generalization that angiosperm seeds have abundant endosperm or cotyledons packed with stored nutrients is misleading. The largest plant family, Orchidaceae, has tiny seeds with rudimentary embryos and virtually no nutritive tissue. In nature, orchid seedlings depend on fungi for their early nutritional needs.

The angiosperm life cycle is often overgeneralized to show just sexual seeds. In some species, such as dandelion, most seeds are asexual. Asexual seed production is termed apomixis.

Contrary to textbook life cycle diagrams, fruits sometimes develop without pollination and fertilization, termed parthenocarpy. It is of substantial economic importance because of the popularity of seedless fruits such as bananas and pineapples.

Contrary to some texts, production of seedless fruit may provide an advantage to certain plant species. If pollination or fertilization fails one year and no fruit are produced, seed-dispersing animals that rely on the fruit may starve or leave the area. Seedless fruit can feed the seed-dispersing animals. The leafy top of a seedless pineapple can form a new plant. Seedless fruit of wild parsnip are preferred by herbivorous insects thus reducing damage to seeded fruit.

Seedless grapes in supermarkets are not seedless because they are sprayed with the plant hormone gibberellic acid. They are genetically seedless. Gibberellic acid is applied to increase the size of the seedless grapes.

Most seedless grapes are not parthenocarpic, because they require pollination and fertilization to set fruit. The grape seeds abort early in development, termed stenospermocarpy.

Seedless fruit crops are not always vegetatively propagated. Seedless tomatoes, seedless cucumbers, and seedless watermelons are grown from seed.

History

Johann van Helmont (1580–1644) was not the first to conclude that plants did not "eat" soil. Van Helmont got the idea for his 1648 potted willow experiment from a nearly identical experiment described in a 1450 book by Nicolaus of Cusa.28 In 1627, Sir Francis Bacon published experiments with terrestrial plants grown in water and concluded that plants got their nutrition from water rather than soil.

George Washington Carver (1864–1943) is often credited with revolutionizing agriculture in the southern United States with his more than 300 peanut inventions. However, none of Carver's peanut inventions was ever a commercial success, nor did Carver invent peanut butter as is often claimed. Carver's main contribution to the peanut industry was his testimony before a congressional committee on peanut tariffs in 1921.

Miscellaneous

An epiphyte is usually defined as a plant that lives on another plant without causing it any harm. This definition is often unrealistic because epiphytes are "nutritional pirates" that can intercept as much as half of the mineral nutrients that the host plant would otherwise receive. The weight of large numbers of epiphytes often causes limb breakage on the host tree. The strangler figs start out as epiphytes but eventually kill their host trees.

The so-called knees of bald cypress are often said to function in obtaining oxygen for the roots or in supporting the tree. However, their function is not known for certain. Several possible functions have been hypothesized.

Poinsettia is not poisonous, as is often stated. Its poisonous reputation was due to an erroneous report in the early 1900s that a child died after eating poinsettia leaves.

Not all deciduous temperate trees are angiosperms. Deciduous gymnosperms include bald cypress, ginkgo, larch, and dawn redwood.

Plant "food" is a misnomer because mineral nutrients are not really food for plants. "Fertilizer" is the correct term.

TEACHING FAST PLANTS

Fast Plants (scientific name: Brassica rapa) are rapid-cycling brassicas. They are members of the crucifer family of plants, closely related to cabbage, turnips, broccoli and other cruciferous vegetables. Bred for over 30 years at the University of Wisconsin – Madison by Professor Paul H. Williams, Fast Plants today require little more attention than continuous fluorescent light, water, and fertilizer. The seeds that you grow in your classroom can be immediately planted or stored for up to 10 years in a refrigerator.

Fast Plants investigations are designed to:

— encourage students to do real science and develop scientific skills

— generate student ownership of learning and investigation

— reach all grade levels

— improve how students understand of biology concepts through hands-on, inquiry-based investigations

Fast Plants activities and manuals are appropriate for all grade levels, from kindergarten to college. Individual activities target different specific grade levels, and each one offers suggestions about how to incorporate hands-on science in your classroom. Fast Plants activities and manuals encompass a wide range of plant biology concepts that fit into most science curricula. Subjects include:

— Ecology

— Environment

— Growth and development

— Heredity and genetics

- — Life cycles
- — Physiology
- — Reproduction
- — Variation
- — Butterflies

Fast Plants materials are designed just for classrooms. The only special equipment necessary for growing Fast Plants is a source of 24-hour fluorescent light that is close to the plants (10 cm from the top of plants). Ceiling lights and ambient/window light provide insufficient light and may result in stunted growth. You can build your own light bank or plant light house from recycled household materials, or you can order *pre-made kits* that require little assembly.

Fast Plants will flower 14-18 days after planting the seeds. Soon after, seed pods will begin to grow. After a total of 35-45 days (the exact time varies depending on the environment: light, water, fertilizer, humidity), the new seeds will be ready for harvest! The amount of time students spend with their plants each day varies, depending on your specific curriculum. Two to three times per week, students should check the plants to make sure the water reservoirs are full.

Their small stature makes Fast Plants suitable for virtually any classroom, even those with very little space available. They can be grown in a space as small as 18"x18", and only require one electrical outlet.

Wisconsin Fast Plants Program

The Wisconsin Fast Plants Program, established in 1986, is a science education outreach program at the University of Wisconsin-Madison that:

— develops instructional materials that use Fast Plants

— facilitates networking between teachers, scientists, and educators

— organizes and leads workshops for teachers around the world

A Life Cycle Concept

Life on Earth is comprised of populations of individuals whose life span varies from a few hours (bacteria) to hundreds or even thousands of years (some trees). It is through the cycle of life of individuals, repeated from one generation to the next, that life of a group of organisms or species is continued on Earth. For many organ- isms, life of an individual begins with fertilization, the time when specialized reproductive cells representing the contributions of a single egg (female) and a sperm (male) come together to form the zygote, or first cell of the new genera- tion.

In higher organisms the zygote divides repeatedly progressing through the stages of growth and development, eventually becoming a mature adult, producing reproductive cells which contribute to yet another generation. The ways in which various organisms complete their life cycles to accommodate living in complex and ever changing environments are extremely varied and a fascinating part of biology.

The growing of rapid cycling Brassica rapa, Rbr, through a life cycle from seed to seed can provide the basis for learning many aspects of biology that are relevant to the students' understanding of themselves as individual organisms among the many others inhabiting the Earth. By looking at the life cycle of Fast Plants from the perspective of the stages of growth and development from seed to seed,

Stage	State	Condition	Dependency
A. seed	• quiescence (dormant embryo)	• suspended growth of embryo	• independent of the parent and many components of the environment
B. germinating seed	• germination	• awakening of growth	• dependent on environment and health of the individual
C. vegetative growth	• growth and development	• roots, stems, leaves grow rapidly, plant is sexually immature	• dependent on environment
D. immature plant	• flower bud development	• gametogenesis — reproductive [male (pollen) and female (egg)] cell production	• dependent on healthy vegetative plant
E. mature plant	• flowering • mating	• pollination — attracting or capturing pollen	• dependent on pollen carriers; bees and other insects
F. mature plant	• pollen growth	• gamete maturation • germination and growth of pollen tube	• dependent on compatibility of pollen with stigma and style

G. mature plant	· double fertilization	· union of gametes · union of sperm (n) and egg (n) to produce diploid zygote (2n) · union of sperm (n) and fusion nucleus (2n) to produce endosperm (3n)	· dependent on compatibility and healthy plant
H. mature parent plant *plus* embryo	· developing fruit · developing endosperm · developing embryo	· embryogenesis — growth and development of endosperm and embryo · growth of supporting parental tissue of the fruit (pod)	· interdependency among developing embryo, endosperm, developing pod and supporting mature parental plant
I. aging parent plant *plus* maturing embryo	· senescence of parent · maturation of fruit · seed development	· withering of leaves of parent plant · yellowing pods, drying embryo · suspension of embryo growth, development of seed coat	· seed is becoming independent of the parent
J. dead parent plant *plus* seed	· death, desiccation · seed quiescence	· drying of all plant parts, dry pods will disperse seeds	· seed (embryo) is independent of parent, but is dependent on the pod and the environment for dispersal

a framework can be developed for understnading the nature of the dependency between organisms and their environment.

Farming Fast Plants

This Farming Fast Plants activity introduces a classroom investigation that is easily adaptable for all grade levels and designed to engage teachers and students as investigators. The activity has the practical outcome of producing an abundant supply of Fast Plants seed for future classroom use and for sharing with other teachers. The central question of the activity is "How many seeds can your students produce from each seed planted?" This activity draws upon many life science principles as they relate to crop production, farming practices and sustainable agriculture.

From the perspective of the teacher and students as "farmers of the Fast Plants crop in the classroom," the activity is rich in investigative learning which leads to an under-standing of the role of the environment and its impact on populations of the student-friendly organisms, Fast Plants.

Farming Fast Plants uses a simple plant-ing design in soda bottles and a Plant Light House made from a paper box and a low-cost energy saver fluorescent circular bulb. Each class-room will have the opportunity to compare its data to other classrooms around the world. An Internet-based discussion group will connect to this site so that teachers and students can communicate their experiences with Fast Plants.

Fast Plants are grown in a hydroponic system, the bottle growing system, or BGS, constructed from a 16-24 oz. soda bottle. Twelve seeds are planted in each BGS and up to nine bottle systems can be placed in one Plant Light House. An alternative, recommended light source is a bank of six 4-foot fluorescent bulbs. Students will tend Fast Plants from sowing seeds through pollinating flowers and harvesting new seeds. The Fast Plants life cycle from planting to seed harvest is 35-45 days. Teachers can encourage students to note any factors that affect the growth and/or health of their plants and change their farming practices accordingly.

Pollinating

The petite Fast Plants will begin to flower about 15 days after sowing. When flowers on more than two Fast Plants are open, your students should begin to pollinate their flowers and continue pollinating every day or two among all open flowers for up to 7 days. Pollen of Fast Plants (rapid cycling Brassica rapa) is relatively heavy and sticky. Unlike many grass and some tree pollens, Fast Plants pollen is normally not carried in the air. Pollinate with beesticks made by gluing a dried bee to the end of a toothpick. Fast Plants are self incom-patible: that is, each stigma prevents germination of its own pollen.

Harvesting

Twenty days or more after the final pollination, the lower leaves of the plants will be withering, and pods will be turning yellow. (Inside the pods, the seed coats will be turning brown.) At this point, remove the nutrient solution from the reservoir and allow plants to dry until crispy brown (approximately 1 week).

Harvest each plant carefully by cutting it off at soil level. Take care not to break off the pods. Number each plant. Harvest seeds from each plant separately by gently rolling the dry seed pods between your fingers over a tray. For each numbered plant, count and record the number of seeds harvested. Count only plump seeds that you think will germinate. Do not count tiny, shriveled "seeds" as these are not truly seeds.

For each bottle growing system (BGS), calculate the average number of seeds harvested for each seed sown. This is your net seed yield (NSY). Then calculate the average number of seeds harvested per each plant harvested. Are the averages different? Why? Finally, calculate the net seed yield (NSY) from all the BGS's in the class to obtain the class NSY. This is the figure you will enter on the Wisconsin Fast Plants website as the NSY from your class.

Place the seeds in labeled envelopes. Include: the seed name, e.g. Fast Plants petite; the number of plants that produced the seeds; date of harvest; total number of seeds produced; your name. Test the viability of your seed cropby germinating 20-50 seeds on wet paper toweling in a plastic bag or petri dish. After 24 hours, calculate the percentage of germination (or "viability") of your seed. Observe the vigor and uniformity of the germination.

For future Fast Plants investigations, store seed envelopes in a cool, dry place, e.g. in a refrig-erator in a moisture-proof, sealed container. Ideally, the container would also contain a drying compound, e.g. indicator silica gel, which can be obtained from a pharmacist or from a camera store. Seed that is stored dry and cool will remain viable for over 10 years.

Farming in Space

This activity originates from NASA's interest in longterm, manned flight and potential colonization of the moon and planets. Plants can be an important part of bioregenerative life support systems in which food is produced and human waste recycled. To this end NASA is supporting the development of experimental equipment designed to grow plants on the Space Shuttle and the International Space Station. At the same time that engineers are designing equipment for plant growth, plant scientists are evaluating various species for their potential and plant breeders are creating plant varieties that may be suitable in life support systems.

An example of one of these systems in which Fast Plants and dwarf wheat will be evaluated experimentally on the space shuttle in the coming years is the Biomass Producation System, BPS, designed by Orbitec. The BPS is a complex piece of equipment with the capability of growing plants in four small chambers in which temperature, light, plant nutrient delivery, CO_2 concentration and relative humidity can be monitored and controlled.

The Farming in Space activity has been designed to coordinate with the flight experiment. It offers teachers and students a chance to examine a number of basic principles and concepts in plant biology and crop production through hands on experiments using a simulated Biomass Production System and the same seed stocks that the researchers will be using during the flight experiments.

The basic experiment is suitable for upper elementary students and higher grades. An important concept in crop production that is the focus of these activities is biomass productivity. Biomass is the amount of living material (mass) produced by a system of living organisms. Comparisons of the ability of wheat and brassica to use the energy of light in the conversion of carbon dioxide, water and mineral elements into plant biomass will be made.

Plant biomass is normally measured as total dry mass (both roots and shoots) of the plant, or it can be a defined portion of the plants such as the dry mass weight of plant tops only. A refinement in our understanding of plant biomass is the concept of harvest index, which is defined as the proportion or fraction of a specially used part of the plant, e.g., seed, fruit or vegetative part in relation to the total plant, including roots. Normally dry mass is used as the basis for estimating harvest index.

Another important concept deals with the efficiency with which various species are able to utilize the energy of light for the conversion of CO_2, water and nutrient into biomass. In this experiment the Energy Conversion Efficiency, ECE, of two species will be compared - wheat a monocot, brassica a dicot. In the Plant Light House, for example (on page 12), total light energy in the system can be estimated by multiplying the wattage of the light bulb in the Light House by the total number of hours that the plants have been growing at the time of their harvest. In this way a conversion efficiency can be determined based on grams of plant biomass for each watt hour of energy.

ECE of plants = total dry mass of plants (roots and shoot) divided by the total watts over the growing period.

Crop Production

The basic experiment will be to grow the two varieties of Fast Plants and two varieties of dwarf wheat for three weeks to follow their development, and to compare their fresh and dry weights. The four hydroponic growing systems, hereafter referred to as the Hydroponic Production Units or HPU's will reside within the Plant Light House (the simulated Biomass Production System). One of the four seed stocks will be grown in each HPU.

The planting design of the overall experiment allows many different kinds of comparisons to be made. Elementary, middle and high school teachers should determine which of the suggested observations and measurements are desirable for their students to make, based on age, time constraints, etc. Although the protocol is written for both sets of plants to be harvested at 21 days, the length of the experiment may vary, depending on environmental conditions in the HPU and on what teachers or students choose to observe. The growing time may be extended for as long as desired, even up to when the dwarf wheats are mature, approxixmately 70-100 days.

Basic Farming in Space Experiment:

1. building a simple, low cost plant growth box, known as the Plant Light House
2. constructing 4 hydroponic nutrient plant systems, HPU's, from 2-liter soda bottles
3. planting four different seed stocks -
   - — dwarf wheat - high yielding, variety, Apogee
   - — dwarf wheat - lower yielding, Super Dwarf
   - — Fast Plants - variety, Basic Brassica rapa, Rbr
   - — Fast Plants - dwarf variety, AstroPlants
4. recording environmental and growth events
5. comparing fresh and dry weights

The experiment is designed to be rich in observations about plant growth, in data taking, simple proportional analysis, and in statistical summation and comparisons between and among the four experimental systems. Growth can be observed and measured using parameters such as height, number of leaves and estimates of root growth. The HPU bottle system allows root growth to be observed easily. At harvest, fresh and dry mass of plant roots and shoots will be measured and may be analyzed to examine various concepts in crop production.

Materials for the HPU

— 4, 2-liter soda bottles

— unpolished cotton string or Watermat® for capillary wicks

— vermiculite, medium grade horticultural

—planting medium, e.g., peatlite, Scotts Redi Earth

— pipette for watering

— Peters 20-20-20 Professional fertilizer

— 1-3 dried bees and toothpicks for making beesticks

— 1 pair of tweezers

Construction of the HPU

1. Cut four 2-liter soda bottles so that the bottoms are 13 cm. tall. These will serve as the reservoirs for the hydroponic nutrient solution. The top half of the bottle will be inverted into the reservoir as the growing funnel and hold the vermiculite and planting medium.

Seed Stocks needed

— 20 AstroPlants seeds

— 20 basic Brassica rapa seeds, Rbr

— 10 dwarf wheat seeds, Apogee

— 10 dwarf wheat seeds, Super Dwarf

Drill or melt a 0.5 mm hole in the bottle cap. Screw bottle cap onto bottle top. Insert a string wick (or other capillary wicking), approx. Invert the bottle top (growing funnel) and place in the reservoir (bottle bottom.) The wick should extend from the reservoir bottom into the inverted funnel produced by the bottle top.

Planting

1. Layer 200 cc. of vermiculite into the funnel and then layer 200 cc. of peatlite on top of the vermiculite. (Or use whatever "soil" you normally use for Fast Plants.)
2. Gently soak the soil and vermiculite with water until it drips from wick at the bottom of the growing funnel. This is called the runoff.
3. Uniformly distibute 10 Apogee wheat seeds in one funnel at the outer edge of the soil up against the clear wall and distribute 10 Super Dwarf seeds similarly into another funnel. Space seeds evenly around the edge approximately 3 cm apart.
4. Gently press the seeds into the soil, but do not bury them. Seeds should now be visible around the perimeter of the bottle through the clear wall of the bottle.

Repeat the procedure for both varieties of brassica seeds, except that two seeds should be dropped at each of the 10 evenly distributed locations around the perimenter. (They will later be thinned to one at each position.) Also, the brassica seeds should be pushed to the wall of the bottle with a forceps or toothpick before pressing them gently into the soil. They should be visible through the wall of the bottle. Each of the four HPUs should now contain a separate variety of plants.

Cover wheat and brassica seeds with a 1 cm layer of vermiculite. Gently moisten from above until water again drips from the the wick at the base of the funnel. Pour off any excess water remaining in the reservoir and replace it with 400 ml of 1/8 strength Peter's Professional fertilizer (hydroponic nutrient solution). Mark the level of the hydroponic nutrient solution on the outside of the reservoir with a marking pen.

Place a label on the completed HPU indicating the date and hour of planting, the variety of seed/plant in the particular HPU, and identify the student/group.

Observing, Measuring and Monitoring

Be prepared to observe your germinating seeds each day, and make appropriate records in your log. Many interesting comparisons can be made between wheat and brassica as well as between the two wheat and two brassica varieties. For example, note the time and way seeds germinate, the root and shoot growth patterns.

Monitor and record the temp inside the HPU's each day as well as the ambient or room temp. If average temperatures within the HPU's reach 30°C/ 85°F, additional ventilation slots can be cut in the top and upper portions of the Light House.

Observe the level of the nutrient solution. The amount used by the plants and lost to evaporation can be measured and graphed. Replace used solution as needed. Algal growth in the nutrient solution can be inhibited by wrapping the reservoir in aluminum foil or dark paper to exclude light.

Brassicas will begin to flower about 14 days after seeding. When flowers on more than two Fast Plants are open, pollination should begin and should continue every two or three days among all open flowers for at least a week. Pollinate with a beestick made by gluing a dried bee to the end of a toothpick. Collect pollen from the flowers of one brassica plant and move it others. Alternatively, pipe cleaners, Q-tips, or very small pieces of cloth (velveteen) could be used for pollinating.

Heads of wheat normally begin to emerge after 23 days. (Wheat is self-pollinated and does not require any pollination activity.) For the basic biomass experiment, we recommed terminating the experiment about 3 weeks after sowing, before the wheat begins to head as flower heads.

1. Twenty-one days after planting, harvest plants from each HPU by cutting them off at soil level. Keep each group of plants separate and label them carefully. Be sure all dry and dead leaves are collected separately from each HPU throughout the growth period and saved for weighing.
2. Weigh the plants from each HPU separately.
3. Fresh weights - At harvesting, quickly place the plants in a preweighed plastic bag. Weigh the total fresh mass of the plants, then subtract the weight of the bag.
4. Dry weight - Plants should be loosely placed in a preweighed brown paper bag and put in a low temperature (200°F) oven for two days or until they reach constant weight (no more weight loss occurring.) For dry weight measurements, a balance capable of measuring milligram or centigram quantities is desirable. (Chemistry classes have such balances.)

The following are aspects of the environment and items in growth and development that could be observed, measured, recorded, analyzed and displayed as a function of time (days after sowing) and then compared.

Environmental monitoring

- light = daily energy input, watts/24 hr cumulative energy input (total watts)
- temperature, daily
- nutrient solution - usage (ml/day)
- appearance of algae, pests, etc.

Developmental events

- germination
- first emergence of root and shoot
- first leaf, second leaf, etc.
- flower buds (brassica) or head (wheat)
- flowers open
- pod elongation
- appearance of branches on stem (brassica), tillers (wheat)
- yellowing of older leaves

Measures of growth (averages for 10 plants)

- plant height
- leaf number
- root length, root number
- number of flowers open
- number of seed pods enlarging
- number of seeds

Measures of biomass (average of 10 plants at harvest)

— fresh weight of tops

— dry weight of tops

— fresh weight of roots

— dry weight of roots

— dry weight of seed (brassica)

Analyses of biomass

— dry weight/fresh weight ratios, tops, roots

— roots/tops ratios

— harvest index of tops, dry

— harvest index of seed (seed weight/total plant dry weight)

— calculate energy efficiency conversion (grams dry weight/watts)

Comparisons (between varieties and species)

— dry weight/fresh weight

— root/top ratios

— total biomass

— harvest indices

— energy efficiencies

Teachers and Students Investigating Plants in Space

Students from around the United States and throughout Ukraine were ground-based participants in the CUE-TSIPS plant science experiment during the Nov. 19-Dec. 5 mission of Space Shuttle STS-87. The students ran simulations of the

B-STIC experiment and faithfully recorded data on plant height, day on which the plants first flowered, the number of seed pods and seeds produced by their AstroPlants.

Teacher communications with the Fast Plants office indicate that the students took their task seriously and were very keen on doing something with NASA. Teachers themselves often used the CUE-TSIPS investigation to coincide with their units on the principles and behavior of plants. There was great interest in the Ukrainian astronaut, Leonid Kadenyuk, and the NASA downlinks of him pollinating and measuring the plants.

Thirty students in the U.S. and thirty-two in Ukraine participated in a live downlink Q & A session with astronaut Kadenyuk on December 1, trying to assertain similarities and differences in the way the plants grew in orbit and on the ground. American students attending the launch at Cape Kennedy on November 19th met the group of nine Ukrainian students who had come for the event.

On the afternoon that the shuttle landed Principal Investigator, Mary Musgrave, sent the information that the Shuttle plants looked normal and that seed pods were forming on the plants that had been pollinated in space.

In Ukraine Hosted by CUE lead scientist for education, Dr. Volodimir Nazarenko, at the Ukrianian State Ecological and Nature Center in Kiev in November 1996, Paul Williams (WFP), Tom Dreschel and Peter Chetirkin (Kennedy Space Center) trained nineteen teachers and scientists from various cities in the Ukraine. Following the visit, 500 more teachers representing 24 regions of Ukraine were introduced to CUE-TSIPS via 57 more workshops. A Ukrainian translation of the CUE-TSIPS manual together with a student workbook was distributed.

From the 20,000 participating Ukrainian students, 5,000 tabulated data sets have been generated and are currently being analyzed in preparation for a national symposium to be held in May of 1998 in Kiev. The CUE program was widely disseminated throughout Ukraine, in 47 broadcasts on national and local TV, 62 radio reports, and more than 100 newspaper and journal articles.

In the United States, 20 lead teachers were trained in March of 1997. These teachers trained an additional 1,073 teachers in 58 outreach workshops. Shorter CUE-TSIPS workshops reached 2,798 more teachers. Another form of outreach in the U.S. was through CUE-TSIPS booths at two national NSTA conventions, at the 1997 NABT convention, and at the 1997 Texas State Fair. Of the 60,000 CUE-TSIPS manuals printed by NASA, 2,000 remained to be distributed at the NSTA convention in April of 1998. CUE-TSIPS participating students of the lead teachers numbered 1,274.

Variation and Fast Plants

Over the next two years, the Wisconsin Fast Plants Program will be developing instructional materials to help teachers look at genetics from several perspectives, e.g., Mendelian, populations, quantitative, and molecular. This article is intended only as an introduction to that effort and addresses some of the underlying ideas behind the concept of biological variation.

If you have grown Fast Plants you will have noticed variation among the individual plants within the group. Variation can range from a little to a lot. This article is designed to help teachers and students understand the basis of the variation they observe in their plantings. Variation is one of the fundamental characteristics of life. All organisms exhibit some variation among individuals.

Understanding the ways that variation is manifested in organisms, how it comes to be expressed through the development of the individual, and how it is transmitted from one individual to the next generation of individuals are central themes in biology.

Working with Fast Plants will enrich a student's understanding of variation. By observing the growth and development of a Fast Plant through the various stages in the life cycle, students will become aware of many visible features, or phenotypes, that make up the organism. Only, however, upon close observation of a population of plants, will they become aware that the characteristics observed on one plant vary more or less on other plants. Such is the nature of variation. The interrelationships suggested in Figure 1 should provide students with numerous ideas for experimentation to probe the basis for the variation observed among their individual Fast Plants.

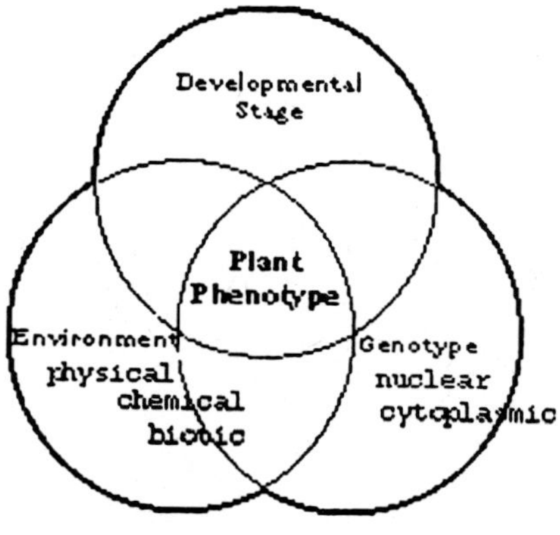

Figure 1: Diagram depicting the interrelationships of genotype, environment, and the development on the plant phenotype

In order to be useful in an experiment the phenotype must be described using terms that are widely understood and easily communicated. For these reasons scientists have agreed upon various standards or descriptors to describe characteristics in the natural world. Descriptors take many forms (Table 1). The choice of how to describe what you observe is important, because it will determine the kinds of descriptors used and establish the basis for recording, analyzing and communicating results

Table 1: Examples of descriptors.

Descriptors	Method of description	Examples
number	1. direct count	1. hair on margin of first leaf
	2. statistical summary of counts	2. n = number counted r = range, x = average
		s = standard deviation
	3. comparator chart with numerical	3. moderately intense purple scale = 6 on a scale of 0 = no
		purple to 9 = very intense purple
size	1. use of a tool to measure	1. height of a plant in mm (estimate) dimension,
		e.g. ruler, calipers
	2. comparator scale	2. short, medium, tall
		compared to a range of
		measure
color	1. visual comparison using standard color chart or	1. no purple (anthocyanin)
	scales	color in plant
	2. describe with words using hue, lightness and	2. very light, yellow-green leaves

	saturation	
shape	1. descriptive language (often Latin)	1. leaf margin, lobed edge
	2. comparator charts	2. leaf spoon-shaped

Environmental Variation

Much can be learned about the role of light, temperature, and nutrients on plant development from experiments in which one or more environmental parameters are changed. Because Fast Plants are highly responsive to changes in the environment, they are ideal for examining the role of the environment on the expression of phenotypic variation.

Although Fast Plants are able to grow within a wide range of environmental conditions, for most investigations it is recommended that they be grown under uniform and ideal conditions. In this way variation arising from sub-optimal conditions of environment will be minimized. The Wisconsin Fast Plants Information Document (WFPID) Understanding the Environment describes how to provide and maintain the various physical, chemical and biotic components of the environment that are most suitable for Fast Plants.

Genotypic Variation

How can students use Fast Plants to investigate the contribution of the genotype to the phenotype? Fast Plants, rapid cycling Brassica rapa, are genotypically variable in that they have a genetically controlled mating system that prevents self-fertilization and favors out-crossing among individuals. As a consequence, even seed stocks selected for uniformity of specific phenotypes and genotypes exhibit considerable variation for other traits.

The Wisconsin Fast Plants Program has developed a number of genetic stocks of rapid cycling Brassica rapa for genetic investigations on the nature and inheritance of variation. Some WFP stocks contain distinctive mutant phenotypes, e.g., anthocyaninless plant, anl, yellow green plant, ygr1, rosette, ros, and male sterile, mst2, that are suitable for Mendelian genetics. Other stocks exhibit phenotypes whose expression may vary continually and which may be quantified as discrete or countable units, e.g., number of hairs, or as estimates of size, e.g. petite dwarf, dwf1, or of intensity of color saturation, e.g., purple anthocyanin. These quantitative phenotypes may be conditioned by a few or many genes and normally require numerical descriptions in which the statistical notations of population size, (n), range (R), arithmetic mean (x), and standard deviation (s) are applied.

Yet other stocks have been developed to combine both simply inherited mutant genotypes and quantitatively expressed phenotypes. An important part of WFP is the continuing development and improvement of seed stocks for uses in genetics. An interesting aspect of Fast Plants is that almost any phenotype that piques a student's curiosity is amenable to genetic analysis. How to investigate these traits of interest will be the subject of future WFPID's.

As your students begin to explore genetic variation using the specialized Fast Plant stocks they should be aware of two types of WFP information documents, the Passports and the Seed Stock Documents (SSD). Passports contain descriptive information on the phenotype, genotype, and genetic background of the seed stock. Included also is information on potential educational and research uses and some technical information.

The Seed Stock Documents contain more complete phenotypic and genotypic information on each WFP stock, including pedigrees, population profiles on particular growth and quantitative characteristics such as cotyledon size, plant height, number of days to flower, hairs on first true leaf margin, and the number of leaves. They also include additional suggestions for educational and research uses including more technical information and references.

Information supporting the effective use of Passports and SSD's can be found in the WFPID Rapid Cycling Brassicas: Phenotypes and Genotypes. This information document contains detailed descriptions of all available. phenotypes and genotypes together with the genetic terminology used with rapid cycling brasssicas.

A group of Louisiana State University undergraduates recently pollinated Brassica rapa in microgravity on the KC-135 aircraft. Four different methods of quantifying pollen transfer were used: number of pollen grains collected by a beestick; number of pollen grains transferred to a stigma; number of pollen grains transferred per unit of surface area; and number of successful ovules developing following pollination.

Brassica in microgravity has not yet been determined, proposed methods must be tested beforehand. The number of pollen grains transferred from anthers to bee sticks during pollination was quantified and compared to ground control tests. Pollen was collected with bee sticks from 19-day old plants with open flowers in either 0-g (on the KC-135) or 1-g environments.

Pollen collected in this manner was quantified by using a hemacytometer to count grains released from the bee sticks by a detergent solution. Total numbers of pollen grains per bee stick were compared statistically using t-tests. In microgravity, bee sticks collected an average of 27,600 grains/ flower. Results concluded that no significant difference occurred in microgravity compared to control.

Trials of all the Brassica species including B. rapa, B. napus, B. juncea, B. oleracea, B. carinata, and B. nigra, as well as R. sativus were planted. These plants were germinated from seed in a petri dish on moist filter paper until they were of a length which could be transferred to pots containing growth media (in the ratio of two sand to one Metromix). These plants were grown until they reached a size in which they could be safely mechanically inoculated with the virus.

To mechanically inoculate the plants, inoculum was prepared by grinding the tissue with phosphate buffer of pH 7.5 until completely crushed. The mixture was filtered through cheesecloth into a beaker contained in an ice bath to prevent the virus from denaturization. The plants were inoculated by dipping a Q-tip or a piece of cheese cloth into the inoculum and gently rubbing it over the leaves. 400 grit carborundum was applied to the leaves before rubbing to cause injury and allow virons to enter cells. The leaves were then rinsed with distilled water to try to remove inhibitors that might be present in plant sap.

The plants were also inoculated using whitefly. The Brassicas were surrounded by infected plants that housed whitefly. After five days, the [Brassicas were separated from the other plants.] The plants were grown in a greenhouse for about three weeks and frequently examined for symptoms. Plants which showed mottling, severe leaf deformity and leaf speckling were judged to have the virus.

4

Photosynthesis and its Applications

Photosynthesis is arguably the most important biological process on earth. By liberating oxygen and consuming carbon dioxide, it has transformed the world into the hospitable environment we know today. Directly or indirectly, photosynthesis fills all of our food requirements and many of our needs for fiber and building materials. The energy stored in petroleum, natural gas and coal all came from the sun via photosynthesis, as does the energy in firewood, which is a major fuel in many parts of the world. This being the case, scientific research into photosynthesis is vitally important. If we can understand and control the intricacies of the photosynthetic process, we can learn how to increase crop yields of food, fiber, wood, and fuel, and how to better use our lands.

The energy-harvesting secrets of plants can be adapted to man-made systems which provide new, efficient ways to collect and use solar energy. These same natural "technologies" can help point the way to the design of new, faster, and more compact computers, and even to new medical breakthroughs. Because photosynthesis helps control the makeup of our atmosphere, understanding photosynthesis is crucial to understanding how carbon dioxide and other "greenhouse gases" affect the global climate.

Applications of Photosynthesis

Photosynthesis and Food

All of our biological energy needs are met by the plant kingdom, either directly or through herbivorous animals. Plants in turn obtain the energy to synthesize foodstuffs via photosynthesis. Although plants draw necessary materials from the soil and water and carbon dioxide from the air, the energy needs of the plant are filled by sunlight. Sunlight is pure energy. However, sunlight itself is not a very useful form of energy; it cannot be eaten, it cannot turn dynamos, and it cannot be stored. To be beneficial, the energy in sunlight must be converted to other forms. This is what photosynthesis is all about. It is the process by which plants change the energy in sunlight to kinds of energy that can be stored for later use.

Plants carry out this process in photosynthetic reaction centers. These tiny units are found in leaves, and convert light energy to chemical energy, which is the form used by all living organisms. One of the major energy-harvesting processes in plants involves using the energy of sunlight to convert carbon dioxide from the air into sugars, starches, and other high-energy carbohydrates. Oxygen is released in the process. Later, when the plant needs food, it draws upon the energy stored in these carbohydrates. We do the same. When we eat a plate of spaghetti, our bodies oxidize or "burn" the starch by allowing it to combine with oxygen from the air. This produces carbon dioxide, which we exhale, and the energy we need to survive. Thus, if there is no photosynthesis, there is no food. Indeed, one widely accepted theory explaining the extinction of the dinosaurs suggests that a comet, meteor, or volcano ejected so much material into the atmosphere that the amount of sunlight reaching the earth was severely reduced. This in turn caused the death of many plants and the creatures that depended upon them for energy.

Photosynthesis and energy

One of the carbohydrates resulting from photosynthesis is cellulose, which makes up the bulk of dry wood and other plant material. When we burn wood, we convert the cellulose back to carbon dioxide and release the stored energy as heat. Burning fuel is basically the same oxidation process that occurs in our bodies; it liberates the energy of "stored sunlight" in a useful form, and returns carbon dioxide to the atmosphere. Energy from burning "biomass" is important in many parts of the world. In developing countries, firewood continues to be critical to survival.

Ethanol (grain alcohol) produced from sugars and starches by fermentation is a major automobile fuel in Brazil, and is added to gasoline in some parts of the United States to help reduce emissions of harmful pollutants. Ethanol is also readily converted to ethylene, which serves as a feedstock to a large part of the petrochemical industry. It is possible to convert cellulcse to sugar, and then into ethanol; various microorganisms carry out this process. It could be commercially important one day.

Our major sources of energy, of course, are coal, oil and natural gas. These materials are all derived from ancient plants and animals, and the energy stored within them is chemical energy that originally came from sunlight through photosynthesis. Thus, most of the energy we use today was originally solar energy!

Photosynthesis, fiber, and materials

Wood, of course, is not only burned, but is an important material for building and many other purposes. Paper, for example, is nearly pure photosynthetically produced cellulose, as is cotton and many other natural fibers. Even wool production depends on photosynthetically-derived energy. In fact, all plant and animal products including many medicines and drugs require energy to produce, and that energy comes ultimately from sunlight via photosynthesis. Many of our other materials needs are filled by plastics and synthetic fibers which are produced from petroleum, and are thus also photosynthetic in origin. Even much of our metal refining depends ultimately on coal or other photosynthetic products. Indeed, it is difficult to name an economically important material or substance whose existence and usefulness is not in some way tied to photosynthesis.

Photosynthesis and the environment

Currently, there is a lot of discussion concerning the possible effects of carbon dioxide and other "greenhouse gases" on the environment. As mentioned above, photosynthesis converts carbon dioxide from the air to carbohydrates and other kinds of "fixed" carbon and releases oxygen to the atmosphere. When we burn firewood, ethanol, or coal, oil and other fossil fuels, oxygen is consumed, and carbon dioxide is released back to the atmosphere. Thus, carbon dioxide which was removed from the atmosphere over millions of years is being replaced very quickly through our consumption of these fuels.

The increase in carbon dioxide and related gases is bound to affect our atmosphere. Will this change be large or small, and will it be harmful or beneficial? These questions are being actively studied by many scientists today. The answers will depend strongly on the effect of photosynthesis carried out by land and sea organisms. As photosynthesis consumes carbon dioxide and releases oxygen, it helps counteract the effect of combustion of fossil fuels. The burning of fossil fuels releases not only carbon dioxide, but also hydrocarbons, nitrogen oxides, and other trace materials that pollute the atmosphere and contribute to long-term health and environmental problems. These problems are a consequence of the fact that nature has chosen to implement photosynthesis through conversion of carbon dioxide to energy-rich materials such as carbohydrates.

Why study photosynthesis? Because our quality of life, and indeed our very existence, depends on photosynthesis, it is essential that we understand it. Through understanding, we can avoid adversely affecting the process and precipitating environmental or ecological disasters. Through understanding, we can also learn to control photosynthesis, and thus enhance production of food, fiber and energy. Understanding the natural process, which has been developed by plants over several billion years, will also allow us to use the basic chemistry and physics of photosynthesis for other purposes, such as solar energy conversion, the design of electronic circuits, and the development of medicines and drugs.

Photosynthesis and agriculture

Although photosynthesis has interested mankind for eons, rapid progress in understanding the process has come in the last few years. One of the things we have learned is that overall, photosynthesis is relatively inefficient. For example, based on the amount of carbon fixed by a field of corn during a typical growing season, only about 1 - 2% of the solar energy falling on the field is recovered as new photosynthetic products. The efficiency of uncultivated plant life is only about 0.2%. In sugar cane, which is one of the most efficient plants, about 8% of the light absorbed by the plant is preserved as chemical energy.

Many plants, especially those that originate in the temperate zones such as most of the United States, undergo a process called photorespiration. This is a kind of "short circuit" of photosynthesis that wastes much of the plants' photosynthetic energy. The phenomenon of photorespiration including its function, if any, is only one of many riddles facing the photosynthesis researcher. If we can fully understand processes like photorespiration, we will have the ability to alter them. Thus, more efficient plants can be designed. Although new varieties of plants have been developed for centuries through selective breeding, the techniques of modern molecular biology have speeded up the process tremendously. Photosynthesis research can show us how to produce new crop strains that will make much better use of the sunlight they absorb. Research along these lines is critical, as recent studies show that agricultural production is leveling off at a time when demand for food and other agricultural products is increasing rapidly.

Because plants depend upon photosynthesis for their survival, interfering with photosynthesis can kill the plant. This is the basis of several important herbicides, which act by preventing certain important steps of photosynthesis. Understanding the details of photosynthesis can lead to the design of new, extremely selective herbicides and plant growth regulators that have the potential of being environmentally safe (especially to animal life, which does not carry out photosynthesis). Indeed, it is possible to develop new crop plants that are immune to specific herbicides, and to thus achieve weed control specific to one crop species.

Photosynthesis and energy production

As described above, most of our current energy needs are met by photosynthesis, ancient or modern. Increasing the efficiency of natural photosynthesis can also increase production of ethanol and other fuels derived from agriculture. However, knowledge gained from photosynthesis research can also be used to enhance energy production in a much more direct way.

Although the overall photosynthesis process is relatively wasteful, the early steps in the conversion of sunlight to chemical energy are quite efficient. Why not learn to understand the basic chemistry and physics of photosynthesis, and use these same principles to build man-made solar energy harvesting devices? This has been a dream of chemists for years, but is now close to becoming a reality. In the laboratory, scientists can now synthesize artificial photosynthetic reaction centers which rival the natural ones in terms of the amount of sunlight stored as chemical or electrical energy. More research will lead to the development of new, efficient solar energy harvesting technologies based on the natural process.

Photosynthesis and environment

How does photosynthesis in temperate and tropical forests and in the sea affect the quantity of greenhouse gases in the atmosphere? This is an important and controversial issue today. As mentioned above, photosynthesis by plants removes carbon dioxide from the atmosphere and replaces it with oxygen. Thus, it would tend to ameliorate the effects of carbon dioxide released by the burning of fossil fuels. However, the question is complicated by the fact that plants themselves react to the amount of carbon dioxide in the atmosphere.

Some plants, appear to grow more rapidly in an atmosphere rich in carbon dioxide, but this may not be true of all species. Understanding the effect of greenhouse gases requires a much better knowledge of the interaction of the plant kingdom with carbon dioxide than we have today. Burning plants and plant products such as petroleum releases carbon dioxide and other byproducts such as hydrocarbons and nitrogen oxides. However, the pollution caused by such materials is not a necessary product of solar energy utilization.

The artificial photosynthetic reaction centers discussed above produce energy without releasing any byproducts other than heat. They hold the promise of producing clean energy in the form of electricity or hydrogen fuel without pollution. Implementation of such solar energy harvesting devices would prevent pollution at the source, which is certainly the most efficient approach to control.

Photosynthesis and electronics

At first glance, photosynthesis would seem to have no association with the design of computers and other electronic devices. However, there is potentially a very strong connection. A goal of modern electronics research is to make transistors and other circuit components as small as possible. Small devices and short connections between them make computers faster and more compact. The smallest possible unit of a material is a molecule (made up of atoms of various types). Thus, the smallest conceivable transistor is a single molecule (or atom).

Many researchers today are investigating the intriguing possibility of making electronic components from single molecules or small groups of molecules. Another very active area of research is computers that use light, rather than electrons, as the medium for carrying information. In principle, light-based computers have several advantages over traditional designs, and indeed many of our telephone transmission and switching networks already operate through fiber optics. What does this have to do with photosynthesis? It turns out that photosynthetic reaction centers are natural photochemical switches of molecular dimensions.

Learning how plants absorb light, control the movement of the resulting energy to reaction centers, and convert the light energy to electrical, and finally chemical energy can help us understand how to make molecular-scale computers. In fact, several molecular electronic logic elements based on artificial photosynthetic reaction centers have already been reported in the scientific literature.

Photosynthesis and medicine

Light has a very high energy content, and when it is absorbed by a substance this energy is converted to other forms. When the energy ends up in the wrong place, it can cause serious damage to living organisms. Aging of the skin and skin cancer are only two of many deleterious effects of light on humans and animals. Because plants and other photosynthetic species have been dealing with light for eons, they have had to develop photoprotective mechanisms to limit light damage. Learning about the causes of light-induced tissue damage and the details of the natural photoprotective mechanisms can help us can find ways to adapt these processes for the benefit of humanity in areas far removed from photosynthesis itself.

For example, the mechanism by which sunlight absorbed by photosynthetic chlorophyll causes tissue damage in plants has been harnessed for medical purposes. Substances related to chlorophyll localize naturally in cancerous tumor tissue. Illumination of the tumors with light then leads to photochemical damage which can kill the tumor while leaving surrounding tissue unharmed. Another medical application involves using similar chlorophyll relatives to localize in tumor tissue, and thus act as dyes which clearly delineate the boundary between cancerous and healthy tissue. This diagnostic aid does not cause photochemical damage to normal tissue because the principles of photosynthesis have been used to endow it with protective agents that harmlessly convert the absorbed light to heat.

There was a color change, but students didn't make the connection between leaves having starch and the production of glucose as a product of photosynthesis. So, is it possible to create an environment in which students are engaged in learning a topic like photosynthesis but are not doing a laboratory activity? Is there some way for students to get content and the history of a topic without a lecture? The following activity is a result of my asking these very questions.

Several assumptions are behind this activity lesson. First, that knowledge is socially and individually constructed, that discussion among students is necessary for students to work out their own understanding, and that a more knowledgeable other is needed to facilitate learning. Second, that students can be engaged in inquiry without being involved in a firsthand investigation of real phenomena. And third, that the nature of science can be somewhat addressed by putting science in a historical perspective. So, if science ideas are built over time as new information is added to our body of knowledge, then looking at the information as if it were clues to a puzzle should help students piece together their own understanding of the phenomena.

Students work in small groups to piece together their own understanding of how a plant gets energy. After they cut the clues out, they sort them into categories, usually according to key words. Students bring different amounts of prior knowledge about the process of photosynthesis to the activity, which they readily share with their groups. In the end, students present how they solved the mystery by providing "evidence" from the clues.

Students leave this lesson having learned the facts about photosynthesis. They readily understand that green plants cannot live without water and air. They also piece together that air is a combination of many gases including carbon dioxide, and if hydrogen is combined with carbon dioxide, glucose can be made.

Students are also aware that over the years many scientists have contributed to the explanation of photosynthesis. And they realize that different scientists approached the question of what plants need to live in different ways and that our knowledge base has changed. Although they are not "experimenting," students do use the process skills of science: observing, classifying, recording, communicating, forming hypotheses, collecting data, and analyzing data. In addition, students are able to explain photosynthesis in words and in symbols. For any group having trouble, the public sharing of information usually corrects any misconceptions.

The best known form of photosynthesis is the one carried out by higher plants and algae, as well as by cyanobacteria and their relatives, which are responsible for a major part of photosynthesis in oceans. All these organisms convert CO_2 (carbon dioxide) to organic material by reducing this gas to carbohydrates in a rather complex set of reactions.

Electrons for this reduction reaction ultimately come from water, which is then converted to oxygen and protons. Energy for this process is provided by light, which is absorbed by pigments (primarily chlorophylls and carotenoids). Chlorophylls absorb blue and red light and carotenoids absorb blue-green light, but green and yellow light are not effectively absorbed by photosynthetic pigments in plants; therefore, light of these colors is either reflected by leaves or passes through the leaves. This is why plants are green.

Other photosynthetic organisms, such as cyanobacteria (formerly known as blue-green algae) and red algae, have additional pigments called phycobilins that are red or blue and that absorb the colors of visible light that are not effectively absorbed by chlorophyll and carotenoids. Yet other organisms, such as the purple and green bacteria (which, by the way, look fairly brown under many growth conditions), contain bacteriochlorophyll that absorbs in the infrared, in addition to in the blue part of the spectrum. These bacteria do not evolve oxygen, but perform photosynthesis under anaerobic (oxygen-less) conditions. These bacteria efficiently use infrared light for photosynthesis. Infrared is light with wavelengths above

700 nm that cannot be seen by the human eye; some bacterial species can use infrared light with wavelengths of up to 1000 nm.

However, most pigments are not very effective in absorbing ultraviolet light (<400 nm), which also cannot be seen by the human eye. Light with wavelengths below 330 nm becomes increasingly damaging to cells, but virtually all light at these short wavelengths is filtered out by the atmosphere (most prominently the ozone layer) before reaching the earth. Even though most plants are capable of producing compounds that absorb ultraviolet light, an increased exposure to light around 300 nm has detrimental effects on plant productivity.

Photosynthetic pigments come in a huge variety: there are many different types of (bacterio)chlorophyll, carotenoids, and phycobilins, differing from each other in their precise chemical structure. Pigments generally are bound to proteins, which provide the pigment molecules with the appropriate orientation and positioning with respect to each other. Light energy is absorbed by individual pigments, but is not used immediately by these pigments for energy conversion.

Instead, the light energy is transferred to chlorophylls that are in a special protein environment where the actual energy conversion event occurs: the light energy is used to transfer an electron to a neighboring pigment. Pigments and protein involved with this actual primary electron transfer event together are called the reaction center. A large number of pigment molecules (100-5000), collectively referred to as antenna, "harvest" light and transfer the light energy to the same reaction center. The purpose is to maintain a high rate of electron transfer in the reaction center, even at lower light intensities.

Many antenna pigments transfer their light energy to a single reaction center by having this energy "hop" to another antenna pigment, and yet to another, etc., until the energy is "trapped" in the reaction center. Each step of this energy transfer must be very efficient to avoid a large loss in the overall transfer process, and the association of the various pigments with proteins ensures that transfer efficiencies are high by having appropriate pigments close to each other, and by having an appropriate molecular geometry of the pigments with respect to each other. An exception to the rule of protein-bound pigments are green bacteria with very large antenna systems: a large part of these antenna systems consists of a "bag" (named chlorosome) of up to several thousand bacteriochlorophyll molecules that interact with each other and that are not in direct contact with protein.

In many systems the size of the photosynthetic antenna is flexible, and photosynthetic organisms growing at low light (in the shade, for example) generally will have a larger number of antenna pigments per reaction center than those growing at higher light intensity. However, at high light intensities (for example, in full sunlight) the amount of light that is absorbed by plants exceeds the capacity of electron transfer initiated by reaction centers.

Plants have developed means to convert some of the absorbed light energy to heat rather than to use the absorbed light necessarily for photosynthesis. However, in particular the first part of photosynthetic electron transfer in plants is rather sensitive to overly high rates of electron transfer, and part of the photosynthetic electron transport chain may be shut down when the light intensity is too high; this phenomenon is known as photoinhibition.

Photosynthetic Electron Transfer

The initial electron transfer (charge separation) reaction in the photosynthetic reaction center sets into motion a long series of redox (reduction-oxidation) reactions, passing the electron along a chain of cofactors and filling up the "electron hole" on the chlorophyll, much like in a bucket brigade. All photosynthetic organisms that produce oxygen have two types of reaction centers, named photosystem II and photosystem I (PS II and PS I, for short), both of which are pigment/protein complexes that are located in specialized membranes called thylakoids.

In eukaryotes (plants and algae), these thylakoids are located in chloroplasts (organelles in plant cells) and often are found in membrane stacks (grana). Prokaryotses (bacteria) do not have chloroplasts or other organelles, and photosynthetic pigment-protein complexes either are in the membrane around the cytoplasm or in invaginations there of (as is found, for example, in purple bacteria), or are in thylakoid membranes that form much more complex structures within the cell (as is the case for most cyanobacteria).

All chlorophyll in oxygenic organisms is located in thylakoids, and is associated with PS II, PS I, or with antenna proteins feeding energy into these photosystems. PS II is the complex where water splitting and oxygen evolution occurs. Upon oxidation of the reaction center chlorophyll in PS II, an electron is pulled from a nearby amino acid (tyrosine) which is part of the surrounding protein, which in turn gets an electron from the water-splitting complex. From the PS II reaction center, electrons flow to free electron carrying molecules (plastoquinone) in the thylakoid membrane, and from there to another membrane-protein complex, the cytochrome *b6f* complex.

The other photosystem, PS I, also catalyzes light-induced charge separation in a fashion basically similar to PS II: light is harvested by an antenna, and light energy is transferred to a reaction center chlorophyll, where light-induced charge separation is initiated. However, in PS I electrons are transfered eventually to NADP (nicotinamid adenosine dinucleotide phosphate), the reduced form of which can be used for carbon fixation. The oxidized reaction center chlorophyll eventually receives another electron from the cytochrome *b6f* complex. Therefore, electron transfer through PS II and PS I results in water oxidation (producing oxygen) and NADP reduction, with the energy for this process provided by light (2 quanta for each electron transported through the whole chain).

Carbon Fixation

Electron flow from water to NADP requires light and is coupled to generation of a proton gradient across the thylakoid membrane. This proton gradient is used for synthesis of ATP (adenosine triphosphate), a high-energy molecule. ATP and reduced NADP that resulted from the light reactions are used for CO_2 fixation in a process that is independent of light. CO_2 fixation involves a number of reactions that is referred to as the Calvin-Benson cycle. The initial CO_2 fixation reaction involves the enzyme ribulose-1,5-bisphosphate carboxylase/oxygenase (RuBisCO), which can react with either oxygen (leading to a process named photorespiration and not resulting in carbon fixation) or with CO_2.

The probability with which RuBisCO reacts with oxygen vs. with CO_2 depends on the relative concentrations of the two compounds at the site of the reaction. In all organisms CO_2 is by far the preferred substrate, but as the

CO_2 concentration is very much lower than the oxygen concentration, photorespiration does occur at significant levels. To boost the local CO_2 concentration and to minimize the oxygen tension, some plants (referred to as C_4 plants) have set aside some cells within a leaf (named bundle-sheath cells) to be involved primarily in CO_2 fixation, and others (named mesophyll cells) to specialize in the light reactions: ATP, CO_2 and reduced NADP in mesophyll cells is used for synthesis of 4-carbon organic acids (such as malate), which are transported to bundle sheath cells.

Here the organic acids are converted releasing CO_2 and reduced NADP, which are used for carbon fixation. The resulting 3-carbon acid is returned to the mesophyll cells. The bundle sheath cells generally do not have PS II activity, in order to minimize the local oxygen concentration. However, they retain PS I, presumably to aid in ATP synthesis. Even though C_4 plants have reduced amounts of photorespiration, the amount of ATP they need per amount of CO_2 fixed is a little higher than in other plants, and therefore their total production rate is similar to that of plants with higher rates of photorespiration.

Some plants living in desert climates, such as cacti, keep their stomates closed during the day to minimize evaporation (stomates are openings in the leaf surface to enhance gas exchange). These plants take up CO_2 during the night when the stomates are open, and temporarily bind the CO_2 to organic acids in the leaf. During the day the CO_2 is released from the acids and used for photosynthesis. Plants using this mechanism of CO_2 fixation are called CAM (Crassulacean Acid Metabolism) plants.

The amount of overall CO_2 fixation in plants growing under optimal conditions is limited primarily by the amount of CO_2 available. Therefore, the increase of CO_2 in the atmosphere will lead to somewhat higher rates of plant growth in environments where the CO_2 concentration limits growth rates. This is usually the case in an agricultural setting, where nutrients and water availability are not limiting. However, also in natural conditions, where limitations other than the CO_2 concentration will generally limit plant productivity, plant productivity has been found to often increase upon increasing the CO_2 concentration.

Photosynthesis and respiration

Virtually all oxygen in the atmosphere is thought to have been generated through the process of photosynthesis. Obviously, all respiring organisms (including plants) utilize this oxygen and produce CO_2. Thus, photosynthesis and respiration are interlinked, with each process depending on the products of the other. The global amount of photosynthesis is on the order of a trillion kg of dry organic matter produced per day, and respiratory processes convert about the same amount of organic matter to CO_2. A large part (probably the majority) of photosynthetic productivity occurs in open oceans, mostly by oxygenic prokaryotes. Without photosynthesis, the oxygen in the atmosphere would be depleted within several thousand years. It should be emphasized that plants respire just like any other higher organism, and that during the day this respiration is masked by a higher rate of photosynthesis.

Diversity of Photosynthetic Organisms

Even though plants are the most visible representatives of photosynthetic organisms, it should be emphasized that many other types of photosynthetic organisms exist. All photosynthetic bacteria other than the cyanobacteria and their relatives use only one photosystem, and for thermodynamic reasons they cannot use water as the ultimate electron donor. Instead, they can use reduced compounds such as H_2S as donor. However, CO_2 fixation occurs in these organisms. Some of these photosynthetic bacteria appear to have retained an evolutionary ancient arrangement of their photosynthetic apparatus, and are of interest for the analysis of evolutionary relationships of photosynthetic systems.

An extensive group of these photosynthetic bacteria, the heliobacteria, was discovered rather recently in the 1980s. The first representative of this group was isolated by the group of Dr. Howard Gest from a soil sample collected on the campus of Indiana University, and this isolation was the result of a fortunate coincidence of serendipitous events. Analysis of the heliobacterial reaction center has helped to lay the basis for the current concept that all photosynthetic reaction centers from the large variety of photosynthetic organisms are related to each other.

The majority of bacteria cannot be maintained in pure culture (that is, without other oganisms). This has essentially limited analysis of photosynthetic prokaryotes to the relatively small group of organisms that can be grown in pure culture. It is likely that the actual diversity of photosynthetic organisms is much larger than is known thus far. Indeed, species with novel photosynthetic properties are reported virtually every year. For example, recently an organism was reported that has chlorophyll d (a chlorophyll that is very rare in nature) as the main pigment. Moreover, several years ago, previously undetected and very small chlorophyll *a/b*-containing prokaryotes were recognized to be the major contributors to photosynthetic production in the open ocean. This emphasizes that much relating to biodiversity and photosynthesis is still to be discovered, and that these discoveries are not limited to tropical rainforests and other ecological settings of large popular interest.

In eukaryotes, photosynthesis takes place in the chloroplast, which has long been known to have prokaryotic features. Chloroplasts are thought to have evolved from a cyanobacterium (or close relative) that was in a symbiotic relationship with a eukaryotic, non-photosynthetic cell and was engulfed inside this cell. The cyanobacterium and the eukaryotic cell presumably were in a mutually beneficial relationship (endosymbiosis), with the photosynthetic organism sharing some of its produced carbohydrates with the host, and the host providing the photosynthetic bacterium with other compounds.

The prokaryote slowly gave up its independence as well as its cell wall, and some of its genetic information was transferred to the nucleus of its eukaryotic host. The resulting chloroplast maintains a small, prokaryote-like circular DNA of its own (DNA is material carrying genetic information); this DNA contains the genetic blueprint to make many of the membrane proteins needed in the chloroplast, which apparently are not easily targeted to and/or transported into the chloroplast. Occasionally, photosynthetic organisms are found where the chloroplast has retained a little more of the original cyanobacterial features. For example, in algae such as Cyanophora paradoxa plastids (called cyanelles) are found that resemble cyanobacteria in their overall morphology as well as in the fact that they are surrounded by a cell wall.

Not all chloroplasts have resulted from a single endosymbiotic event, but apparently from multiple events that occurred independently. Chloroplasts from higher plants and many green algae probably all result from the same endosymbiotic event, whereas chloroplasts from red and brown algae and from diatoms are the result of one or more other events. The situation is even more complicated in cryptomonads, a type of algae, and chlorachniophytes, photosynthetic amoebae, which apparently are the result of an endosymbiotic event of a eukaryotic alga in a eukaryotic host. The nucleus of the endosymbiont has been mostly degraded, resulting in a chloroplast enveloped by four membranes.

Chlorophyll is used by all photosynthetic organisms as the link between excitation energy transfer and electron transfer. Of particular note is the rate with which these transfer reactions need to occur. As the lifetime of the excited state is only several nanoseconds (1 nanosecond (ns) is 10^{-9} s), after absorption of a quantum, energy transfer and charge separation in the reaction center must have occurred within this time period. Energy transfer rates between pigments are very rapid, and charge separation in reaction centers occurs in 3-30 picoseconds (1 picosecond (ps) is 10^{-12} s).

Subsequent electron transfer steps are significantly slower (200 ps - 20 ms) but, nonetheless, the electron transport chain is sufficiently fast that at least a significant part of the absorbed sunlight can be used for photosynthesis. However, in the presence of excess light, damage may occur, which may originate from the formation of chlorophyll in "triplet state". In a triplet state two electrons in the outer shell have identical rather than opposite spin orientation. This triplet chlorophyll readily reacts with oxygen, leading to the very reactive singlet oxygen, which can damage proteins. To counter this damaging reaction, carotenoids are usually present in close vicinity to chlorophylls.

Many carotenoids efficiently "quench" triplet states of chlorophyll, thus avoiding formation of singlet oxygen. Chlorophyll in its free form is very toxic in the light in the presence of oxygen, because a close interaction with carotenoids is not always available under such circumstances. Therefore, all chlorophyll in a cell in aerobic organisms is bound to proteins, generally with carotenoids bound to the same protein.

Structure Determinations

Because of the strict requirements of positioning of pigments and electron transfer intermediates to allow efficient electron transfer and minimal damage, the structure of pigment-protein complexes involved in photosynthesis is critical. With the exception of specific antenna complexes (such as phycobilisomes in cyanobacteria and chlorosomes in green bacteria), pigment-binding proteins are usually hydrophobic membrane proteins. This initially hampered attempts to elucidate the structure of these complexes, as membrane proteins do not readily form the well-ordered crystals that are needed for high-resolution X-ray diffraction studies.

However, in the 1980s the first structure of a membrane protein complex, the photosynthetic reaction center from a purple bacterium, was determined at high resolution (about 3 Å; in comparison, the distance between neighboring atoms in a molecule is about 1 Å). Investigators from the Max Planck Institute in Martinsried (Germany) who were involved with this work, most notably Hartmut Michel and Johann Deisenhofer, received a Nobel Prize in chemistry for this research. Since then, the structure of various reaction centers and antenna complexes has been determined at resolutions between 2 and 4 Å.

Similarities Between Reaction Centers

Surprisingly, structural comparison of reaction centers from different photosynthetic systems showed that these reaction centers are basically similar to each other in terms of their overall three-dimensional structure. The basic reaction center unit consists of a protein complex with 10 transmembrane helices originating from either two identical protein subunits or from two similar polypeptides of common evolutionary origin. Each of these polypeptides contribute five membrane-spanning helices, and bind 2-3 chlorophylls (or, in the case of anoxygenic bacteria, bacteriochlorophylls).

The fourth membrane spans from each subunit are held together by two chlorophylls, which are the chlorophylls in the reaction center that can be oxidized (give up an electron) upon excitation. Directly associated with the reaction center are proteins that bind antenna pigments. In the case of PS I and similarly organized reaction centers from green and heliobacteria, the antenna portion, with six transmembrane helices, is attached to the N-terminal end of the reaction center proteins.

Photosynthesis has been studied in significant detail and photosynthetic systems are used frequently for development and application of advanced technologies, because photosynthetic systems are fairly well understood, are complex, and often undergo rather unusual biochemical reactions. Some examples are provided below.

Rapid electron transfer reactions

A major difficulty in measuring enzyme kinetics at relatively short time scales (less than 1 ms) is that "traditional" enzyme reactions require a mixing of substrate and enzyme, which usually takes a relatively long time. Kinetic analysis of light-driven reactions such as photosynthetic electron transport have a great advantage in this respect: reactions can be triggered simply by a light pulse, which can be even shorter than 1 ps. Moreover, many of the components participating in electron transfer have different absorption spectra depending on whether they are in the oxidized or reduced form.

Using laser spectroscopy methods or more standard optical spectroscopy, it is relatively simple to follow the electron around on a timescale between 1 ps and several ms. The primary charge separation occurs in several ps, and reactions become gradually slower as they involve components that are further away from the reaction center. Because of the fast speed of early reactions, the electron and the "electron hole" are physically separated rapidly by a large distance (the electron generally has traveled about 2 nm to the other side of the membrane within 1 ns after charge separation), so that back reactions (charge recombinations) are not favorable anymore.

Unpaired electrons on reactants that are transiently formed during redox reactions involving transfer of a single electron in many instances can be detected using electron paramagnetic resonance (EPR) and derived techniques (including ENDOR, electron nuclear double resonance, and ESEEM, electron spin echo envelope modulation). Many of these techniques can be used to kinetically follow redox reactions, and provide detailed information regarding electron spin distributions etc. Therefore, photosynthetic membranes and reaction centers have a prominent place as experimental systems in biochemistry and biophysics.

Reaction centers are essentially an assembly of cofactors, held in the appropriate position and orientation by the protein environment. Several groups have used the natural system as a model to design organic molecules where the equivalents of the different cofactors are linked together by covalent bonds of various lengths. The result is the creation of a number of sophisticated molecules that serve as "artificial reaction centers".

The more advanced molecules consist of two chlorophyll-type molecules linked together (one serves as the electron donor, the other as the acceptor), with the electron-accepting molecule linked to two quinones, which serve as electron acceptors in the natural system. The electron donating chlorophyll analog is linked covalently to a carotenoid, which can donate an electron to the oxidized chlorophyll. Upon excitation of the chlorophyll, a charge separation occurs resulting in an oxidized carotenoid and a reduced quinone. This charge-separated state is formed with high efficiency.

Such molecules can be introduced into liposomes (artificial membrane vesicles) in a specific orientation, and when these are excited by light, a charge separation will occur across the liposome membrane. This results in an electric potential or proton gradient across the liposome membrane, which may be used for a variety of purposes, including ATP synthesis.

Genetic modification and protein engineering

Because of the ease of detailed functional analysis of reactions and their rates in photosynthetic systems, reaction center complexes are frequently used to determine the consequences of small alterations in the polypeptides on the functional characteristics of the cofactors. Changes at single amino acid residues in the reaction center complex are sufficient to introduce large changes in the properties of cofactors, which in turn leads to altered electron transfer rates and efficiencies.

Single amino acid changes at specific sites in the protein are easily introduced by genetic modification techniques, and resulting functional changes can be studied. An elegant example of such an approach is the modification of the midpoint redox potential of the bacteriochlorophyll in the reaction center of purple bacteria. The midpoint redox potential is correlated with the ease with which an electron is given off after excitation and is taken up by the oxidized bacteriochlorophyll. Jim Allen, JoAnn Williams and coworkers at Arizona State University found that creating or deleting hydrogen bonds between the protein and the bacteriochlorophyll changed the midpoint redox potential of this bacteriochlorophyll in a rather predictable manner. In this way, reaction center complexes can be built with different oxidizing strengths, and effects on reaction rates and ultimately the effectiveness of alternate electron donors can be determined.

Mutational analysis of photosynthesis proteins is simple in several bacterial systems. The reasons why this is so in selected cyanobacteria and purple and green bacteria are that

1. foreign DNA is taken up by the cell spontaneously or is introduced easily by other means such as electroporation ("electric shock"),
2. once the DNA is inside it is incorporated into the organism's genome at one predictable and specific site by means of a process named homologous double recombination, and
3. the organism can be propagated without relying on photosynthesis, for example using an added carbohydrate source.

Genetic approaches involving directed mutagenesis as described above have proven to be very useful in studying photosynthetic electron transfer and will be of increasing relevance for the design of photosynthetic organisms for biotechnological uses. By this method the function of a large number of genes has been probed, and the role of individual domains and residues has been determined. Genomic sequencing projects are very useful in this respect, and the complete DNA sequence of one photosynthetic organism is already known. From the DNA sequence, the potential of the organism can be determined.

Genetic modification of higher plants

Globally, improving plant productivity by genetic means has been an important goal for many years. Even though initially it was hoped that crop productivity could be boosted by "improving" the photosynthesis process, it has become increasingly apparent that improved productivity will be best accomplished by genetic modification of crop plants to introduce insect or pathogen resistance, or to yield improved vitality under marginal conditions (for example, at high salinity, which has become a significant factor in many agricultural areas because of continued irrigation). A pertinent example is the development of varieties of cotton and other crops that express a pro-toxin from a bacterium, Bacillus thuringiensis, that is converted to a toxin in the midgut of particular insects such as caterpillars but not in other life forms. This allows efficient biological control as long as the insects do not develop resistance to this compound.

Genetic modifications to intrinsically and significantly improve the photosynthesis process have not yet been successful. The reason for the apparent inability to "improve" the photosynthesis process itself presumably is related to the fact that photosynthetic systems have evolved over a relatively long period of time, and that the selection factors have not changed significantly in recent history. This has led to the emergence of a very effective photosynthetic apparatus that is difficult to improve upon by simply changing some amino acid residues or by introducing or deleting some genes. If relatively simple changes could have significantly improved the photosynthesis process per se, Mother Nature would have already found these as natural mutations are rather frequent.

However, it is possible that significant progress in this area can made in the future, if new design paradigms for enzyme function and specificity can be developed. For example, if protein structures (particularly the structure of the active site) can be better modeled and predicted, one should be able to further improve upon the RuBisCO specificity of CO_2 vs. oxygen. It is also important in this respect to determine what the rate-limiting step in the process is under natural conditions. Even though more effective light capture by crop plants might be considered by introduction of antenna pigments that absorb in the green and yellow region of the light spectrum, light capture and the light reactions usually are not limiting plant productivity in agricultural settings. Therefore, such modifications in a plant will result in increased productivity only in light-limiting settings.

Photosynthetic Characteristics of Vertical Distribution Seaweeds

Since seaweeds play an important role as producers in a marine ecosystem, they are one of the key organisms in teaching marine ecology. Additionally, they are appropriate materials in teaching the diversity and unity of plants. In spite of such importance, there have been only a small number of studies on the use of seaweeds in teaching biology or on the development of student laboratory exercises.

In Japan, people are familiar with seaweeds because they eat many kinds. However, there is very little subject matter concerning algae, especially seaweeds, in biology education at schools. Under the Japanese new science curriculum standards, there are no chapters on algae at elementary school level and little time can be allotted to study seaweeds at junior high school level. Thus, Japanese students have only a few opportunities to study algae, especially seaweeds, during the nine years of compulsory education.

Although some seaweeds have been shown to be useful materials for experiments in teaching photosynthesis, no laboratory exercises using living seaweeds for teaching photosynthesis currently appear in Japanese junior high school science textbooks. There are several reasons why seaweeds have rarely been used as teaching materials. Firstly, most science teachers are not familiar with using seaweeds. Secondly, for most science teachers in schools don't find it easy to obtain fresh seaweeds, especially in inland schools; and thirdly, if fresh seaweeds can be obtained it might be difficult to keep them fresh until use.

Conditions for culturing seaweeds in junior high school science laboratories and ways to use these cultured seaweeds for detecting photosynthetic activity qualitatively in junior high school science classes. The red seaweed Mastocarpus yendoi (Gigartina mamillosa) Masuda et Yoshida was found to be very useful material for many laboratory exercises in biology at the primary and secondary levels because it can be cultured for about a month under controlled conditions and also under room conditions. The alga is a good experimental material for teaching photosynthesis, because it allows students to realise that not only green plants, but also some other plants whose colours are not green can photosynthesise.

The zonation (vertical distribution) of plants is an interesting topic in ecology. So far, the topic has been taught only using terrestrial plants. However, the vertical distribution of seaweeds is observed in seashore communities and is useful for teaching the zonation of plants. This phenomenon is closely related to the photosynthetic characteristics of seaweeds and is also useful for teaching the relationships between the photosynthetic characteristics of seaweeds and environmental factors such as light.

There is an apparent vertical distribution (zonation) of seaweeds in seashore communities, in which green ones occur at the higher position, brown ones at the middle, and red ones at the lower position of the intertidal and subtidal zones. For many years, this phenomenon has been thought to be explained by the theory of complementary chromatic adaptation, which came from Engelmann's experiments in the 1880s and has now been shown to be inaccurate. Actually, the growth of seaweeds is limited by the spectral distribution (light quality) as well as by the intensity of light (light quantity).

The zonation is caused by the differences in the photosynthetic pigments that each seaweed group possesses. Yokohama showed the different photosynthetic responses of a green seaweed occurring at an upper position in the intertidal zone and a red seaweed occurring at 20 m in depth. The green one could not photosynthesise under green light at the same rate as under white light. On the other hand, the photosynthetic rates of the red seaweed under green light and white light were the same.

Living Seaweeds in Teaching Photosynthesis

In Japan living seaweeds are thought to be too difficult to use in laboratory exercises for teaching photosynthesis in secondary schools. However, this seems merely to be speculation because there have only been a small number of studies on introducing seaweeds into laboratory exercises related to photosynthesis. Jinno and Fujita used seaweeds to detect photosynthetic activity by an improved Indigo Carmine Method and introduced the experiment in senior high school biology classes. However, they did not consider how to prepare materials for laboratory exercises in an inland school. They also did not discuss how the experiment could be introduced into junior high school science classes. In addition, their laboratory exercise was not a quantitative experiment.

Furthermore, since these seaweeds can be cultured under classroom conditions for at least two weeks, they can be used in laboratory classes during that entire period. These seaweeds occur in the upper or middle positions of intertidal zones and can tolerate considerable temperature changes so could be sent with seawater in a bottle by post from a coastal area to an inland school.

These seaweeds, therefore, can be used as well as Cladophora rudolphiana, which could be cultured using a commercial artificial seawater under laboratory conditions and could be used for measuring photosynthetic rates quantitatively. With the exception of a few matured fronds of both seaweeds, there were no considerable differences in the photosynthetic activities of fresh fronds collected at different sites during the period from April to September. This is the best season to collect these seaweeds, because the low ebb occurs in daytime and the habitat of these seaweeds can easily be accessed.

Teaching zonation (vertical distribution) by using seaweeds

The difference in their photosynthetic responses to white and green light appears to be related to the difference in the colours of their fronds. This is because of the difference in their accessory photosynthetic pigments. Most green algae do not have any accessory photosynthetic pigments that can absorb green light. On the other hand, red algae contain phycoerythrin as an accessory photosynthetic pigment, so they can absorb green light and use the light energy for photosynthesis. In deeper sea areas, only blue-green light can penetrate. Thus, red seaweeds can grow in such areas where ordinary green seaweeds cannot grow. This is one of the causes of the vertical distribution of seaweeds and could be an interesting topic in plant ecology at the secondary level.

In the laboratory exercise developed, students are required to measure photosynthetic rates of seaweeds under white light and green light quantitatively. There are some methods and equipment to measure photosynthetic oxygen evolution from seaweeds quantitatively.

Future Directions

Light energy is cheap, clean, and essentially inexhaustible. With limited supplies of fossil fuel and increasing concern about CO_2 emissions, further development of technologies that make use of solar energy is inevitable. Current silicon-based technologies for the harvesting of solar energy require a very energy-intensive production process and even though they have improved significantly over the years in their efficiency, further development of photosynthesis-based technologies for energy collection is certainly warranted.

However, photosynthesis and related processes can be applied to many more areas than just solar energy conversion. Realizing that novel designs and applications of light-mediated processes have enormous promise in the next decade and beyond, Arizona State University has started an initiative, Project Ingenhousz, named after the 18th century physician who discovered that light is needed for oxygen evolution by plants, and that only green parts of the plant carry out this process.

The goal of the initiative is to capitalize on research progress and ideas in this area, and to more effectively interface academia, where many of the discoveries are made, with the private sector, where such discoveries are worked out further and applied. For example, there are a myriad of possible applications of artificial reaction centers and related molecules in nanotechnology. Many synthetic pigments also have found biomedical uses in tumor detection, as they -for unknown reasons- tend to accumulate preferentially in tumors and are highly fluorescent and thus easily detectable in a patient whom is being operated on to surgically remove a tumor.

In the biotechnology field, photosynthetic organisms are likely to play an increasing role in (over)production of enzymes, pharmaceuticals, nutraceuticals, etc., which until now are produced primarily by genetically modified heterotrophic microorganisms such as yeast and selected bacteria. A major advantage of photosynthetic organisms is that no fixed-carbon source needs to be added for growth and, therefore, production costs are lower and the chances of contamination with other microorganisms are less.

There are several ways to modify organisms to have them (over)produce useful compounds. One is to introduce specific genes under a strong promoter, leading to high expression of these genes and to synthesis of a "new" enzyme. Another way is to delete genes so that substrates will accumulate. For this to be optimally successful the metabolic pathways of an organism need to be fairly well understood, and genomic DNA sequences are an important step in this direction.

A third way to produce a new compound is to utilize an existing enzyme and to modify the site where the substance to be converted (the substrate) binds, so that a different substrate can be bound and a different product can be formed. With any of these approaches, selection for randomly generated combinatorial mutants with specific properties also has been proven to be effective. With an increasing arsenal of genomic sequences, and with improving knowledge regarding determinants of protein structure and cofactor binding, any of these three approaches are very promising.

Another potential application of photosynthetic organisms is in bioremediation. Bioremediation is the clean-up of environmental (soil or water) pollutants by biological means. An example is the biological breakdown of toxic organic compounds into innocuous products. Also, remediation of nitrate from drinking water supplies is becoming an increasingly pressing issue. The advantage of using photosynthetic organisms is that no external energy source needs to be provided for growth of the organism if it is in the light, making these organisms very suitable for remediation of aqueous surface environments.

Another utilization of photosynthetic organisms is to have these organisms use solar energy to produce clean-burning fuels. Even under natural conditions some photosynthetic systems such as algae can produce hydrogen, which probably is the cleanest fuel as it reacts with oxygen to produce water. However, the cheapest and most universal electron donor of all, water, upon oxidation in PS II forms oxygen, which is not very safe in combination with hydrogen. For this reason methods have been sought to temporally separate oxygen evolution and hydrogen production in algae; in the laboratory this can be achieved by sulfur deprivation, which preferentially inhibits photosynthesis.

Another option would be to use photosynthetic organisms for methane production. Even though methane upon combustion will form CO_2, the overall atmospheric CO_2 balance would not be disturbed as an equal amount of CO_2 will have been taken out of the atmosphere upon methane production by the photosynthetic organism. Research in photosynthesis in all its facets has proven to have opened many doors in a variety of disciplines, ranging from biophysics to plant physiology. Progress has been driven by an interdisciplinary approach to this complex, yet fascinating, spectrum of problems, challenges, and opportunities. Photosynthesis is the basis of our food and energy supply, and innovative utilization of solar energy is likely to be of increasingly critical importance in the future. This, together with novel uses of photosynthetic principles for other purposes, make it likely that photosynthesis and its applications will help to shape an increasingly broad area of exciting discoveries and innovative ideas.

5

Applied Ethnobotany

Ethnobotany has been defined as the discipline concerned with the interactions between people and plants. There are many aspects of Ethnobotany, including the ways that people name and classify plants, the values placed on them, their uses and their management. It reaches across the natural and social sciences. Plants have always been of central significance to human welfare and always will be. Plants provide people with food, fuel and medicine, as well as materials for construction and the manufacture of crafts and many other products. Their chemical and genetic constituents are being increasingly explored for human benefit. They are major parts of the physical worlds which people inhabit and in which they construct their realities.

They lie at the base of food-webs, supporting most other forms of life. The central role of plants in the everyday lives of rural people is obvious in developing countries, with the daily round of activities revolving around agriculture, the care of domestic animals, the gathering of fuelwood, the cooking and eating of largely plant-based food, the construction of buildings and fences, the use of herbal medicine, and so on.

Ethnobotany can be applied for many practical purposes, among which McClatchey and his co-authors have listed land-use development, agriculture, forestry, cultural conservation, education and the development of the health food and herbal medicine industries. Applied Ethnobotany draws on both personal (including traditional) and scientific forms of knowledge, allowing comparisons and integration for the benefits of conservation and sustainable development. In the past, ethnobotanical studies have all too often been just academic exercises or have served only external interests, with the results benefiting neither local people nor conservation.

The fundamental strengths of applying the approaches and methods of Applied Ethnobotany are that:

— They allow the knowledge, wisdom and practices of local people to play fuller roles in identifying and finding solutions to problems of conservation and sustainable development.

— Local people are involved fundamentally in investigations so that there is a better chance of 'buy-in'.

— Realistic case-studies of ways of balancing conservation with use become available to inform the evolution of national and other higher level policies.

Among the particular challenges to which Applied Ethnobotany can contribute are :

— Conservation of plants (including varieties of crops) and other forms of biological diversity.

— Botanical inventories and assessments of the conservation status of species.

— Sustainability in supplies of wild plant resources, including of non-timber products.

— Enhanced food security, nutrition and healthcare.

— Preservation, recovery and diffusion of local botanical knowledge and wisdom.

— Reinforcement of ethnic and national identity.

— Greater security of land tenure and resource ownership.

— Assertion of the rights of local and indigenous people.

— Agreements on the rights of communities in protected areas.

— Identification and development of new economic products from plants, for instance crafts, foods, herbal medicines and horticultural plants.

— Contributions to new drug development.

The betterment of rural livelihoods is a complex task and it is not suggested that Applied Ethnobotany is a universal panacea. Natural resource issues are only part of wider livelihood issues, and botanical issues only part of natural resource issues. There will always be uncertainties about how people will perceive their future options and the livelihood strategies that they will adopt. However, what is certain is that most rural people in developing countries will contin-ue to be heavily reliant on local wild plants.

Further, it is the poorest people, in particular, who will remain most dependent on resources of wild plants and who stand most to gain if these resources are managed in sustainable ways. Applied Ethnobotany can therefore play a significant part in the battle to relieve poverty.

Many people have been consulted to produce the present synthesis, which certainly will require revision with time and as other experiences are incorporated. Each course or programme is expected to differ in detail, moulded as appropriate to the contexts of particular departments, universities and countries or regions. On the other hand, it is noteworthy that findings of the consultations undertaken for the present project show an unexpected degree of agreement about the contents of courses and programmes in Applied Ethnobotany and on how they should be taught. There appears to be an emerging consensus. Ethnobotany is sometimes seen as a 'soft' subject, but, actually, it can and should be intellectually demanding for both staff and students.

As Janice Alcorn has commented : "The ethnobotanical field worker observes the living system of which plant use is a part. Careful observation is not, however, an easy job. It requires looking at human activities and organisations from a plant's viewpoint and looking at plants and plant communities from a culturally informed as well as a scientific perspective. Only by looking at the material in this way can the ethnobotanical field worker recognise links between the subunits investigated by researchers in different disciplines. Methods of different disciplines reveal different aspects of the system under study ... . It is up to the fieldexperienced worker to integrate the data and spot new areas requiring investigation."

Ethnobotanists are faced with a continuing learning process throughout their careers. There is much to gain from the sharing of experiences and ideas within countries and internationally, though barriers of language remain a challenge, as between anglophone and francophone Africa. Networking is an invaluable tool. No-one has all the answers. Progress in developing courses or programmes in Applied Ethnobotany will depend greatly on the sharing of experiences and the learning of lessons by those who are practically involved.

It is anticipated that Ethnobotany will become a powerful field of scientific activity in the 21st Century. Unusually for a modern academic subject, there are particular opportunities for innovative contributions from ethnobotanists from developing countries. The advantages of such ethnobotanists can include personal experience of the problems that rural people face, intuitive appreciation of local cultures, and knowledge of local languages. Ethnobotanical research requires relatively little equipment and is cheap compared with many other fields of science.

Ethnobotany is a key subject for conservation and sustainable development. Capacitybuilding in Applied Ethnobotany is urgently needed in developing countries because of the intimate links between rural people and local plants. This is not to say that Applied Ethnobotany is not also useful as a taught subject in industrial countries, including to train people able to explore the many, largely hidden, economic dependencies of people in such countries on plants and the implications of consumer cultures for conservation. Furthermore, some ethnobotanists from industrialised countries will become involved in collaborative research with colleagues in the developing world.

ETHNOBOTANY: SCOPE AND STATUS

Ethnobotany: Past and Present

The first published use of the term 'Ethnobotany' was by John Harshberger in 1896, referring to a botanical culture revealed through archaeological research in the Mancos Canyon, Colorado, USA. From this start, the scope of the subject has expanded to include studies of modern cultures, greater interdisciplinarity and, more recently, greater attention to its applications to conservation and sustainable development. It is a science that has been rapidly evolving, a state of affairs that will likely continue for some time.

Many early studies, as some still are today, were largely or entirely descriptive, being concerned essentially with documenting the local names and uses of plants. Attention was commonly directed towards more indigenous communities rather than peasants (i.e. non-indigenous local people), not infrequently with a bias towards medicinal plants. By and large, these studies have proved of little practical value to the local people who provided the information. For example, many studies of medicinal plants in Polynesia have been insufficiently interdisciplinary and with inadequate attention to local concepts of medical conditions to be of much value for devising improvements in healthcare. Not infrequently, Ethnobotany has been used as a means of extracting knowledge of the uses of plants, especially as medicines, from communities, with the aim of developing new commercial products elsewhere.

Over the last decade in particular, Ethnobotany has tended to become more analytical, quantitative, cross-disciplinary and multiinstitutional. Ethnobotanists are now much more engaged with questions of conservation, sustainable development, cultural affirmation, and the intellectual property rights of local and indigenous people. A growing inclusion of ecology is leading to new insights into the origin and dynamics of tropical ecosystems. Several stages in the historical progress of the subject in Africa have been recognised:

— an initial emphasis on recording vernacular names and uses;

— a broadening to include more work on nutritional and chemical analyses of edible and wild plants;

— investigations into the quantities of materials used and/or the frequency of use;

— quantitative studies of human impacts on plant resources, particularly those entering commercial trade; and

— valuations of plant resources.

Worldwide, some of the major developments have been:

— A widening of Ethnobotany from a focus on indigenous people to embrace all sections of humanity.

— A greater use of anthropological methods to comprehend better how, and why, people classify, value, and give symbolic significance to plants.

— A growing awareness that ethnobotanical knowledge should be appreciated as part of wider knowledge-systems or 'cognitive matrices'.

— Greater scientific rigour in terms of setting and testing hypotheses, and quantification.

— More emphasis on participatory research aimed directly at the identification and resolution of practical problems of conservation and sustainable development.

— Greater recognition of the intellectual property rights of local and indigenous people, especially respect for secret medical knowledge and acknowledgement of the need to provide a fair return of benefits to the local level when research aims at the identification of new commercial products.

Wade Davis has expounded on some of the challenges facing contemporary ethnobotanists : "Ethnobotanists must record not only lists of plant uses but a vision of life itself.

This is the second and much more difficult task - to understand not just how a specific group of people uses plants but how that group perceives them, how it interprets those perceptions, how those perceptions influence the activities of members of that society, and how those activities, in turn, influence the ambient vegetation and the ecosystem upon which the society depends."

Apart from its theoretical significance, Ethnobotany is emerging as a subject of great practical value. Its application can lead to a strengthening of cultural diversity and conservation, greater sustainability in the exploitation of plant resources, and the development of new plant products. It has helped in Latin America (and doubtless elsewhere) to change the image of local people so that organisations that make decisions about development have more respect for the cultures and authority of rural communities, resulting in a search for ways to collaborate under conditions of respect and equality.

Ethnobotanical research can sometimes be a form of cultural rescue. It enables the recording and documentation of traditional knowledge about the empirical uses of plants - knowledge which is widely disappearing. The rescue and documentation of traditional knowledge can contribute to the strengthening of indigenous cultures. It can result in the demonstration of the value of cultural diversity within the context of the processes of globalisation, modernisation and integration of indigenous peoples into national societies.

The People and Plants Initiative was started in 1992, as a partnership between WWF, UNESCO and the Royal Botanic Gardens, Kew. Its aim has been to build capacity in Ethnobotany among individuals and institutions in the developing world. It has tried to contribute to the development of Applied Ethnobotany and its practical adoption around the world. Activities have included the training of young ethnobotanists, support for the development of networks and courses, and the dissemination of case-studies and methodologies through the production and distribution of publications and videos. There have been national or regional programmes with co-ordinated series of activities in several countries in Africa, Asia, Latin America, and the South Pacific.

Ethnobotany is closely related to several other subjects. One of these, Economic Botany (known as Plant Resources in China), has been established longer. It concentrates on plant products and their uses. The core components of courses in Economic Botany cover categories of plant product, such as wood, resin and fragrances, with less attention given to the social and cultural dimensions of using and managing plant resources than is the case with Ethnobotany. In practice, there can be considerable overlap in the contents of courses in the two subjects.

Economic Botany is similar to Wild Plant Utilisation, a full programme of which is taught at Northeast China Agricultural University. Ethnoecology, a term introduced in 1954 and more concerned with the ecological basis of human relations with the environment, is less focused on botanical aspects of the environment than Ethnobotany or Ethnobiology. Conservation Biology is more strictly concerned with conservation than Ethnobotany. In practice, courses in the subject often have inadequate coverage, not only of plants, but also of the social, cultural, economic and communication aspects of conservation.

These deficiencies are unfortunate, even if the prime interest of a conservation biologist is to protect species of charismatic animals, because the retention of suitable habitat generally requires support from the local populace, and this support is more likely to be forthcoming if conservationists pay attention to the needs of local people for plant resources, so important to their livelihoods. Medical Botany, once a major part of the education of doctors in Europe, is still taught in some countries, for instance to students of integrated medicine in China, and in more than 30 universities and colleges teaching Traditional Chinese Medicine in the same country.

Ethnobotany is a universal subject in terms of its theory, but it will contribute little to the intellectual life of a country or to the resolution of practical problems, unless it becomes well embedded within educational and training institutions, and in practice. This means the emergence of a critical mass of national ethnobotanists who are knowledgeable, active and ethical. Thus, the development of courses and programmes within countries is vital.

In India, Ethnobotany emerged as a distinct discipline in the early 1970s, when much documentation of the uses of plants by tribal groups in Central India was undertaken under the leadership of Professor S K Jain, Director of the Botanical Survey of India. The work was later extended elsewhere, for instance into the south of the country. A training course in Ethnobotany was initiated in 1988. Respect for Ethnobotany, as a significant subject for development, grew from the mid-1990s, with greater emphasis on applications to rural problems. Research in Ethnobotany has contributed greatly towards developing approaches for the enhancement of the use of indigenous knowledge in rural development.

Interest in Ethnobotany has also been growing rapidly elsewhere in the subcontinent. Ethnobotanical research started in Nepal in about 1970 and has since become a popular subject of research. As in India, there has been movement in other countries of the subcontinent during the 1990s, away from just documentation of local uses of plants towards more participatory approaches to the identification and solving of problems of plant conservation and sustainable use.

Ethnobotany as a taught subject

For the purpose of discussion, a distinction is made between a course and a programme. A course is taken to be a relatively brief period of study, for example a one-week course for professionals or a module within a programme (e.g. a unit of Ethnobotany within an undergraduate programme in Botany). A programme is longer in duration, being a subject of graduation or else a tailored package of several courses designed to give an effective education in Ethnobotany within the context of a wider degree programme.

There is no doubt that the number of courses in Ethnobotany is increasing. A survey of the teaching of Economic Botany in the USA, undertaken in 1963, found 110 universities offering single courses in this subject, though only 5 at graduate level. A growing demand from students was reported. There were no courses actually entitled Ethnobotany, which at the time had yet to be regarded as a distinct academic subject in its own right. There were no specialised programmes in Economic Botany, but the author drew special attention to two universities of special merit, Harvard - with progressive teaching by Richard Schultes involving laboratory and fieldwork and access to good research facilities - and Iowa State - which offered the most in-class lecture time.

A subsequent survey in 1996, not restricted to the USA, showed that, by then, Ethnobotany had often become recognised as a distinct subject. A major finding was a growth in the number of programmes in Economic Botany or Ethnobotany from 2 in 1963 (Harvard and Iowa) to 30 in 1996. It was noted that Ethnobotany, especially concentrating on medicinal plants, was becoming fashionable. It was also found that there was a trend away from teaching these subjects to just students of Botany, with an increase in the number of students enrolled registered in non-botanical departments or inter-disciplinary programmes.

The 1996 survey identified 135 institutions worldwide offering courses in Economic Botany or Ethnobotany. The largest number was in North America (70 courses; 23 programmes), the equivalent figures for other regions being South America (7; 5), Europe (6; 1), Asia (3; 0), Australia (1; 0) and Africa (0; 0). A similar predominance of courses in the USA was also a finding of a small internet survey of Ethnobotany courses conducted in 2001 by Florent Bernard and Mark Nesbitt of the Royal Botanic Gardens, Kew, and one of the present authors, Alan Hamilton: 19 out of the 35 courses or programmes detected were in the USA.

Neither of these surveys should be regarded as definitive, both likely underestimating the number of courses outside North America. Nevertheless, it is probably true that there are many more courses in the USA than in any other country, a reflection of the large number of universities and students, and the popularity of interdisciplinary subjects. Judging by a remark that many of the courses are 'shallow' and by descriptions of the courses on their websites, it is evident that many courses in Economic Botany and Ethnobotany in the USA are intellectually undemanding, being aimed at general 'liberal arts' students. The first programme devoted to Ethnobotany in the UK was launched in 1998. It is a 1-year MSc programme taught collaboratively by the Department of Anthropology of the University of Kent at Canterbury, the Durrell Institute of Conservation and Ecology and the Royal Botanic Gardens, Kew.

A survey of 1995 confirmed the leading position of Mexico within Latin America as a centre for the teaching of Ethnobotany, noting the contributions of the Universidad de Chapingo and the Centro de Investigación Cientifica de Yucatán, the latter linked to researchers from the Universidad Nacional Autónoma de México (UNAM). The same survey identified two universities in Central America providing significant courses on useful plants, namely the Universidad Nacional Autónoma de Nicaragua-Léon (UNAN) and the Universidad de Panamá.

A survey published in 1997 confirmed that there were very few ethnobotanical courses in Africa, even though it was estimated that about 1500 students were currently learning something about the subject. There were no courses at that time in East Africa, where, more recently, there have been some significant developments. The most adventurous efforts have been in Uganda, where the Department of Botany, Makerere University, has initiated a full three-year undergraduate programme in Ethnobotany. This is possibly the first such programme in the world. Unfortunately, the programme at Makerere is only open to private students, the level of fees being such as to likely deter many potential students from applying.

The Department of Botany at Makerere is also considering starting an MSc programme in Ethnobotany. The Faculty of Forestry and Nature Conservation at Makerere includes a course in Ethnobotany in its BSc (Forestry) programme and it is likely that Ethnobotany will also be included in two MSc programmes being developed, one in Agroforestry and the other in Rural Resources and Development (a joint programme with the Faculty of Agriculture).

The Department of Botany, Kenyatta University, plans to start an MSc programme in Ethnobotany in the near future, while the Department of Botany, Nairobi University, is considering starting an undergraduate course in the subject. Both of these departments in Kenya currently teach elements of Ethnobotany in other programmes, as is also the case with the Department of Botany of the University of Dares Salaam in Tanzania and the Department of Crop Science and the Faculty of Forestry at Sokoine University of Agriculture in the same country. There is no full course in Ethnobotany in Tanzania.

Ethnobotany has been introduced widely into undergraduate and postgraduate curricula in Botany in universities and colleges in India, but so far no specific programme leading to the award of a degree or diploma specifically in the subject. Recently, the University of Tribhuvan in Nepal has created an elective course in Ethnobotany, and many students in the country have opted to do research for their dissertations on the subject . There are no ethnobotanical courses within programmes of forestry in Pakistan, although components of the subject are covered as parts of 'Plant Taxonomy' and modules on forest utilisation.

Ethnobotany, as a taught subject for graduates, was first established in China in 1987, in the Department of Ethnobotany of the Kunming Institute of Botany, Chinese Academy of Sciences. About 25 students have studied or are currently studying for MSc or PhD degrees. More recently, a number of other institutions have started to teach the subject, including the Southwest Forestry College , the National University of Pharmacy, Inner Mongolia Normal University (where the teaching of Ethnobotany to graduates in the Mongolian language commenced in 1998) and many medical colleges and universities.

Each university or college initially designed its own course, but there is now movement towards adoption of a common curriculum following a workshop held under the auspices of the present project in August 2001. Ethnobotany is not a major taught subject in universities in Malaysia, but is increasing in importance. Ethnobotany is not offered as a specific subject in the major forestry schools in Malaysia.

Ethnobotany urgently needs development as a taught subject and professional discipline. Lists of perceived weaknesses can make daunting reading. It has been suggested that all of these are due to its youthfulness. Part of the problem is not so much to due to weaknesses in Ethnobotany peripse, but rather to the frequent failure of ecologists, geneticists and other specialists to acknowledge the contributions that Ethnobotany has made to their subjects. The perception that Ethnobotany is not a 'hard core science' is a reflection, in part, of methodological weaknesses in conservation more widely. Much conservation, as practised on the ground, is based on personal experience or intuition, rather than with its directions and activities being firmly supported by evidence.

There is often little monitoring of success, or evaluation of effectiveness. Results are rarely widely disseminated. There is a need to find more effective ways of operating. A comparison has been made with medicine, a discipline similar to conservation in that action is often required urgently in the absence of precise information. The practice of medicine is said to have undergone an 'effectiveness revolution' in some countries in recent years through improvements in the criteria upon which strategies in public health, or for the treatment of individual patients, are based. The People and Plants Initiative is currently exploring ways to establish a network charged with identifying and disseminating more effective practices in Applied Ethnobotany.

Specific ways of improving standards, include:

— Exchanges of case-studies, analyses and ideas between ethnobotanists.

— Support and develop an ecosystem-based approach to conservation and sustainable development, as a basic orientation for the development of Applied Ethnobotany .

— Promote standardisation in the levels of rigour expected of courses and programmes in Applied Ethnobotany, within countries and internationally. Achievement of a measure of standardisation will give potential employers better ideas of what to expect of graduates and should enhance the mobility of graduates in the job market.

— Raise awareness of the value of Applied Ethnobotany within universities and educational ministries, and among potential students and employers. Awareness-raising among potential students and employers needs to proceed simultaneously. There is considerable concern among students in Ethnobotany in East Africa about their prospects of employment.

— Promote greater rigour in research in Ethnobotany, including through the formal stating and testing of hypotheses on people/ plant relations.

— Strengthen an existing trend towards greater quantification. A survey of ethnobotanists active in Africa revealed that only 15% appeared to use statistics in their teaching.

— Increase 'hardcore scientific elements' such as Phytochemistry. This might increase the acceptability of Ethnobotany as a 'real science' in some universities, making it easier for courses and programmes to be approved.

The People and Plants Initiative is promoting Applied Ethnobotany as a distinct form of Ethnobotany because Ethnobotany has a major role to play in conservation and sustainable development.

In advocating Applied Ethnobotany and an ecosystem-based approach to conservation and sustainable development, people/ plant relations are so central to human livelihoods that courses or programmes in Ethnobotany could potentially cover a vast range of topics. Unless there is focus, almost anything could be taught - hence, the low opinion in which the subject is held in some quarters.

The centre of attention is the local ecosystem of people and nature, the local level being selected because it is here that people are active and at which practical on-the-ground management is achieved. The potential implications of local actions on wider ecosystems are demonstrated, as well as the effects of external influences on the local. Since biological diversity has a geographical dimension, and since sustainable development must be based on responses appropriate to local environments, it is clear that both conservation and sustainable use are dependent on the existence of an appropriately matching cultural diversity.

Embarking on ethnobotanical research can be daunting because of the complexity of ecosystems and the vast number of ethnobotanical questions that could be asked. Janice Alcorn has suggested that one of the best ways of entering the 'ethnobotanical matrix' is to focus on plants used by local people, asking: "What good is this plant?" .

The real-life interactions of people with plants often do not conform neatly to the ways that academic disciplines and related professional fields are organised. The reality of rural socio-ecology in developing countries is that agricultural systems are not strictly dissociated from forestry systems, nor are concerns about health divorced from wider social and environmental affairs. A professional understanding of the constraints governing access and use of plant resources requires a knowledge of Sociology, Anthropology and Economics as much as Botany and Ecology.

People living in rural communities in developing countries may obtain food, shelter, medicine, fuel, fodder and other resources from plants that are 'wild' as well as from those that are cultivated, straddling the domains of the forester and the agriculturalist. There is often less distinction between food and medicine than is normal in the West. Individual wellbeing is felt to be closely connected to the social and spiritual worlds, requiring appreciation by researchers of local worldviews and religious beliefs, as well as of more material factors.

The training of ethnobotanists must obviously extend across the boundaries of disciplines, as traditionally defined. Fields of knowledge in academia have tended to become increasingly specialised over recent years. This is a reflection, in part, of the huge quantities of information on a vast diversity of specific topics that exist today and a growing specialisation of occupations, especially within industrial societies. Disciplines and related professions concerned substantially with plants have shared in the information explosion, sometimes with dramatic consequences.

On the one hand, scientific knowledge about plants has contributed to the introduction of high-yielding varieties of crops and thus to the explosion in the size of the human population. However, on the other hand, benefits from science have accrued disproportionately to people living in richer, industrialised and largely urban countries, or to more privileged people in the developing world.

Scientists have paid comparatively little attention to the problems of conservation and development faced by the majority of humankind, especially the many poor people who live in developing countries. The search for answers to many of the problems of conservation and sustainable development associated with rural people in developing countries requires a more holistic and participatory approach to research than has conventionally been the case. Research approaches need to correspond more closely to the multi-dimensional realities of people's lives. Fundamental requirements are acknowledgement of the knowledge and wisdom of local people and their close engagement in the identification of problems and potential solutions.

Applied Ethnobotany, an interdisciplinary subject, is well placed to surmount the divisions imposed by the narrowness of many modern academic fields and professions concerned with human livelihoods and the environment. Centres of economic strength and scientific endeavour, notably in Europe and North America, have contributed disproportionately to the shaping of modern academia and the professions all over the world. Aspiring teachers are encouraged to carry out investigations of the histories of these and other plantrelated subjects in their own countries. They should analyse their appropriateness, as currently taught and practised, to meet the challenges of conservation and sustainable development.

Future of Botany

Scientific Botany, as it emerged in Europe during the Renaissance, was closely tied to medicine and pharmacy. Written records of the uses of plants, especially as medicines, date much further back in China, Ancient Greece, India and, comparatively recently, the medieval Arab world. The first botanic gardens in the western tradition were physic gardens attached to schools of medicine. They were created for the use of students and for the production of medicines. The teaching of Botany in China, as a formal subject, began in the early part of the 20th century and only during the last 50 or so years in much of Africa.

The Age of Discovery and the spread of the European empires were accompanied by a new interest in collecting and cataloguing all types of plants . Knowledge of the natural world was seen in a general philosophical way as a key ingredient in the acceleration of human 'progress'. More immediately, there was intense interest in finding plants of economic worth for national or personal enrichment. Many botanical gardens and arboreta in the tropics, such as Pamplemousses on Mauritius and Peradeniya in Sri Lanka, originated as testing grounds for crops or as holding grounds for plants in transit. Major botanical gardens in the colonial homelands, such as the Royal Botanic Gardens, Kew, formed the hubs of international networks of collection and testing.

Many specialist branches of Botany have emerged over the last 200 years, including Anatomy, Cytology, Ecology, Genetics, Molecular Biology and Physiology. Ecology, the science concerned with the study of living beings 'at home', emerged as a distinct discipline in the late 19th century, founded on older traditions of natural history. The need to take account of the major roles of people in shaping the structure, floristic composition and dynamics of vegetation in Europe became rapidly apparent, but the equivalent massive influence of people on tropical vegetation, including tropical forest, has been recognised only more recently.

Ecologists working in the tropics have tended to concentrate their research on types of vegetation thought to be more natural. Ethnobotany has been instrumental in showing that agricultural and 'wilder' types of vegetation are often thoroughly interlinked through economic and cultural ties . A major trend in Biology, including Botany, over the last decades has been a significant expansion in some countries in the teaching of Microbiology, Molecular Biology, Genetics, and related subjects. The loser has been 'Basic Botany', more or less synonymous with 'whole plant Botany' (as it has been called).

Basic Botany, covering fields such as Anatomy, Ecology, Morphology, Systematics and Taxonomy, has been in serious decline in the USA. Systematic Botany has virtually disappeared as a taught subject in British Universities and many students are no longer taught to identify plants . The same is reported from the Netherlands and Spain.

One consequence is that Departments of Botany have often been merged with Departments of Zoology into Departments of Biology, within which 'whole plant Botany' has tended to receive even less attention than 'whole animal

Zoology'. The result is graduates in Botany or Biology who have little ability to work professionally with 'real plants'. "The production of botanists who can't tell a composite from an orchid or leaf anatomy from stem anatomy is unconscionable. And common. ... Regardless of speciality, botanists should have a broad background in all major phases of botany".

It is reported from the UK that the decline in 'whole plant Botany' at universities is further reflected in schools. Also in the UK, there has been a reduction in the popularity of Biology, both in schools and universities. A consequence is that the requirements for entry to departments of Biology in universities have been lowered. Lock believes that the decline in the UK is not related to job prospects, of which few pupils are said to have any idea. He suspects that it is rather more to do with the image and nature of the subject. 'A level' Biology (taught at senior secondary level) has apparently come to be seen as boring. He believes that GCSE syllabuses (taught at junior secondary level) no longer place stress on those things that make living things intrinsically interesting - their forms, anatomy, variety, location, behaviour and ecology.

Biology has become too similar to Chemistry or to exercises in processing data. Two comments made by experienced educators at a meeting of the Linnean Society in April 2002 help to explain why many students are losing interest in field Botany: "I've watched generations of pupils being completely turned off Biology by the national curriculum"; "Botany is not 'cool' - it takes too many years to master". The teaching of Botany, whether at school or university, does not have to be boring or seem irrelevant.

Gabriell Paye has developed an approach to teaching Botany in high schools in Boston, USA, starting from a reference that students can relate to - useful plants in their own cultures. Activities include ethnobotanical interviews (learning about plants from family, friends and neighbours), learning how to collect and identify plants, and studies of plants as sources of food and medicine, including simple tests of the ingredients and physiological activities of bought products. She reports that, when she taught Botany using a traditional textbook approach, the interest and information retention levels among students were much lower. "In contrast, by entering the world of science through a personal experience of ethnobotany, students gain a real sense of how important plants are in their lives. I find that when they are fuelled by this enthusiasm, they are more willing to then delve into other aspects of botany."

No analysis of trends in the teaching of Botany in developing countries, but, there has sometimes not been the drastic decline in 'whole plant Botany' evident in the developed world. Basic Botany is still a major component of programmes in Botany in China, Nepal, Pakistan and Uganda. However, there has been a recent decline in the number of students taking science at A-level in Uganda, probably reflecting a perception among students of a lack of opportunities for employment and the absence of science teaching in virtually all private schools (the number of which has grown greatly during recent years).

The reduction in Biology in schools in Uganda means that it has become harder to find eligible candidates for programmes in Botany or Ethnobotany. The relative resilience of Basic Botany, in at least some developing countries, certainly has advantages for Applied Ethnobotany. However, developing countries have their own, often severe, educational constraints. Not least of these are shortages of finance and, sometimes, of highly trained staff. National policies in poor countries often favour an emphasis on mass education, especially as delivered through primary schools, squeezing resources for universities even further than would otherwise be the case.

There are no government grants available for postgraduate training in Uganda. There has been a recent major expansion of private schools in many developing countries catering for the inadequacy of state-supported systems. Many of these do not teach science, mainly because of the expense involved in setting up and running laboratories. There is a serious problem of graduate unemployment in many developing countries and better students tend to opt for subjects such as Medicine, in which there is a perceived greater chance of employment. Botany is often the loser. Given the central importance of plants to development and conservation in developing countries, it is evident that there should be a place for Botany as a major taught subject.

However, many Botany programmes need to change to make them more relevant. In the words of Dr Patrick Mucunguzi of the Botany Department, Makerere University, Uganda: "Botany needs to be taken to the community". Although Microbiology and related fields are fashionable in well-resourced countries, it is difficult for researchers in developing countries to make major contributions in these fields.

Equipment is often obsolete or not functioning, and sometimes supplies of water and electricity in laboratories are intermittent. However, Applied Ethnobotany is relatively cheap, and there are many opportunities for practical work. The task today is to develop Applied Ethnobotany to a more advanced state and to persuade officials in universities and governments that the subject is worthwhile. This is best achieved through examples of its successful application.

Forestry

Modern Forestry originated in Germany where the first forestry school was established in 1789. This tradition of forest management developed and spread around the world. Becoming known as Scientific Forestry, it became the predominant influence in forestry education and practice in many countries for 200 years. The primary aim of Scientific Forestry is to maximise the yield of money from a forest, especially through the production of timber. 'Scientific foresters' are trained to select species or provenances of timber trees of economic worth and to manage them systematically. They learn how trees should be planted or encouraged to regenerate, how their growth can be promoted, and their optimal times of felling.

Scientific Forestry was introduced into India in 1864 with the appointment of the first Inspector General of Forests, from Germany and thereafter spread to other colonial territories. It was introduced into Uganda in 1929 following an advisory visit by a forestry official from India. In Britain, forestry received little systematic attention from the government until after the First World War, an event instrumental in raising awareness of the need for a home-grown 'strategic reserve' of timber. The Forestry Commission was founded in 1919 and has since become a major landowner. Conifers, such as sitka spruce Picea sitchensis, were favoured for planting, given their high potential rates of growth and their ecological suitability for planting on the poorer quality of land which tended to become available.

Although British forestry policy in the tropics was normally centrally concerned with timber, this was not entirely to the exclusion of other considerations. Forest Reserves were established in upland areas to protect water catchments and the needs of villagers were recognised by allowing them to collect 'minor forest products', for their own use, free-of-charge or with payment of small fees. The roles of forests and foresters have been radically re-thought in many countries during the last 20 years. Forests have increasingly come to be seen as serving multiple functions. There have been upsurges of interest in social, community and participatory forestry, in non-timber forest products (NTFPs) and, generally, in trying to find ways to engage all stakeholders, especially local communities, in forest management.

The history of graduatelevel forestry education in Uganda provides an example . A Forestry programme was started at Makerere University in 1970, initially taking students from the whole of East Africa. The curriculum concentrated on Scientific Forestry for the next 20 years and it was only in 1990 that a 'people element' started to be seriously introduced. In Pakistan, the importance of medicinal plants has become recognised by the Pakistan Forest Institute, with the Biological Sciences Research Division becoming engaged in a variety of research and promotional activities, including surveys of use and trade, and cultivation trials.

Several factors have been responsible for these developments. In some cases, there can be a questioning of the authority of Forest Departments, especially when they have come to exercise control over very extensive territories. Ninety-three per cent of the forest area of India is under government control. The political legitimacy of Forest Departments can be diminished when foresters are suspected of benefiting personally from their positions of power, a major issue in some countries.

Another cause of change has been a growing realisation that governments cannot control the often serious problems of forest loss and degradation which are occurring in their countries without the support of local people. There is also a better general understanding of the values of forests, apart from as sources of timber, and non-utilitarian values have become better appreciated by officials. The older generation of foresters frequently labelled products from forests, other than timber, as 'minor forest products', a term which has contributed to a failure to recognise their significance to local people, or the impact of their collection on the forests. Even timber harvested by non-mechanical means could be ignored.

Forestry, like Biology, is proving increasingly unattractive to students in some industrialised countries. There is a perception that Forestry is more physical than intellectual, and more of a male than a female occupation: "In Britain and many other countries there is a common perception that forestry comprises nasty men with nasty chain saws cutting nasty straight lines of nasty exotic species." An equivalent decline is not reported from at least some developing countries, such as Pakistan and Uganda, where degrees in Forestry are still seen as relatively likely to lead to jobs in the context of generally high graduate unemployment .

The growth of social and environmental forestry in Uganda has attracted an increasing proportion of female students, many having previously been put off, it is said, by an image of forestry as "difficult manual work in thick forest" . Forestry today needs to demonstrate its appeal to values that have wide resonance in society. It should generate intellectual excitement and attract bright people. The incorporation of Applied Ethnobotany into Forestry curricula and its use as a tool by professional foresters will help move the discipline in the right direction. Work with communities to evolve improved methods of managing trees and other plants has many potential benefits for conservation and sustainable development.

Agriculture

Agriculture provides the great bulk of food supporting people on Earth. Despite a very high percentage of terrestrial primary production being devoted to this cause, 700-800 million people still lack adequate access to food. It is not hard to predict that demands for food will rise sharply, not least because the size of the human population itself is predicted to grow, from its present 6 billion to 8.3 billion in 2025. There is considerable disagreement about how best to meet this challenge, a problem compounded by the likelihood of considerable environmental uncertainty, for example due to climatic change.

The area under cultivation could expand by 20-40% by 2020 . There have been dramatic changes in agriculture in many parts of the world over recent centuries and decades. Some of these followed the opening up of the world by European exploration and colonisation from about 1500, for example, with maize and the potato being introduced into the Old World, and wheat and sugarcane into the Americas.

Science has become a major force for change over the last 150 years, during which time advances in chemistry and biology, including genetics and plant physiology, have led to significant developments in soil science, crop-breeding and pest-control. The last 50 years, in particular, have seen a major intensification of agriculture in some regions, involving the introduction of high yielding varieties of crops, much use of agricultural machinery and major increases in inputs of water, chemical fertilisers, pesticides and fossil energy. Such agriculture is referred to as 'intensive', though ironically it is often called 'conventional' by agriculturalists.

The practice of agriculture involves continuing learning by farmers. Individual research and suggestions from friends and neighbours must have always been normal parts of farming life. The first records of provision of more formal agricultural advice are associated with pre-industrial states, such as those of Mesopotamia (dating to c.1800 BC), Ancient Egypt, Ancient Greece, the Roman Empire and Imperial China (from 600 BC). The major motivation appears to have been the desire by the state or of powerful factions within it to enhance their interests, a parallel with the way that agricultural research and education have developed in more modern times.

Powerful forces driving agricultural research and education over the last 150 years have included the desires to attain higher yields or financial profits from crops, these forces themselves being based on the aims of providing high or reliable incomes to farmers (e.g. in the European Union), food security (again in the EU) or hard currency through the sale of exports (many tropical countries, some of which have economies heavily reliant on one or a few 'export crops').

Agricultural education can be designed for different 'levels' in agricultural systems. In practice, as it has evolved over the last 150 years, a 'conventional' model of agricultural development has emerged which sees science as the source of innovation, technology as the application of science, and development as a result of the transfer of new technologies to the farmer. If there is a problem, then science will find the answer. Three levels of agricultural education have emerged from this thinking, namely those designed respectively for the training of agricultural scientists, extension workers, and farmers.

'Extension education', as a general educational concept, dates back to around 1850, when the universities of Oxford and Cambridge in England began to consider how they could serve the educational needs, near to their homes, of the rapidly growing populations in industrial urban areas . From this beginning, extension services have become a common feature of more wealthy societies, being developed not only for agriculture but for many other aspects of life, such as the environment, care of old people, family planning and so on.

'Extension science', at least as an academic field, has tended since the 1970s to move away from a conventional model of 'how do we get them to do want we want' towards a participatory approach. In the case of farming, this means that farmers are supposed to be more involved in defining the types of research undertaken and the contents of information packages provided to them. One of the foundations of modern developments in agricultural research and education was the establishment by 1800 of agricultural societies throughout much of Europe.

Members of these societies, known as 'improvers', were generally aristocrats, their agents, or 'men of science'. They were motivated by the desire to improve their wealth or to apply science to agriculture. Agricultural science evolved rapidly during the 19th century, with notable contributions by Justus von Liebig at Giessen in Germany and through the initiation in 1843 of agricultural experiments at Rothamsted in England. The Royal Agricultural Society of England was founded in 1838 with the aim of promulgating the results of scientific research.

The agricultural colleges which then became established in Europe served a small minority of young landowners and farmers. The first agricultural college in the English-speaking world was the Royal Agricultural College, opening in England in 1845, many of its later students leaving with their diplomas to fill posts in the Colonial Agricultural Administrations .

Farmers vary in their openness to agricultural advice or new technologies. Some farmers who are more 'progressive' tend to be those with more education, exposure to the mass media and access to resources. The greatest successes with agricultural extension services have been where conditions have been most favourable for industrial agriculture - as has proved to be the case over much of Western Europe and North America, with their high levels of financial resources and often good quality soils, and in irrigated areas of Asia. The Green Revolution, a term used for the major changes in Asia resulting from intensification of agriculture, helped turn India from being an importer of food to self-sufficiency. The earlier years of extension services could be particularly productive, because then there could be special opportunities to apply new technologies starting from traditional bases.

Greece is an example, with the first 15 years of extension services after their introduction in 1950 being especially fruitful. Until recent decades, agricultural research and extension have generally been regarded as public goods and these services have been provided by governments or charitable societies free-of-charge or for nominal payments. Other kinds of organisation have since become increasingly engaged, notably agriculture-related commercial companies, agricultural commodity marketing boards (concerned to assure the supply and quality of their products), agricultural development projects, and non-governmental organisations.

The private sector has taken an increasing role in the breeding of new varieties of crops, the development of agricultural chemicals, and in making of these available to farmers. The private sector today accounts for 80% of the global market in the breeding and distribution of seeds, though the public sector remains predominant in some countries such as India and Japan. Globally, the private sector has become increasingly dominated by a few multinational companies during the last decade. Government extension services have often been reduced, or payments required for their services (particularly in the North, as in the Netherlands).

Large parts of the world have benefited little, or not at all, from modern developments in agricultural research, education and extension. These are especially those rain-fed agricultural areas which lie in countries with few financial resources, including almost the whole of Africa, large parts of Asia and Latin America, and sub-stantial parts of Europe. Indeed, some of these places have suffered from deteriorating environments, as periods of fallow in systems of shifting agriculture have been reduced, more land has been cleared of forest, soil erosion has increased, and soil fertility declined.

Despite its successes, intensive agriculture is not without its problems. Some of these are social. They include a massive erosion of local rural cultures, including knowledge of plants and their uses. Many millions of rural people have been displaced from their previous places of abode through the consolidation of land-holdings and the introduction of mechanisation. Often moving to rural areas which are marginal for agriculture or to city slums, many of these people or their descendants now live precarious existences on the edges of survival. Environmentally, there are many problems with intensive agriculture, such as worries concerning its massive use of water, energy and chemicals, and its side effects of loss of soil fertility and structure, soil erosion, damage to human health, and pollution.

Since 1970, the worldwide rate of application of nitrogen fertilisers has increased by seven times and contributions from humans are now the same as all natural inputs to the nitrogen cycle. Half to two-thirds of nitrogen fertilisers now enter nonagricultural ecosystems with serious consequences for terrestrial, freshwater and marine ecology . The full financial costs of industrial agriculture are currently little met by farmers or consumers, but rather passed on to others, including future generations.

Accordingly, farmers and the public are little aware of the deleterious consequences of their farming practices or patterns of consumption. High-input farming is often favoured through financial incentives, as in North America and the European Union. Apart from causing local environmental degradation, this is an obstacle to agricultural development in developing countries, where progressive farmers are faced with high tariffs for their exports and may even be undercut in their home markets through the dumping of 'food aid'.

The concept of 'sustainable agriculture' is today gaining ground. This refers to new approaches to agricultural research, education and extension. Sustainable agriculture is based on recognising and building on locally-available resources and natural processes, including encouraging nutrient recycling and biodiversity, and limiting the use of external inputs of agrochemicals and non-renewable energy. A basic principle is full participation of farmers and rural people in all processes of problem analysis and technology development, adaption and extension.

Ethnobotany can certainly make important contributions to the development of more sustainable agriculture. This is most obviously so in the case of low input agriculture, where the 'conventional' approach of 'telling farmers what to do' has not been very successful, and where there is general recognition of the desirability of applying participatory methodologies for the identification and solution of problems. Systems of low input farming have to be intimately adapted to the local environment; local knowledge is a crucial ingredient in formulating potentially successful pathways of change. The case for Ethnobotany in the development of intensive agriculture is perhaps less obvious, given that industrial farming has resulted in a major reduction in plant diversity (large areas of uniform, virtually weed-free, crops) and that most industrial farmers know relatively little about their local plant worlds, at least in comparison with their more traditional colleagues.

Industrial farms are biologically much simpler than traditional farms. Even so, there are considerable advantages to involving industrial farmers fundamentally with research. It has been found in the Netherlands that many farmers currently following industrial practices are coming to recognise the value of more sustainable agriculture. They wish to learn more about the details of the natural world as they seek to enhance and benefit from the biological diversity on their farms.

Knowledge of Ethnobotany can be useful to agricultural scientists and extension workers for them to better:

- Learn about the perceptions, values and knowledge of farmers about their crops and other plants.
- Be able to co-experiment with farmers on new practices, including crop breeding.
- Facilitate exchanges of information between farmers.

Medicine

Traditional Medical Systems (that is Chinese Traditional Medicine, Tibetan Medicine, Mongolian Medicine, Tai Medicine and Uguar Medicine) have become recognised officially in China after the establishment of the People's Republic. The Chinese government also recognises the usefulness of Traditional Medical Knowledge (folk medicine as practised in homes and villages) but discourages Shamanistic Medicine. There are, today, 36 universities teaching traditional medicine in China.

In 1967, a society was formed in Japan to support Kampo, Traditional Japanese Medicine. It now has 10,000 members and 200 preparations have been cleared for prescription by the National Institute of Health as well as by insurance companies. In 1970, the Indian Parliament passed the Indian Central Council Act, establishing a Central Council for Ayurveda. This was followed by the accreditation of courses at colleges and universities.

An initiative by WWF at Dolpo, Nepal, to encourage sustainability in the harvesting of medicinal plants, linked to the strengthening of Tibetan medicine, is being watched with interest elsewhere in the country. There are research centres in all three East African countries charged with the study of traditional medicine, including its potential to contribute to national systems of healthcare. They are the Centre for Complementary Medicine and Biotechnology in Kenya, the National Chemotherapeutics Laboratory in Uganda, and the Institute of Traditional Medicine, Muhimbili Medical Centre, Tanzania .

The medical establishment in the UK, as embodied in the British Medical Association, has traditionally opposed 'alternative medicine', but in 1988 the Royal Society of Medicine recommended bridge-building with other traditions. In Mexico, there have been efforts to educate doctors about traditional medicine, register traditional medical practitioners, and provide herbal remedies for sale to communities. The TRAMIL network in the Caribbean and Central America is undertaking research aimed at authenticating and recommending herbal medicine to treat common ailments.

Individual doctors and some governments have adopted, or are considering for adoption, integrated (syncretic) medicine, drawing on Western and other traditions. In fact, even in Western Europe, there are long established variations in the degree to which herbal treatments are used in conventional medicine. For example, they are much more part of normal practice in Germany than in the UK. The impetus towards integrated medicine can stem from desires for greater medical effectiveness, financial limitations, or the wish to affirm local cultures.

Resistance to co-operation can stem from any of the traditions, but most often from the Western. The involvement of governments is important because this can lead to a more systematic approach. Actually, it is common practice around the world for some Western-trained doctors to recommend herbal or other 'alternative' treatments and for some practitioners of other traditions to prescribe Western drugs. An excellent example of integrated medicine has been set by China, where, from the days of Chairman Mao Tse-tung, a goal has been set of developing a national medical system drawing on the best of Western Medicine and indigenous medical traditions.

The approach has been empirical and pragmatic, and today integrated knowledge has become fully implemented throughout the country. Experience of introducing herbal medicine into an orthodox setting in the UK has been described by Sue Eldin and Andrew Dunford. Their approach to integration involves regular discussions between the general practitioners, practice nurses and a herbalist. They report that the herbalist deals with an increasing number of 'heartsink patients' (representing about 50% of consultations). These patients have problems that are not easy to define or treat through Western Medicine.

Applied Ethnobotanists, working on their own or with sympathetic Western-trained doctors or other specialists, have many potential roles to play in the development of improved systems of healthcare and related issues of conservation and sustainable development. They include contributions towards:

— Documentation and understanding of non- Western systems of health and healing.

— Training physicians to work with traditional medical practitioners.

— Identification of treatments, based on local medical traditions, to recommend for wider adoption. Such work helps reduce consumption of pharmaceutical drugs, which can be very expensive in developing countries. It can also lead to the substitution of imported medicinal plants or pharmaceutical drugs with locally-based medications.

— Development of healthcare systems and practices which draw on both Western and other types of medicine.

— Research into active principles in plants, including for the benefits of national healthcare and economies. This can lead to the discovery of new drugs. If discoveries are based on local medical knowledge, then research should be undertaken according to recognised ethical standards, with a fair and appropriate distribution of the benefits of research and commercialisation to relevant parties.

- The recording of toxic traditional medicines so that traditional healers might be persuaded to substitute safer plants or reduce the quantities administered.
- Increased national autonomy regarding the planning and management of health policies.
- Understanding changes in economies, societies and cultures relating to the management and use of medicinal plants.
- Identification of species of plants in need of conservation. Particular attention needs to be given to plants in trade, for which the danger of over-harvest is greatest.
- The establishment of schemes to conserve, sustainably harvest, or cultivate medicinal plants.

Courses and Programmes in Applied Ethnobotany

The challenges of interdisciplinarity Ethnobotany is multidisciplinary in that knowledge and skills pertaining to many disciplines are needed by ethnobotanists. It is interdisciplinary, especially as an applied subject, in that synthesis between the disciplines is essential to ensure successful identification and resolution of real-life problems of conservation and sustainable development .

Interdisciplinarity presents considerable challenges for staff and students. If several members of staff, with varying backgrounds, are responsible for delivering the bulk of the teaching of a course or programme in Applied Ethnobotany, each concentrating on his or own area of speciality, then all of them must make every effort to select those aspects of their subjects which are most relevant to Applied Ethnobotany and take every opportunity to explain connections. It is not enough to leave synthesis to the students. If this happens, then many students will fail to make the necessary connections and they will not become useful applied ethnobotanists.

A course or programme in Applied Ethnobotany should provide an education which will assist its graduates to identify and find answers to problems in the real world. Such problems rarely fall neatly into the discrete disciplines into which modern academia is divided. Applied ethnobotanists should have an understanding of relationships between the botanical, ecological, social, economic and political dimensions of managing plant resources and conserving botanical diversity.

A successful course in Applied Ethnobotany will often involve staff drawn from different departments or faculties. They must learn how to communicate with one another . Those involved should not be discouraged by initial problems. Experience in the initial development of an interdisciplinary approach shows that this can be unstable and unproductive for several years due in large measure to differences in philosophical outlook between disciplines, including in underlying paradigms . There are barriers of terminology. Modern fields of knowledge are often so specialised and ridden with jargon that they are almost impenetrable to others.

They tend to emphasize specialisation rather than lateral thinking. The range of materials which could usefully be covered in courses in Applied Ethnobotany is immense, especially considering the many contributory disciplines. The problem has been paraphrased as 'breadth versus depth'. The danger is that graduates may end up knowing a little about a lot and be masters of nothing. While there are strategies to help deal with this, an element of 'what to leave out' is probably unavoidable. There is, therefore, a need to identify the core competences required of an Applied Ethnobotanist.

The educational challenges encountered in Applied Ethnobotany are actually reflected in many professional fields (such as Forestry and Medicine) concerned with finding practical answers to human problems. Programmes in Forestry have been expanded in their coverage of topics in recent years to accommodate new subject matter now seen as essential. The world today is subject to rapid ecological, economic and cultural change. All professionals have to be adaptable and learn how to cope with a constantly shifting agenda, including finding ways to cope with the modern explosion of ideas and information. There is often less security in jobs and more individuality in career-trajectories than in the past.

Learning today must be seen, even more than before, as a matter for continuing pursuit throughout life. Staff teaching courses in Applied Ethnobotany are just as much faced with these challenges as are their students. As with Forestry, much learning will be self-learning, and courses and programmes should be structured to encourage this . Major aims of courses and programmes in Applied Ethnobotany, as with Biology, should be to teach students how to think, how to identify problems, how to explore them and how to acquire information or assistance from specialists, as necessary for the tasks in hand. As with

Forestry, there are major roles for in-service professional courses and professional networks.

A more problem-orientated approach to learning than is conventional has been advocated for interdisciplinary subjects. The idea is to develop professional competency through acquiring the ability to recognise problems and apply solutions in real social contexts in which there can be considerable uncertainty, instability and conflict. It is a recognition that every problem in professional practice is unique and requires an open-minded and fresh approach, rather than merely applying standard techniques in a mechanical way. While some lectures may still be given, for example covering basic theory and concepts, most learning in a problem-orientated programme is self-directed or tutor-facilitated in small groups. The emphasis is on action and interpretation rather than on theory and memory. Students build the ability to learn through exercises in solving problems under the guidance of experienced practitioners.

While certainly there should be elements of problem-orientated self-learning in interdisciplinary subjects, there can be considerable constraints to embracing this approach whole-heartedly. They include the need for exceptional degrees of competency and commitment from staff, who must devote more time and effort to support individual students than is conventionally the case. Costs also increase, especially if there is much individual fieldwork. The commitment of several departments to this approach may be needed, which may be difficult to achieve.

The extra effort required of students can be a major challenge if they are faced with economic difficulties, which is often the case. Furthermore, students may find it hard to cope with a full-blooded problem-orientated approach if they are used to learning by rote, all too common in education in some countries. Brown, referring to the ideas of Ramsden and Schön , has written of theories of learning which can underpin approaches to the education of professionals: "Ramsden defined learning as applying and modifying one's own ideas.

It is, he maintained, not the passive receipt of authoritative knowledge. Learning in a professional context may require a slightly broader definition because much of what is learned may not be consciously 'known'. When asked how to identify a particular species of tropical tree few experts will be able to produce a list of defining characters. Most will simply recognise a tree from its 'Gestalt'. This is an example of what Schön has termed 'knowing-in-action', one of the essential components of skilful professional practice. Knowing-in-action is revealed in the spontaneous skilful execution of a complex task, but it can rarely be made explicit. It does not therefore constitute the conscious appli-cation of ideas or theories. This view of the way that professionals may work undermines the traditional epistemology of professional education.

It suggests that professionals rarely 'solve' problems, but may simply recognise them and apply appropriate solutions. However, most problems in professional practice are not routine but are unusual, often unique. Standard actions produce unexpected results that the professional has respond to. Schön claimed that the essential counterpart to 'knowing-in-action' is the capacity of the skilful practitioner to respond intelligently to the unexpected. Their actions are modified on the basis of reflection, leading to revision of the personal ideas that underpinned the 'knowing-in-action'.

A constant cycle spontaneous action followed by reflection and modification of personal conceptions of the problem constitutes what Schön saw as professional artistry. There are obvious parallels between this view and Ramsden's description of learning as the application and modification of personal ideas."

Many of the challenges of interdisciplinarity faced in Applied Ethnobotany are paralleled Conservation Biology, a related field. Conservation Biology is concerned specifically with biological conservation. The point of departure when devising courses or programmes Conservation Biology therefore differs somewhat from that of Applied Ethnobotany.

There is likely to be more emphasis on topics, such as loss species and genetic diversity, and loss and fragmentation of habitats. There will likely be more attention given to 'traditional' conservation measures, such as protected areas, ex situ conservation, and re-introductions of species. Given that the starting point lies in the biological world, the logic of the approach of conservation biologists tends to begin by stressing the need for biological inventories and the preparation of 'Red Lists' endangered species.

Taxonomy is seen as a basic discipline and, accordingly, the shortage of taxonomists is particularly bemoaned. In contrast, Applied Ethnobotany is embedded in an ecosystem-based approach to conservation and sustainable development, with an emphasis on the management plant resources. Natural and human systems are seen as thoroughly intertwined. Thus, the perceptions, values, uses and methods management of plants by all those people who are stakeholders in a particular ecosystem become fundamental considerations.

Being mostly motivated by an interest plants and animals, there is a tendency for conservation biologists to focus on aspects of prob-Skills seen as desirable include the abilities to communicate with the public, assess the interests of stakeholders, communicate across disciplines, and work in interdisciplinary teams. It is recommended that curricula in Conservation Biology should cover such matters as written and oral communication, explanations of the science and values of biodiversity to the lay public, group decision-making, interpersonal skills, group planning, leadership, and advocacy .

As mentioned earlier, a course is taken to be a relatively short unit of study and a programme a subject of graduation. There is no international consistency in the structure of tertiary-level education or in the nomenclature used for degrees. The term 'undergraduate programme' used for one leading to the degree of BSc or equivalent. Such a programme will typically be of threeyear's duration and include only limited periods of individual research. MSc programmes are commonly two years in length, composed half of group learning and half of individual research, though one-year programmes are also found.

Assuming that the value of Applied Ethnobotany is realised, an initial question is whether it is sufficient for its teaching merely to be incorporated into courses or programmes in other subjects or whether it should be taught as a subject in its own right. It is common to teach elements of Ethnobotany within other courses, such as 'Taxonomy' in Botany programmes, 'Community Forestry', 'Non-Timber Forest Products', 'Agroforestry' or 'Natural Resource Management' in Forestry programmes, or 'Pharmacology' in Schools of Medicine. Such teaching is useful, but is it enough?

The overall rationale of Applied Ethnobotany is unlikely to be appreciated by students if its subject matter is only encountered scattered throughout other courses. A dedicated course or programme in Applied Ethnobotany will help students to think across the boundaries of traditional disciplines, greatly enhancing their abilities to address reallife problems. General programme in Applied Ethnobotany should be open, in principle, to students from a wide range of backgrounds. This should be a major consideration in the design of programmes and the setting of prerequisites for entry. Applied Ethnobotany can be a very useful specialisation for postgraduate students, not only botanists, but graduates in a variety of other disciplines, including Agriculture, Anthropology, Forestry, Medicine, Pharmacology, Sociology, as well as others.

On the other hand, there can be value in tailoring undergraduate courses in Applied Ethnobotany to the requirements of particular programmes, such as Agriculture, Forestry and Medicine. There will be substantial common elements in such courses, whatever the discipline, and, if two or more departments in the same university are contemplating the introduction of courses in Applied Ethnobotany, then greater efficiency may be achieved through providing common taught components.

There are many possible types of courses and programmes in Applied Ethnobotany. The three considered most generally useful are:

— Programmes of one to three years duration.

— Courses in undergraduate programmes, commonly with about 60 hours of teaching including 20-30 lectures and a limited amount of fieldwork.

— Short professional courses of five days to three months duration, preferably leading to the award of a certificate or diploma.

These could be run, for instance, for members of government departments and NGOs who wish to upgrade their knowledge. Professional courses should have well defined purposes and should normally be entirely or substantially field-based. There can be scepticism about the value of undergraduate programmes in Ethnobotany, as expressed, for example, by staff at two universities in Kenya. The principal argument is that the students will 'specialise' too early, reducing their opportunities for employment.

There are actually only two undergraduate programmes in Ethnobotany worldwide, these being mounted by the Department of Botany, Makerere University and Mbarara University of Science and Technology, both in Uganda. The thinking which led to the development of the programme at Makerere should be a matter of reflection for academics working in botany departments elsewhere in developing countries. The historical context at Makerere is that graduates in Botany have typically become teachers of Biology or been employed by research institutes. However, in 1991, the entire education of aspiring teachers of Biology became transferred to the School of Education.

The Department of Botany was no longer involved, and the opportunities of jobs for its graduates accordingly reduced. Furthermore, in the mid-1990s, the Department of Botany undertook a survey of its graduates and found that most of those who had recently become employed were working either in research centres or in natural resource management. A common experience reported by the latter group was that most of the problems they encountered were community-related and yet, they complained, they had received no training for such work. Some members of staff of the department then decided to review, fundamentally, the purpose of an education in Botany within their national context. It was this that led to the development of the undergraduate programme in Ethnobotany, a subject conceived as being 'Botany for the People'. Traditional Botany is still being taught in parallel by the department.

Students completing postgraduate programmes in Applied Ethnobotany should be equipped to start work as professional ethnobotanists, though some may proceed to doctoral level. Apart from its value to the students themselves, and hopefully to those communities which participate in their research, an added benefit of doctoral research is the provision of casestudies which can be used in teaching.

A survey in East Africa has demonstrated that, at present, there is little connection between the pursuit of research at doctoral level in Ethnobotany and acceptance by the universities more generally of the value of Ethnobotany as a taught subject. Choices of topics for doctoral research in East Africa overwhelmingly reflect the interests of individual members of staff. The key institutional factor regarding the acceptability of a research topic is its perceived potential to produce results considered to be 'major contributions to science'.

Each course or programme in Applied Ethnobotany needs defined purposes. These will be decided through internal processes within departments and universities. These discussions will be better informed if reviews exist of the status and potential applications of Ethnobotany within the country or region. Developers of courses and programmes are advised to consult members of relevant government departments, industries, research institutes and non-governmental organisations, discussions which could lead to the added benefits that they will become involved in teaching and of raising the chances of employment for the graduates.

Courses and programmes in Applied Ethnobotany will typically be attached to particular departments and faculties, even though members of other departments and faculties may be involved in their teaching. Courses can be mounted by a variety of departments. Currently in Brazil, courses in Ethnobotany are taught within departments of Botany, Health, Horticulture and Pharmacology. As mentioned elsewhere, a single course might serve several departments, though with special components designed for the needs of particular categories of student.

Courses and, even more so, programmes, will benefit if members of different departments and faculties are involved in the teaching. Cooperation is not always easy to achieve. Universities vary in the degrees to which they recognise the value of interdisciplinary subjects such as Ethnobotany. The fundamental educational philosophy of a university is likely to be reflected in the basic structures regulating teaching and the degree of flexibility possible between departments. When the desirability of co-operation between departments or faculties is unrecognised institutionally, then there may be added difficulties in timetabling.

The ways that students and courses are funded can affect the abilities of departments and faculties to co-operate. In the case of Makerere University, Uganda, fees paid by students vary in amount by faculty, but are paid centrally, causing complications if there is a demand that they be distributed between faculties according to their contributions to interdisciplinary teaching. The problem is further compounded because some students at Makerere receive government grants, while others are entirely self-supporting. The latter group includes all students registered for the programme in Ethnobotany in the Department of Botany. Questions have arisen as to how the Department will pay for the time of lecturers of other departments and the rates at which they should be paid.

The level of fees can be a deterrent for private students. There is a trend towards an increasing number of self-financed students in many countries, a reflection of a global expansion in tertiary-level education and the incapacity or unwillingness of governments to bear the entire costs. The level of the fee payable by students to enrol in the programme in Ethnobotany at Makerere is a large sum in the local context. It may be noted that even then, the total of fees received does not meet all the costs of the programme, which has been subsidised from the core funds of the Department of Botany and some voluntary teaching by members of other departments.

Many academics have not heard of Ethnobotany and know nothing of its potential usefulness. It is suggested here that proponents of Applied Ethnobotany emphasise its value for conservation and sustainable development. They should point out just how important plants are in local cultures, and the economic necessity of maintaining the base of plant resources. They should emphasise that plants are essential elements in all aspects of public health, including nutrition and the curing or prevention of ailments. They should be able to demonstrate that Applied Ethnobotany can contribute to the study of native plants and the conservation of traditional botanical knowledge. They should be able to provide examples of how Applied Ethnobotany can contribute to the relief of poverty and to social justice. Well-documented case-studies should be ready to hand.

In some cases, universities within countries share common syllabuses. For example, the same curriculum is followed by all four agricultural universities and six agricultural colleges in Pakistan. In such cases, the introduction of a new course must normally be agreed at a higher level than that of a single institution. This particular impediment has been surmounted by Dr Khan Bahadar Marwat of NWFP Agricultural University in Pakistan in the case of Ethnobotany, through his achievement in establishing, for his university alone, a Department of Weed Science. Two elective courses in Ethnobotany, at elementary and more advanced levels, have been included in the programme.

Some members of staff may not appreciate the merits of working with colleagues from other departments. They may not think beyond their particular subjects or even their own specialities within them. They may be intellectually enmeshed in particular par- adigms - sometimes unconsciously - and this may limit their perceptions about the nature of scientific or other modern academic knowledge and the types of education or research that are 'authentic'. They are likely to be only vaguely aware of approaches and methods used in other subjects.

'Traditional botanists' often have little awareness of the importance of culture, land ownership and rights of access to natural resources for determining how 'wild' plants are used and managed. They know little about connections between agricultural and 'wild' ecosystems, and many do not appreciate the significance of human actions for moulding 'natural' vegetation. Sociologists and economists often fail to realise the roles of biological and ecological variables in determining relationships between people and plants, including the restraints that they impose over how plants can be used and managed.

Conventional economists can adhere to the erroneous theory that natural resources are infinite or are perfectly substitutable with man-made capital. Use of a questionnaire to ascertain the use of firewood collected from a national park in Tanzania was initially rejected by a department of Zoology because questionnaires were regarded as not being part of the toolkit of a zoologist.

In principle, programmes in Applied Ethnobotany should be open to students from a wide range of backgrounds, though clearly requirements for enrolment should differ between undergraduate and postgraduate levels. A programme in Applied Ethnobotany is best regarded as a specialisation within Botany, though of an interdisciplinary nature. Non-botanists should be allowed to enrol, but they should have a genuine interest in plants, because otherwise they will probably find it impossible to reach professional competency. It is a common experience that students of Ethnobotany are somewhat older than the average.

A decision to study Ethnobotany, as a major subject, is a deliberate choice, rather than merely just one further step up an educational ladder in the same subject. Students are often attracted to Ethnobotany by its inter-disciplinarity, and concerns for the environment and the welfare of poor rural people. Advantages of a broad admissions policy to a programme are that students are more likely to be well motivated and that everyone will benefit from the contributions of students hailing from a diversity of backgrounds.

The recommendation of an open-minded approach to admission to a programme should not be mistaken as a call to be 'soft'. A lack of rigour in admissions policy could lead to current or potential students questioning the strengths of courses and also doubts on the part of potential employers. Each department must establish its own entry requirements, which may be institutionally constrained as, for example, in Brazil, Cuba and Mexico, in which it is normal for students to take written examinations for entry to postgraduate programmes.

Other requirements which have been suggested for entry to postgraduate programmes include attainment of specified standards in undergraduate degrees, work experience and expressions of interest. The latter could be demonstrated through interview, or the submission of ideas for the individual research which the student will be required to undertake. A flexible approach to admission to an elective course in Ethnobotany has been adopted by Fatima Jinnah Women's University, Rawalpindi, Pakistan. This course, entitled 'Ethnobotany and its Application to Conservation in Environmental Science', was introduced in 1999 and is open to students from many disciplines, including Economics. There is no requirement for a background in Botany.

In contrast, entry to the undergraduate programme in Ethnobotany run by the Department of Botany, Makerere University, Uganda, stipulates passes in two science 'A-levels' (advanced secondary school qualifications), one of which must be in Biology, Chemistry or Agriculture. Greater flexibility is exercised in the case of mature-aged applicants. Experience has suggested that the requirements for normal entrants are over-prescriptive, and they are likely to be revised.

Student assessment

Many methods can be used to assess the performance of students. For courses at undergraduate level, there is likely to be an emphasis on written forms of assessment, such as essays, practicals (including fieldwork), and final papers.

Students taking programmes should be assessed for their practical skills and personal aptitudes as well as their knowledge. Certificates of Attendance or Adequate Performance are desirable for professional courses to give pride in achievement and to provide evidence of attainment relating to opportunities at work.

Courses and programmes should be evaluated periodically to achieve incremental improve- ments and for accountability. Evaluators should consult the teaching faculty, students, the administrative staff of universities, and members of relevant external organizations. Once a programme is well established, there should be occasional surveys of the employability of graduates and their effectiveness in their occupations.

The nature of staffing for courses and programmes in Applied Ethnobotany will depend upon the availability of interested individuals, the extent of their knowledge, their competency as teachers and the structural arrangements of universities, for instance relating to the ease of co-operation between departments and faculties.

It is likely that, for the present, the majority of staff involved will not have been trained primarily as applied ethnobotanists, but rather will have studied traditional subjects such as Anthropology, Botany, Ecology, Economics, Forestry, Medicine, Pharmacology and Sociology. Few will have been trained outside their own discipline . If a course or programme is taught by staff, each with a background in a traditional discipline, then it is vital that they do not just teach their 'own' subjects in isolation, leaving integration to the students.

Lecturers should make every effort to think across disciplines and encourage the same in students through provision of models, analyses and case-studies. Making the effort to learn beyond a relatively narrow discipline in which one has been trained and feels competent is a challenge, easier to handle if colleagues encourage one another to broaden their horizons. There will commonly be a need for staff development. One approach to developing expertise among staff is for a department to encourage doctoral research in Applied Ethnobotany, with the hope that the students, once graduated, will join the faculty .

The teaching of courses at undergraduate level is demanding, even though less detailed knowledge is needed compared with the postgraduate level, and the length of the teaching period is relatively brief. Courses will often be taught by one or a few lecturers. The challenge is to cover the broad range of the subject in a truly interdisciplinary way. The temptation should be avoided in departments of Botany to leave the entire teaching of a course in Applied Ethnobotany to a taxonomist, unless the person concerned has the necessary interdisciplinary knowledge and expertise in teaching. Courses in Ethnobotany are frequently taught by taxonomists, as in Malaysia .

Visiting lecturers can contribute greatly to courses or programmes in Applied Ethnobotany, bringing in fresh perspectives and special expertise. The use of such lecturers is infrequent. Miguel Alexiades and William Bailey of New York Botanical Garden have served as visiting lecturers on courses in Ethnobotany in Brazil. Javier Caballero of the Botanical Garden of the Universidad Nacional Autónoma de México (UNAM) has taught Quantitative Methods in Ethnobotany around the world, including on behalf of the People and Plants Initiative. Sonia Lagos-Witte of the TRAMIL programme has served in Brazil, Colombia, Honduras, Indonesia and Nicaragua.

Ultimately, the initiation and success of courses or programmes in Ethnobotany will generally rely on the enthusiasm and energy of one or a few people who recognise the value of the subject and are committed to making its teaching a success. Their presence is critical for encouraging other members of staff and for promoting wider contacts. The key role of such 'energisers' is no different here than for the stimulation of intellectual activity generally.

Surveying the history of Botany in the USA, the Botanical Society of America concluded that "Most botanists attribute their original interest in plants to another botanist or teacher able to convey the beauty and intellectual excitement of plant studies". Analysing the development of Ethnobotany in departments of Botany and Forestry in East Africa, John Kessy has drawn attention to two contrasting schools of thought and approaches to teaching. This is a contrast widely mirrored elsewhere, including in the USA.

One school of thought is composed of teachers who are conservative in nature and content with traditional approaches, seeing Ethnobotany as essentially the same as Economic Botany, considered to be the study of the uses of plants. The other school - the 'daring school of thinkers' - has accepted that Ethnobotany can play a major role in conservation and sustainable development, and has tried to start innovative courses or programmes. Members of this school believe that Botany and Forestry have much to contribute to the future of their countries, but that they need to be overhauled to respond satisfactorily to modern challenges. Materials needed, or useful, for a course or programme include:

— Rooms for lectures, seminars and tutorials, with equipment such as blackboards, projectors, etc.

— Slides, videos, etc.

— Laboratories with microscopes, chemicals, etc.

— Computers and accessories, including word-processing and database programmes and access to the internet.

— An herbarium and equipment for collecting plants.

— An ethnobotanical collection.

— A map collection and cartographic facilities.

— Field equipment, especially for recording information (e.g. notebook, pencil), the demarcation of plots and marking of plants, the measurement of position (e.g. altimeter, compass, inclinometer, geographical positioning system (GPS), etc.), size (tape measures, callipers, etc.), height (e.g. inclinometer) and weight (balances of different capacities).

— Money. The lack of adequate finance is a crucial issue in developing countries . Money is needed inter alia to pay staff, purchase equipment and consumables, obtain literature and support needy students. Funding can be even more of a critical issue with short professional courses than with undergraduate courses or postgraduate programmes because there may be no provision in regular budgets.

Access to literature is crucial for both staff and students. Lists of required reading and background literature should be given to students. Students should be required to search out literature on unfamiliar subjects for themselves because the ability to do so will be invaluable to them later in life, including if they become professional applied ethnobotanists. There is a need for 'readers' (collections of relevant papers) for participants in short professional courses.

There may be potential gaps in the literature which local experts in Applied Ethnobotany should consider writing. If interesting research has been undertaken, but is unavailable in a suitable form, then, with the permission of the researchers (if required or ethically desirable), lecturers can perform a useful service through its proper documentation for students. Reviews of the status of Ethnobotany in countries and regions are extremely useful for giving orientation in Applied Ethnobotany, including in relation to its teaching. Similarly, national or regional directories of Ethnobotany are valuable reference materials.

The People and Plants Initiative has prepared reviews of the status of Ethnobotany for Africa and Malaysia. There is also a need for basic texts, honed to the needs of particular countries and courses. There is a severe shortage of literature in most developing countries, for instance in Africa. The People and Plants Initiative has tried to help through producing and widely distributing publications and videos dealing with various aspects of Applied Ethnobotany. Some lecturers teaching Ethnobotany are relying heavily on these materials.

Electronic information is today assuming greater importance, although many ethnobotanists in many developing countries, including in Africa, lack access to the internet. The age of the computer and the development of the internet have only further widened the gaps in technology and information between industrialised and developing countries. Computers are often in very short supply in universities in developing countries and the cost of access to the internet can be prohibitive. (The dollar costs of internet access can be much higher in the developing world than in industrialised countries.) Course organisers should endeavour to find ways of increasing the accessibility of computers and the internet to staff and students.

Many methods can be used in the teaching of Applied Ethnobotany, including lectures, seminars, tutorials, field and laboratory studies (demonstrative, or involving individual or group work), required reading, literature studies, and individual research. The choice of method may be constrained by institutional limitations, the abilities of staff or the availability of finance, equipment or access to transportation. Different educational methods are appropriate to different aspects of courses, suggesting, for instance, that the fundamentals of theory in Botany, Ecology and Anthropology are best delivered in lectures, but that interactive seminars might be more useful for the teaching of Ethics. The designers of courses and programmes will need to decide the level of detail to be covered in particular topics, always bearing in mind the need to maintain interdisciplinarity and the potential limitations of students possibly drawn from a diversity of academic backgrounds.

Elective courses may be offered within programmes to students with particular interests. Courses, mounted strictly for aspiring foresters, agriculturalists or other such specialised groups of students, will certainly have some common content, but should have a bias in some sections towards aspects of Applied Ethnobotany of particular relevance to their discipline.

Lecturers should identify aspects of contributory subjects, such as Anthropology, Botany, Economics and so on, which are particularly relevant to Applied Ethnobotany, rather than just teaching them in the 'standard' way. It is reported from East Africa that many students, even in regular Botany programmes, shy away from some subjects (e.g. Plant Taxonomy and Systematics), because they are taught too theoretically and with too much use of specialised language. A more practical orientation, even in traditional programmes - let alone for students of Applied Ethnobotany - is thought likely to be more attractive to many students.

It is strongly recommended that the teaching of the Social Sciences be tailored specifically to meet the needs of applied ethnobotanists. Concepts, such as theories of human behaviour, need to be applied to real-life issues of natural resource management . Connections between socio-economic and ecological systems must remain at the centre of attention. This is similar to the challenge of teaching social issues in courses in Conservation Biology, in which case, it has been recommended, there should be a focus on the political, economic and cultural origins and patterns of human use of natural resources.

As with Conservation Biology, students need to be versed in policy issues. They should know about the wider political, legislative and economic dimensions which influence local relationships between people and plants. They should be aware of strategies used around the world for conservation and the promotion of more sustainable use of plant resources, and be able to analyse their suitability within their own national contexts. There should be studies of how traditional local institutions governing conservation and the use of natural resources have sometimes been replaced by the institutions of the state, and about the possibilities of reviving or establishing local institutions to complement initiatives of the state.

Many mature-age students of Applied Ethnobotany are deficient in the basic sciences, such as Biology, Chemistry, Anthropology and Sociology. It will also be the case that most students, entering postgraduate programmes directly after graduation, will lack familiarity with some of the basic topics of Applied Ethnobotany. Most students, previously specialising in Social Science, will know little of Botany, and those coming from the Sciences lit- tle of Social Science. It is suggested that staff organise special tutorials, seminars and lists of required reading to help students with deficiencies to catch up.

Many students lacking a background in Botany can find Ethnobotany rather daunting, because so much detailed knowledge seems to be required. This is why an interest in plants is deemed essential for all students. It might be thought that students who have already covered certain topics in their previous education might be permitted to skip more basic classes in these subjects. In most cases this would be a mistake.

Unfortunately, subjects such as Taxonomy in programmes in Botany are often taught inadequately. Furthermore, Applied Ethnobotany requires a more practical orientation and a more interdisciplinary approach than is normal in traditional courses. Organisers of courses will have to decide the level of detail in which Chemistry and other, largely laboratory-based, subjects are covered. It should be noted that Applied Ethnobotany should be focused on field issues and that many students taking programmes in Applied Ethnobotany may have little interest in, or aptitude for, Chemistry or laboratory research.

On the other hand, there are merits of learning about methods of laboratory analysis relevant to Applied Ethnobotany and it is said that a good coverage of Chemistry will make the subject more acceptable in some universities, appearing more genuinely 'scientific'. A possible approach is to mount optional courses in laboratory-based techniques and associsated theory relevant to Applied Ethnobotany.

Ethical issues have gained prominence in Ethnobotany in recent years and need to be studied in courses and programmes. There are many sub-topics, including regarding the purposes and beneficiaries of research, the forms of relationships between ethnobotanists, members of local communities and other collaborators, and how rights to land or access to plant resources can be justified.

Victor Toledo has written that many scientists assume that their work is somehow 'superior' to common pursuits. He mentions that raising questions about the ultimate aim of Ethnobotany can lead to radical ideological questions relating to the universal character or political neutrality of science. Is it right, he asks, for ethnobotanists to approach people as "mere objects of research" (just as they might do plants), establishing a "partial and asymmetric relationship" - a result of "an encounter between a dominant and a dominated culture"? He notes the strong interest today in the discovery of new commercial products based on plants or knowledge of the uses of plants held by local people. He mentions that this tendency is encouraged by the ever-growing dominance of capitalism and the readiness of companies and other inventors to patent new products. How can benefits derived from new discoveries be shared justly and equitably with local people or for conservation, and what forms should such benefits take?

The ability to work effectively in the field requires many competencies on the part of applied ethnobotanists. They must have background knowledge relevant to the case in hand, the ability to work effectively with other people, knowledge of useful approaches and methods, and appropriate attitudes and behaviour. Some of this can be learnt, some is intuitive, and much depends on experience and a continuing willingness, and ability, to learn and reflect. There are protocols for working with communities and theories about ways to involve people and deal with environmental disputes.

It has been recommended that students of Ethnobotany should be required to take language training even in the case of more elementary courses. However, this would seem to be a context-specific matter, given the problems caused by variations in linguistic background between students and in selection of languages to learn in multilingual countries.

The ability to do things is fundamental for work in Applied Ethnobotany. Some of the most vital skills are also the most difficult to teach and learn. These fall into two interconnected sets - the ability to work effectively with other people, including in interdisciplinary teams, and the ability to recognise priorities and contribute to their solving. Skills in communication are essential for applied ethnobotanists, just as they are for others involved in the management of natural resources.

Good ethnobotanical work often depends on collaboration between different specialists; the education of the ethnobotanist should therefore be concerned with learning how to form and work in teams. Applied ethnobotanists need to be able to maintain effective communication with local people throughout the entire process of research, from the initial identification of issues, through the gathering of information and analysis of results, and to the identification of recommendations for follow-up action.

The ability to recognise priorities and contribute systematically to their solution is partly a matter of leadership, and the ability to mobilise fellow researchers and communities. Qualities required include the abilities to obtain adequate background knowledge of a site and its wider context, to observe and obtain information and opinions from local people, to select logical sequences of activities to tackle the issues identified, and to form teams of people with appropriate skills. The ability to identify and solve practical problems, working collaboratively with other people, is an art for which some students will inevitability come better equipped than others. In common with the education of foresters and other environmental managers, this is a matter of life-long learning.

The incorporation into curricula of case-studies, role-playing exercises and participation in real-world situations can help develop these skills. Specific educational tools that have been suggested include research projects that integrate social and ecological issues, workshops and seminars involving interactions with members of outside agencies, the involvement of professionals from outside groups in student graduate committees, and student internships with agencies and organisations. The subjects of problem-solving and communication should not be relegated to elective courses, as is sometimes the case in schools concerned with natural resource use.

There are several skills associated with the acquisition and production of written materials which ethnobotanists should acquire. They include the abilities to use libraries, journals and the internet, to make inquiries of databases, write scientifically, and to produce informative diagrams and maps. Fieldwork should form an essential component of courses and programmes in Applied Ethnobotany , just as it should in Botany, Biology and Conservation Biology. Fieldwork was seen as a 'crucial' component of undergraduate programmes in the Biological Sciences by 79% of university departments which responded to a survey in the UK.

Unfortunately, the serious shortages of finance and transport in many developing countries limit the amount of fieldwork that may be possible. Opportunities for fieldwork will anyway be greater with postgraduate programmes than undergraduate courses. Postgraduate programmes should include a period of group fieldwork of one to three weeks duration, perhaps based at a research station, and an extensive period, typically of about a year, devoted to supervised individual field research.

Specific suggestions for field visits during general undergraduate courses in Ethnobotany include: visits to various types of ecosystems to gain some familiarity with their plants, ecology and human relations; ethnobotanical walks with local people; surveys of plant products in homes; visits to markets and plant-based industries; interviews with traditional doctors; visits to (and perhaps the creation of) ethnobotanical gardens; and visits to herbaria. Specific research methodologies should be taught through instruction in class and through practical experiences. Descriptions of methodologies specific to particular topics should be fully integrated into relevant lectures, seminars and field exercises. Emphasis should be placed throughout on how to collect and analyse data of good quality.

A very large number of methodologies can potentially be used in Applied Ethnobotany -- a reflection of its interdisciplinary nature. Many of them are described or mentioned in materials produced under the People and Plants Initiative. Some methodologies in Applied Ethnobotany are more specifically ethnobotanical, while others are borrowed or adapted from contributory disciplines.

In the case of 'standard' techniques associated with contributory disciplines, lecturers and students need to acquire the ability to reflect on whether the methods should be used in their 'standard' forms or whether it is better to adapt them, especially in relation to the contributions that local knowledge can make to deciding what, where and how to record. The results of such reflection, transformed into practice, will often be an improvement in the usefulness of the data and a saving in time. Even decisions on the categories of information to note on plant specimens collected as vouchers, possibly regarded as a rather simple and standard matter, will benefit immensely from knowledge of the ways that local people perceive the parts and values of plants, and of their knowledge of geography and ecology.

The sampling of vegetation or plants to determine their distributions and other features requires selection of the locations and sizes of sample plots, and of features to record within them. Selection of all of these variables can benefit from local knowledge, for example through inquiry about local perceptions of vegetation types and their origin, the distribution of vegetation types or plants of interest, and the features of particular types of plants regarded as being of significance. In contrast to 'standard' methodologies in ecology, the applied ethnobotanist will often want to record plants that have been harvested, perhaps now represented only by dead or sprouting stumps.

In the case of programmes, it is strongly recommended that these should include a course dedicated to scientific methodology, including the setting and testing of hypotheses and associated statistical methods. The potential advantages of quantification include repeatability, representivity and generation of new hypotheses. Apart from improved quality of data, a further advantage of quantification is that the results of research can be more convincing to some potential beneficiaries, especially more educated people, whether in communities, government departments or other agencies. The biggest challenge in quantification is said to be in making sense of ethnobotanical knowledge.

Quantitative techniques should be applied sensitively. Statisticians ignorant of field realities can propose sampling strategies for research in Applied Ethnobotany which may seem admirable from the mathematical viewpoint, but are impractical under field conditions or take inadequate account of local knowledge. Applied ethnobotanists are faced with the task of finding practical answers to real-world problems. They must be able to cope with complexity and must allocate time to various research tasks with the aim of establishing a convincing overall picture.

The use of quantitative techniques in Applied Ethnobotany will therefore not always be absolutely perfect from the perspective of the statistical purist, yet they may be adequate for applied purposes. The applied ethnobotanist needs to retain an holistic perspective, best achieved through setting aside periods for reflection and discussion in between periods of more intensive collection of information or data. Certainly, those teaching 'Quantitative Methods in Applied Ethnobotany' or involved in the examination of students should have had experience of Ethnobotany applied to real problems.

There is a danger that the production of figures somehow 'proves' that the information is reliable. Sarah Laird (pers. comm.) has compared the relative reliability of quantitative and qualitative methods of gathering information during research into the values of plants to local people in Cameroon. She writes that "many results obtained using quantitative, particularly rapid techniques, are valuable as indicators of community relationships with plants, but often fail to reveal important categories of use and more complex perceptions and relationships to nature.

Basic problems - such as the ability for older individuals to identify species from herbarium specimens, which lack the characteristics used locally for identification such as smell, architecture and colour, or limits to the researcher's knowledge of local classification and use - are often buried within, and warp, so-called 'quantitative' data sets. Although greater quantification can help in efforts to improve standards in Ethnobotany, without a strong qualitative ground in local culture and use, quantitative methods can distort as much as reveal local relationships." Applied Ethnobotanists must also be aware that, unless care is taken, quantification may create barriers to communication with local partners, mystified by unfamiliar terms and academic approaches to problem-solving.

Applied ethnobotanists should approach their work with an understanding of their abilities and limitations - confident yet humble. They should realise that many local people will have much more knowledge of most aspects of local plant worlds and societies than researchers could ever discover. At the same time, they need to be cognisant of the contributions that they themselves can (and should be able to) bring to dialogues with local people. These are likely to include wider perspectives of issues of conservation and sustainable development, knowledge of relevant national and international policies and national regulations, access to published scientific information and outside specialists, and knowledge of methodologies used in the natural and social sciences.

Many of the assumptions brought by applied ethnobotanists when they start work at a new site or on a new problem will likely prove to be false or misleading. Previous assessments of the distribution and conservation status of species of plants, based on available scientific knowledge, may well prove inaccurate in the light of local knowledge . Preconceived views of priorities in conservation and sustainable development may well differ radically from those of local people.

Above all, researchers need to respect local cultures, even if there are facets of them with which they do not agree, or find uncomfortable. This can be just as much of a challenge for national researchers, some of whom will have cultural backgrounds different from those of their local collaborators, as it can be for researchers from other countries. Applied ethnobotanists do not need to sacrifice their own beliefs and motivations (without which they would hardly have embarked on challenging journeys), but rather should share them with local people as the foundation for honest discourse.

6

Teaching and Learning in Plant Biology

In contemporary society, it's very obvious that as a result of the rapid explosion of knowledge in biology, due to the achievements of molecular biology and biotechnology, many new content areas and technologies are involved in the teaching of biology. This means that graduates are part of a society in which knowledge will be rapidly changing as we go through the 21st century, and they will need to be able to cope with these changes. It is also the case that they will certainly have to be prepared to change their professional focus during their working life.

In order to be successful, they must have the ability to access and generate new knowledge in a purposeful fashion, and to move beyond simple content knowledge to critical analysis and an understanding of emerging trends and issues. They should be able to solve real life problems, to communicate with one another, to see relationships within what they have learned, to perceive their field of study in the broad perspective and to develop flexibility and adaptability to continue learning in their disciplines throughout life, including practical skills and personal skills. That is common to all the major universities around the world.

The implementation of contemporary education theories and strategies in the teaching process will facilitate students developing the above generic skills. Three years ago the plant biology course in most of the universities in China was usually divided into two or three courses, including botany, plant physiology and plant systems and evolution. With the explosion of knowledge in biology, particularly achievements in molecular biology and biotechnology, much new content and many new courses should be included in the discipline of biology, However, because of limited study hours, we must combine some related courses and compress some concepts.

More importantly, designing the curriculum should depend on the system of the course, i.e. the structure and physiology are adaptive in plants, so it's unreasonable to separate them into different courses. The recent research indicates that the trend in the development of the discipline in plants is integrative. Based on this background, under the program of reform of biology courses which was supported by MOE (Ministry of Education) of China, we have redesigned a new course in plant biology and following two main strands: individual plant development and plant systems and evolution, we have developed a new course syllabus.

Plant biology is intended to introduce some of the broad and fundamental issues in plants, and is designed to be an integrated course, including morphology and the anatomy of plants, and metabolism and bioenergetics in plants, with the emphasis being on the relationships and adaptability between the structures and functions in plant. Plant systems and diversity is one of the main content areas relating to angiosperm classification. The tight relationship between plants and their environment and the way in which they influence one another are important contents of this course, as is the protection and utilizing of plant resources involved in plant biology.

Plant biology is usually taught as a two semester compulsory course. At present, the teaching method I use is conventional lectures which are given by multimedia. We made the courseware for the plant biology lectures. In laboratory classes, there are individual and teamwork tasks. Before the examination, there are consultations and tutorials, but few people meet with us, the majority of students not asking academics issues in plant biology. Instead, they are focusing on how to pass the examination. Although students who have got good 'A-level' grades can remember the definitions of terms, they do not adequately understand the concepts involved and commonly they forget the knowledge soon after the examination.

The project of teaching/learning is a good way to train students in practical skills, and the topics we offer cover the main contents and experiment skills of the course. Students make plans to complete these tasks by themselves, the teacher supervising if needed. In terms of assessment, apart from reports of experiments mid-semester and the final closed-book examination, the practical test is a necessity for all students. If someone can't pass it, he/she will not be permitted to participate in the final examination, meaning that they will have to study this course again.

All the recent research in science education in universities suggests that we would like 'teaching intent' and 'learning outcomes' to be consistent. When we design plant biology courses, the teaching intent is to get students to grasp the theories and skills of plant biology, to establish good knowledge backgrounds for higher level courses, to develop the ability to solve real problems using the theories and skills learned in classes, to understand the concept that plants are forever evolving and have done so since the origin of life, and to develop an inquiring and open approach to the study of plant biology.

Through the examination, practical tests, field trip reports and questionnaires, these surveys showed that students understand the basic theories of plant biology, including the structure and function, growth and development in plant; learn the basic skills, including observation of microstructure, collecting and identifying species; and improve their technique in producing biology slides. Ninety percent of students can pass the examination, but after the examination the knowledge they learned is quickly forgotten; and after two semesters 70-80% students can't do the field trip work.

The characters in current teaching are discipline-centred, teacher-centred teaching, and the student learning is passive surface learning. A wealth of evidence has been reported to support the concept that under the discipline-centred teaching, the needs, concerns, and requirements of teacher and student are not considered because the course is driven by, and depends mainly on, the disciplinary content that must be presented. The teacher transmits information.

In the teacher-centred style, the teacher is regarded as the authoritative expert, the main source of knowledge, and the focal point of all activity. The student is the passive recipient of the information already acquired by the teacher. The teacher selects from the discipline the information to be taught, studied, and learned. In this environment, surface approaches to learning are very common, the students reduce what is to be learnt to the status of unconnected facts to be memorized. The learning task is to reproduce the subject matter at a later date .

In fact teaching and learning should be inseparable, in that learning is a criterion and product of effective teaching. In essence, learning is the goal of teaching. Science teaching requires attention to both the content of the course and the process of moving students from their initial state of knowledge and understanding to the desired level. In fact, teaching is part of a whole that comprises the teacher, the learner, the disciplinary content, the teaching/learning process, and the evaluation of both the teacher and the learner.

The contemporary major theoretical development is the move towards the constructivist perspective and view of how people learn science. The major practical development is the move towards student-centred approaches and student active science as an appropriate teaching technology, which is seen as compatible with the constructivist view of learning. Student-centred teaching focuses on the student and, in particular, on the cognitive development of the student.

The teacher's goal is to help students grasp the development of knowledge as a process rather than a product. The focus of classroom activities and assignments is on the student-centred process of inquiry itself, not on the products of inquiry. Students create their own conceptual or cognitive models. Content, teaching style, and methods are adapted to aid the cognitive and intellectual growth of students.

Student-centred teaching combines an understanding of the way that humans process information with other factors that affect learning such as attitudes, values, beliefs, and motivation. If we adopt student-centred teaching, we would therefore expect that the learning style of students will convert to active, deep and lifelong learning. If students are to become independent, lifelong and active learners, the program of teaching strategies needs to include methods and tasks which are interesting, motivating and require the students to be involved in both team and individual learning tasks.

Concept Mapping

There are many academic and technical terms in plant biology, and especially, there are some concepts that are very difficulty and confusing for students to understand. Concept mapping is a very useful tool for solving these problems. Concept maps can give a schema of the main concepts. There are many notes and linkages in the life cycle, and they can be used to help me to establish whether or not the students understand the concepts that link various pieces of information together. They can be used to explain why I am focusing on the sporophyte and the gametophyte generations, meiosis and fertilization as parts of the life cycle. In this way students can see how particular pieces of information fit into the overall schema.

The completed concept map; can be used to help students know what it is they have learned and what it is they still do not understand, and can be used as an assessment tool. The linking concepts such as mitosis and meiosis can tend to relate to the content I teach in my lectures. So concept mapping is a powerful tool to help the understanding of some confusing and difficult concepts in the course. I think concept mapping is really suitable for plant biology. I'd like to use it more.

Other possible ways to use it might be that students are asked to draw the concept maps before and after teaching a new topic in plant biology. In this way the lecturer can find out what the students' preconceptions are and what might be their misunderstandings and weaknesses. This can lead the instructor to work out the best way to teach that topic, and thus to modify his/her lecturing content and teaching methods correspondingly.

Problem-based learning

During recent decades, problem-based learning has become very common in teaching science in western countries. PBL is a curriculum design and teaching/learning strategy that simultaneously develops higher order thinking and disciplinary knowledge bases and skills by placing students in the active role of problem solvers confronted with a situation that reflects the real world. So PBL is a very effective method to develop learner critical thinking, self-directed and lifelong learning, problem solving and teamwork skills. It is well documented in the literature that PBL is a very good teaching strategy. It has worked very well in several fields, for example medicine and engineering.

There are many real life problems that need to be solved in the plant biology field and we met such a problem in the university three years ago. A farmer came from the Jinshan county of Hubei province, asking for help, because he did not harvest any plums last year. Students will be divided into groups, each group having 5-7 people. Firstly, they should gather the relevant information from textbooks, the library, Internet, journals and staff of the department. It may be necessary to have an interview with the farmer.

There are many factors which influence fruiting including harsh climates, the development of flower organ abnormality, diseases and insect pests and the nutrition of the soil. So students should investigate using the knowledge and skills they have learned to successfully integrate interdisciplinary knowledge. They must analyze and figure out the main reason behind the plum trees not fruiting, and finally they should make a plan to help the farmer so that next year he can get plums.

It's very obvious that PBL facilitates self-directed and lifelong learning skills, problem solving, analytical and critical thinking skills, integration of interdisciplinary knowledge, teamwork and interpersonal skills. Unfortunately, some problems also exist with this approach. Typically, it is time consuming, and it is difficult to create suitable problems for first year students. It requires the students having integrated knowledge and teamwork skills, but these are exactly what first year students lack.

Implementation problems

Students are accustomed to the conventional teaching methods, where they are used to getting knowledge just by memory. They are not used to taking as much responsibility for their own learning and will complain about the extra efforts needed and be reluctant to use these learning approaches. Therefore it's very important to make the transition smooth for students. Limitation of hours is a common problem, but a good way to solve this problem may be by using WebCT. However this may elicit the next problem, that is financial and facilities problem.

Setting up WebCT involves systems engineering, and will need cooperation between the academic staff and computer engineers. Besides, possibly, it will not be easy to convince my colleagues to agree with, and use, these new teaching strategies in plant biology, It needs time to communicate with one another and discuss these new ideas. There may also be some handicaps from the level of the whole university. Currently the present system of university administration is not flexible enough to accommodate such change, and it is not easy to make a special policy for modifications of plant biology.

Improving Plant Biology Courses

Nowadays, in the theoretical development, the constructivist perspective and viewpoint of how people learn science have been in the ascendancy. In practical development, student-centred approaches and student active learning have been adopted as an appropriate teaching technology, which is seen as compatible with the constructivist view of learning. Nevertheless, strategic plans for developing effective teaching and learning environments are rarely found. A single teaching strategy is never appropriate to all learning contexts, nor is a single teaching method superior to another in all situations (particularly in terms of student performance).

Effective teaching means designing the teaching/ learning context so that students have every encouragement to react with the level of cognitive engagement. The information society tends to organize itself around patterns of cognition. Therefore, the pivotal emergent property conditioning the future of these different societies is learning. Students are seen to have to construct their own knowledge, and learning is a process of inconsistent movement itself, which cannot be replaced by a teacher. First of all, think about students' requirements and approaches to learning, and how their learning motivation is produced.

In the teaching process, we can arouse student's review of their prior understanding of concepts and knowledge, then put forward new problems and facilitate their enthusiasm of learning further. To do this most successfully we can cite examples of crucial problems in real world, and thus mobilise their enthusiasm for learning. For example, when teaching the practical protection of plant diversity, the existence of the problem of sandstorms in Beijing is first referred to, before focusing on the implications for the need for the protection of plant diversity in the area.

Learning outcomes depend on an interaction between the characteristics of the student, the teaching style and methods of the teacher, and the policies and practices of the department and institution , so teaching and learning are very complex processes. In China, the botany course has maintained a traditional pattern for a long time, in its teaching objective of training botanists. The teaching content is now considered dated, since it basically concentrates on classical morphology and taxonomy.

Nowadays, the plant science field is developing rapidly, and new offshoot disciplines and research fields come forth continually. The 'web' will be a foundation that students use to learn the professional courses further and thus will be useful in training biology-based professionals of the highest calibre. To reflect fully the new developments in plant science, the reproduction, growth, development or evolution, the phylogeny and the maintenance of plant species diversity are added. At the same time, the detailed description of plant groups is reduced to create a more balanced course.

At the moment, the constructivist perspective has been introduced, and the teaching technology of student-centred learning has been applied. Most of teaching strategies have been related to and have been used by turn, for example, case study analysis, small group investigation tasks, problem-based teaching approaches, role play activities, simulations, interactive teaching/learning sessions, discussion questioning, programmed instruction, independent learning tasks, community activities, etc. Barnett and Griffin calls for teaching to become more research-like, while Hattie and Marsh suggest that marrying teaching and research by enhancing the relationship between them is a desirable aim of universities. In field practice and laboratory work, some grouping experiments and researching practices are designed for students and are accomplished by themselves.

Although it is as above, it is fractional and not a systematic application, so it is clear that there are many shortcomings in the teaching process still. Learning is a hard and difficult process that depends on teachers as much as learners. On the base of elaborate teaching plan, it is urgent that the constructivist ideas and student-centred learning strategies are applied more widely and further.

Improving Teaching and Learning

In teaching content, part of plant diversity included the correlative knowledge of plant taxonomy, ecology and biogeology, but it has been integrated and reorganised according to the clue of current state, history, evolution and maintenance of diversity. In teaching strategies, although some modern methods have been carried out, there is fractional, not systematic application. At present, there has not been a moment to be lost in improving of teaching strategies.

There are some teachers who complain about the reduction in hours for basic courses, with the development of teaching and learning reform in high education. As long as we think over, we can find out that the traditional lectures consume a great deal of hours for infusing material knowledge. Students are not satisfied with traditional content and methods, which are to study characteristic of groups dryly and to observe plant material with magnifier passively, even some students said that to memorize many plants is taxonomist's thing, but they need to realise diversity only. They desire to learn more from the course actively.

A review of the literature indicated that most lectures were ineffective, presenting too much detail and too little illustrative material, and offering few opportunities for active involvement by the students: To accept our role as coach/facilitator as opposed to the familiar lecturer, while the teaching hours of traditional lectures are reduced, some modern strategies must be applied more widely. On the basis of constructivist perspective, firstly, the teaching content is researched carefully and the inner relationship within the knowledge is thought out. Then, the concept maps and learning problems are designed systemically.

Finally, the lectures are developed continuously by means of the concept maps and learning problems. Through the development of problems and concepts step by step, the students can achieve the deep approaches. Numerous studies have shown correlations between students' deeper approaches to learning and higher quality learning outcomes. Otherwise, the strategies of problembased and case study are useful for parallels between motivation at work and for learning and promoting synthesis of multidisciplinary perspectives.

A major goal of biology teaching is enhancing students' biology learning. In teaching practice, we often pay attention to more knowledge than skills, and students gain very detailed knowledge. However, with rapid developments in biology, knowledge is exploding so that we cannot give students all the knowledge they need in university. Students need to achieve self-directed and lifelong learning skills, and integration of relevant knowledge, they are active learners.

Learning is a process that the concepts change continuously and of selfconstruction by students. We cannot force them to do it, but can help them to do it by using concept maps. Ability to apply knowledge requires a stable conceptual framework . Generally speaking, the concept map reflects inner relationship between knowledge and correlation between concepts, it is useful to forming systematic knowledge 'web' in the brain so that students can apply this knowledge and concepts flexibly.

Modern development of biology desires the integration of knowledge and concepts strongly. Biggs argues that meaning is constructed through learning activities and, therefore, teaching and learning must be about conceptual change. Concept maps have been described as working as 'spark plugs' or catalysts for discussion because students have something to start with . The concept mapping approach was summarised as six steps by Kinchin.

Concept mapping is seen by some as a method that encourages the acquisition of 'a habit of changing habits'. For teachers to change their 'habits of teaching' will, in many cases, require a fundamental shift in their basic assumptions about teaching and learning . As a part of teaching, content of plant diversity is designed into a concept map. On the basis of reconstruction of teaching contents the problem of plant diversity is illustrated by the four aspects: current state, history, evolution and maintenance of diversity, and is involved in the four levels: gene, individual, community and ecosystem. In real teaching, the concept map will be introduced step by step. After all content of plant diversity is learned, the whole map will be displayed and linked completely.

Problem-Based Learning

Problem-based learning is a curriculum design and a teaching-learning strategy and is about learning subject knowledge in the context of using and developing process skills. It is powerful because it is a learning environment that embodies most of the principles; it forces the students to learn the fundamental principles of the subject in the context of needing it to solve a problem; and it offers an opportunity to practice and to use many processing skills. Students learn concepts and how to apply them while working with the cases, they reconstruct prior knowledge and continue learning from there and finally, they take responsibility for their own learning and are trained to actively seek information, structure and present it.

In the face of the problem in the real world, students' epistemic motivation are enhanced easily, they can take part in the teaching activities on their own initiative and their self-directed, cooperative and thinking skills are trained. On the other hand, the knowledge in their brain is reconstructed and integrated. In designing a problem, we must simultaneously focus on two aspects when students devote their attention to solving problems as an active role as a practitioner:

1. to develop both higher order thinking; and
2. academic knowledge bases and skills.

Learning is conceptualised as inter-psychological process of participation in social practices, and it is not reserved for activities and interactions intentionally organized for learning. First of all, the selective problem must be one in the real world and be complex enough so that epistemic motivation and enthusiasm to learning further are facilitated enormously, thinking and cooperative skills are trained deep, and knowledge and concepts are integrated as soon as possible.

The degraded problem of the ecosystem has a concern in each of us, and it is a fatal topic in China, so it is selected as an important problem to probe in the process of learning. This problem is involved in complex concepts and theories, and integration of them. For example, degradation of ecosystem, biodiversity, competition, disturbance of ecosystem, ecological stable state, and moderate disturbance hypothesis, etc. .

Case study is different from problem-based learning, it tell a real and complete story, is usually interdisciplinary, has academic and professional significance, and has social implications. As the teaching strategy is interesting, relevant, motivating for students, it is used in teaching process widely. Algal blooms is a significant problem in procreative practice and academia, it has occurred many times historically in the world. Its appearance would often bring tremendous tragedy to aquatic animals and plants, furthermore, affect production in aquaculture.

The occurrence and prevention of algal blooms is involved in complex and interdisciplinary issues. In China, students have been used to the teaching strategies of how to deal with examinations in middle school, so how the teachers control and develop the teaching process gradually will be the most important key of achieving the teaching aim. The Piagetian model of intellectual development thinks that each individual must learn in a manner to adapt to his or her present level of development for advancing to the next level of development. Research showed that pupils' prior knowledge could significantly influence classroom teaching and learning.

Teachers should be aware of students' prior knowledge and misconceptions, because they are strong predictors of student achievement in science, and the teacher should examine why these misconceptions occur . Before classes, it is necessary that the background of students is researched. Under the circumstances that we realize the foundation of students adequately, students are led to our objective through different strategies to be carried on in order. Of course, the teaching process is always dynamic. For the first year students, they need to be introduced step by step, it may be the best way that the different teaching strategies are used by turn.

Physiological and Molecular Plant Biology (Bachelor of Science)

Physiological and Molecular Plant Biology involves the study of plant biology, biochemistry, genetics, gene transfer technology and microbiology. What distinguishes Physiological and Molecular Plant Biology from other plant-related programmes at Massey University is that you will study the structure and function of plants at the cell through to whole plant level. You may want to use genetic and DNA technology to understand systematics or plant physiology. Useful subjects at school are Chemistry, Biology and Maths with Statistics.

Physiological and Molecular Plant Biology undergraduates become research technicians with Crown

Research Institutes, teach at schools and polytechnics, or perform technical and advisory work. Post-graduates may become plant scien-tists with Crown Research Institutes or private companies, or lecturers at universities. Careers may also include science management, administration and science policy.

Pant Biology (Bachelor of Science)

Plant Biology combines the study of the structure and function of plants with investigations of how the whole plant and its environment (natural or managed). What distinguishes Plant Biology from other plant-related programmes at Massey University is that you are more likely to focus your study at the whole plant level. You may be interested in bioinformatics (analysis of DNA sequences) which assists in understanding biodiversity and enables input into conservation issues. Useful subjects at school are Chemistry, Biology and Maths with Statistics.

Plant Biology undergraduates become research technicians with Crown Research Institutes, technicians with government departments (eg Department of Conservation) and regional authorities, teach at schools and polytechnics, or perform technical and advisory work. Postgraduates may become scientists with Crown Research Institutes or private companies, or lecturers at universities. Careers may also include science management, administration and science policy.

Plant Protection (Bachelor of Science)

Plant protection encompasses the study of living organisms - pathogens, pests and weeds - that are harmful to the productivity and/or quality of plants. What distinguishes Plant Protection from other plant-related programmes at

Massey University is that you will focus your study at the pest, disease and weed problems that affect crops and what can be done about them. You may be concerned about the threat posed by pesticide use and whether genetic engineering of resistant plants provides the ultimate answer. Useful subjects at school are Chemistry and Biology.

Plant Protection undergraduates become research technicians with Crown Research Institutes, technicians with government departments (eg MAFQual), teach at schools and polytechnics, or perform technical and advisory work with agricultural chemical companies, industry organisations such as the New Zealand Apple and Pear Marketing Board. Postgraduates may become scientists with Crown Research Institutes or private companies, or lecturers at universities.

Horticultural Science (Bachelor of Science)

Horticultural Science involves the study of plants and developing new technologies so as to be in control of their yield, quality and timing. What distinguishes Horticultural Science from other plant-related programmes at Massey University is the focus upon plants grown as a commercial crop, dealing more with the science that underpins the commercial use of plants than business management.

You may want to know how to use plant breeding, DNA technology, tissue culture or environmental physiology to create high value, premium quality food for world markets. Useful subjects at school are English, Chemistry, Biology and Mathematics.

Horticultural Science undergradu-ates become technicians with Crown Research Institutes or government departments, teach at schools and polytechnics, and undertake advisory work. Those with postgraduate qualifications can become scientists with Crown Research Institutes or private companies, or lecturers at universi-ties.

Forestry (Bachelor of Applied Science)

Forestry combines science and business in the production, processing and marketing of wood. What distinguishes the Forestry major from other plant-related programmes at Massey University is that you can study combinations of Silviculture, Natural Resource Management, and traditional Agriculture. You may wish to plan and evaluate forestry diversification proposals in terms of profitability, risk and resource use

Horticulture (Bachelor of Applied Science)

Horticulture involves the study of plants and how we can be in economic control of their yield, quality and timing. What distinguishes the Horticulture major from other plant-related programmes at Massey University is the focus upon plants grown as a commercial crop, dealing more with the business and technology aspects than pure science. You may want to know how to avoid chemicals in orchards, evaluate horticultural business proposals, or schedule crops for export. Useful subjects at school are English, Chemistry, Biology and Mathematics.

Horticulture undergraduates may own their own horticultural business or manage them for others; control packhouses; provide technical advice and products to the production sector; be involved in marketing and distribution internationally; or teach at schools and polytechnics. Postgraduates may become consultants, scientists with Crown Research Institutes or private companies, or lecturers at universities.

Forestry undergraduates are well placed to participate in the changes associated with diversifying our land use from traditional agriculture to forestry. Local government (eg Regional and District Councils), forest companies and service industries including banks and merchandise retailers, employ our graduates.

Landscape Management (Bachelor of Applied Science)

Landscape Management combines art and science with creativity and analysis. What distinguishes the Landscape Management major from other plant-related programmes at Massey University is that you will study natural or managed landscapes from the point of view of plants and the environment, and how we as people can gain aesthetic pleasure. You may want to know how to sustain, develop, improve and manage landscapes for towns, cities and private homes. You may be concerned about the conservation of plant species in natural areas, or protecting important or sensitive landscapes. Useful subjects at school are English, Biology, General Science and Mathematics.

Landscape Management undergraduates often create their own businesses, particularly in garden design and maintenance. They may also work with local authorities, parks, sports clubs, private gardens, or as teachers and consultants.

Ecology (Bachelor of Science)

Ecology is where science and nature meet, and involves the study of plants, animals and microbes, as well as earth and physical sciences, genetics, DNA technology, behaviour, biogeography, mathematics and physiology. What distinguishes Ecology from other plant-related programmes at Massey University is that you will study whole ecosystems (natural or managed) where plants, animals and microbes interact. You may want to know how stream or forest systems work, examine changes in populations over time, or protect endangered plants and animals. Useful subjects at school are Chemistry, Biology and Maths with Statistics.

Undergraduate degrees in Ecology lead to careers with central and local government (eg Regional and District Councils), Crown Research Institutes, environmental or conservation organisations, school teaching, technical and advisory work. Postgraduate qualifications allow you to consider research and management positions with the Department of Conservation or the Ministry for the Environment.

One year of full-time equivalent study, taken part-time. Available at Palmerston North (Turitea) and Extramurally. Horticulture combines art, science and business in the production, marketing, use and improvement of fruits, flowers, vegetables and ornamental plants. What distinguishes the Certificate in Horticulture from other plant-related programmes at Massey University is the one-year full-time equivalent duration of study, compared with the three-year duration of a degree. The programme is designed for part-time extramural study.

Students who may decide to study horticulture beyond the certificate will be able to credit papers to the BApplSc degree. Useful subjects at school are General Science. The Certificate is intended to meet the needs of those with horticultural aspirations including those who are about to commence a career in horticulture, are currently employed in the horticultural industry, work in the horticultural service industry, are considering a career change to horticulture, or have horticulture as a major interest.

The Certificate allows students to specialise in one of five areas (cut flowers, fruit, landscape management, nursery, vegetables) of horticultural endeavour. This specialisation, along with instruction in business management, botany, soils, engineering and plant diseases and pests, provides a sound educational basis for careers as:

— producers/managers in the cut flower, fruit, nursery and vegetable industries;

— landscape contractors and managers;

— sales and technical employees in the service industries - examples are with seed, plants, fertilisers, agricultural chemicals;

— technicians in organisations which use plants in their research and development programmes.

Graduate Diploma in Rural Studies

The Graduate Diploma in Rural Studies is a highly flexible programme designed primarily for mid-career people seeking to further their knowledge in the agricultural, horticultural, forestry, natural resource and related subject areas. What distinguishes the Graduate Diploma from other plant-related programmes at Massey University is both the 1-year full-time equivalent duration of study and, it being targeted at those who are at mid-career. Hence candidates will typically have either already completed a university degree in any subject area or have relevant career experience. For those with an interest in plants, you can customise a course of study to include your specific areas of interest.

7

Gene Expression and Signal Transduction

Plant Biologists may be forgiven for taking abiding satisfaction in the fact that Mendel's classic studies on the role of heritable factors in development were carried out on a flowering plant: the garden pea. The heritable factors that Mendel discovered, which control such characters as flower color, flower position, pod shape, stem length, seed color, and seed shape, came to be called genes. Genes are the DNA sequences that encode the RNA molecules directly involved in making the enzymes and structural proteins of the cell. Genes are arranged linearly on chromosomes, which form linkage groups-that is, genes that are inherited together. The total amount of DNA or genetic information contained in a cell, nucleus, or organelle is termed its genome.

Since Mendel's pioneering discoveries in his garden, the principle has become firmly established that the growth, development, and environmental responses of even the simplest microorganism are determined by the programmed expression of its genes. Among multicellular organisms, turning genes on (gene expression) or off alters a cell's complement of enzymes and structural proteins, allowing cells to differentiate.

Various internal signals are required for coordinating the expression of genes during development and for enabling the plant to respond to environmental signals. Such internal (as well as external) signaling agents typically bring about their effects by means of sequences of biochemical reactions, called signal transduction pathways, that greatly amplify the original signal and ultimately result in the activation or repression of genes. Much progress has been made in the study of signal transduction pathways in plants in recent years.

Genome Size, Organization, and Complexity

As might be expected, the size of the genome bears some relation to the complexity of the organism. For example, the genome size of E. coli is 4.7×10^6 bp (base pairs), that of the fruit fly is 2×10^8 bp per haploid cell, and that of a human is 3×10^9 bp per haploid cell. However, genome size in eukaryotes is an unreliable indicator of complexity because not all of the DNA encodes genes.

In prokaryotes, nearly all of the DNA consists of unique sequences that encode proteins or functional RNAmolecules. In addition to unique sequences, however, eukaryotic chromosomes contain large amounts of noncoding DNA whose main functions appear to be chromosome organization and structure. Much of this noncoding DNA consists of multicopy sequences, called repetitive DNA. The remainder of the noncoding DNA is made up of single-copy sequences called spacer DNA. Together, repetitive and spacer DNA can make up the majority of the total genome in some eukaryotes. For example, in humans only about 5% of the total DNA consists of genes, the unique sequences that encode for RNAand protein synthesis.

The genome size in plants is more variable than in any other group of eukaryotes. In angiosperms, the haploid genome ranges from about 1.5 $\times 10^8$ bp for Arabidopsis thaliana (smaller than that of the fruit fly) to 1×10^{11} bp for the monocot Trillium, which is considerably larger than the human genome. Even closely related beans of the genus Vicia exhibit genomic DNA contents that vary over a 20-fold range. Why are plant genomes so variable in size?

Studies of plant molecular biology have shown that most of the DNA in plants with large genomes is repetitive DNA. Arabidopsis has the smallest genome of any plant because only 10% of its nuclear DNA is repetitive DNA. The genome size of rice is estimated to be about five times that of Arabidopsis, yet the total amount of unique sequence DNA in the rice genome is about the same as in Arabidopsis. Thus the difference in genome size between Arabidopsis and rice is due mainly to repetitive and spacer DNA.

Until recently, the total number of genes in an organism's genome was difficult to assess. Thanks to recent advances in many genomic sequencing projects, such numbers are now becoming available, although precise values are still lacking. According to Miklos and Rubin, the number of genes in bacteria varies from 500 to 8,000 and overlaps with the number of genes in many simple unicellular eukaryotes. For example, the yeast genome appears to contain about 6,000 genes. More complex eukaryotes, such as protozoans, worms, and flies, all seem to have gene numbers in the range of 12,000 to 14,000. The Drosophila (fruit fly) genome contains about 12,000 genes. Thus, the current view is that it takes roughly 12,000 basic types of genes to form a eukaryotic organism, although values as high as 43,000 genes are common, as a result of multiple copies of certain genes, or multigene families.

The best-studied plant genome is that of Arabidopsis thaliana. Chris Somerville and his colleagues at Stanford University have estimated that the Arabidopsis genome contains roughly 20,000 genes. This estimate is based on more than one approach. For example, since large regions of the genome have been sequenced, we know there is one gene for every 5 kb (kilobases) of DNA. Since the entire genome contains about 100,000 kb, there must be about 20,000 genes. However, 6% of the genome encodes ribosomal RNA, and another 2% consists of highly repetitive sequences, so the number could be lower. Similar values likely will be found for the genomes of other plants as well. The current consensus is that the genomes of most plants will be found to contain from 20,000 to 30,000 genes.

Some of these genes encode proteins that perform housekeeping functions, basic cellular processes that go on in all the different kinds of cells. Such genes are permanently turned on; that is, they are constitutively expressed. Other genes are highly regulated, being turned on or off at specific stages of development or in response to specific environmental stimuli.

Prokaryotic Gene Expression

The first step in gene expression is transcription, the synthesis of an mRNA copy of the DNA template that encodes a protein. Transcription is followed by translation, the synthesis of the protein on the ribosome. Developmental studies have shown that each plant organ contains large numbers of organ-specific mRNAs. Transcription is controlled by proteins that bind DNA, and these DNAbinding proteins are themselves subject to various types of regulation. Gene regulation in eukaryotes is far more complex than in prokaryotes. The added complexity of gene expression in eukaryotes is what allows cells and tissues to differentiate and makes possible the diverse life cycles of plants and animals.

In prokaryotes, genes are arranged in operons, sets of contiguous genes that include structural genes and regulatory sequences. Afamous example is the E. coli lactose (lac) operon, which was first described in 1961 by François Jacob and Jacques Monod of the Pasteur Institute in Paris. The lac operon is an example of an inducible operon-that is, one in which a key metabolic intermediate induces the transcription of the genes. The lac operon is responsible for the production of three proteins involved in utilization of the disaccharide lactose. This operon consists of three structural genes and three regulatory sequences. The structural genes code for the sequence of amino acids in three proteins: β-galactosidase, the enzyme that catalyzes the hydrolysis of lactose to glucose and galactose; permease, a carrier protein for the membrane transport of lactose into the cell; and transacetylase, the significance of which is unknown.

The three regulatory sequences control the transcription of mRNA for the synthesis of these proteins. Gene i is responsible for the synthesis of a repressor protein that recognizes and binds to a specific nucleotide sequence, the operator. The operator, o, is located downstream (i.e., on the 3'side) of the promoter sequence, p, where RNA polymerase attaches to the operon to initiate transcription, and immediately upstream (i.e., on the 5'side) of the transcription start site, where transcription begins. (The initiation site is considered to be at the 5' end of the gene, even though the RNA polymerase transcribes from the 3' end to the 5' end along the opposite strand. This convention was adopted so that the sequence of the mRNA would match the DNA sequence of the gene.)

In the absence of lactose, the lactose repressor forms a tight complex with the operator sequence and blocks the interaction of RNA polymerase with the transcription start site, effectively preventing transcription. When present, lactose binds to the repressor, causing it to undergo a conformational change. The lac repressor is thus an allosteric protein whose conformation is determined by the presence or absence of an effector molecule, in this case lactose. As a result of the conformational change due to binding lactose, the lac repressor detaches from the operator. When the operator sequence is unobstructed, the RNA polymerase can move along the DNA, synthesizing a continuous mRNA. The translation of this mRNA yields the three proteins, and lactose is said to induce their synthesis.

The lac repressor is an example of negative control, since the repressor blocks transcription upon binding to the operator region of the operon. The lac operon is also regulated by positive control, which was discovered in connection with a phenomenon called the glucose effect. If glucose is added to a nutrient medium that includes lactose, the E. coli cells metabolize the glucose and ignore the lactose. Glucose suppresses expression of the lac operon and prevents synthesis of the enzymes needed to degrade lactose. Glucose exerts this effect by lowering the cellular concentration of cyclic AMP (cAMP). When glucose levels are low, cAMP levels are high. Cyclic AMP binds to an activator protein, the catabolite activator protein (CAP), which recognizes and binds to a specific nucleotide sequence immediately upstream of the lac operator and promoter sites.

In contrast to the behavior of the lactose repressor protein, when the CAP is complexed with its effector, cAMP, its affinity for its DNA-binding site is dramatically increased (hence the reference to positive control). The ternary complex formed by CAP, cAMP, and the lactose operon DNA sequences induces bending of the DNA, which activates transcription of the lactose operon structural genes by increasing the affinity of RNA polymerase for the neighboring promoter site. Bacteria synthesize cyclic AMP when they exhaust the glucose in their growth medium. The lactose operon genes are thus under opposing regulation by the absence of glucose (high levels of cyclic AMP) and the presence of lactose, since glucose is a catabolite of lactose.

In bacteria, metabolites can also serve as corepressors, activating a repressor protein that blocks transcription. Repression of enzyme synthesis is often involved in the regulation of biosynthetic pathways in which one or more enzymes are synthesized only if the end product of the pathway-an amino acid, for example-is not available. In such a case the amino acid acts as a corepressor: It complexes with the repressor protein, and this complex attaches to the operator DNA, preventing transcription. The tryptophan (trp) operon in E. coli is an example of an operon that works by corepression.

Eukaryotic Gene Expression

The study of bacterial gene expression has provided models that can be tested in eukaryotes. However, the details of the process are quite different and more complex in eukaryotes. In prokaryotes, translation is coupled to transcription: As the mRNA transcripts elongate, they bind to ribosomes and begin synthesizing proteins (translation). In eukaryotes, however, the nuclear envelope separates the genome from the translational machinery. The transcripts must first be transported to the cytoplasm, adding another level of control.

Eukaryotes differ from prokaryotes also in the organization of their genomes. In most eukaryotic organisms, each gene encodes a single polypeptide. The eukaryotic nuclear genome contains no operons, with one notable exception. Furthermore, eukaryotic genes are divided into coding regions called exons and noncoding regions called introns. Since the primary transcript, or pre-mRNA, contains both exon and intron sequences, the pre-mRNA must be processed to remove the introns.

RNA processing involves multiple steps. The newly synthesized pre-mRNA is immediately packaged into a string of small protein-containing particles, called heteronuclear ribonucleoprotein particles, or hnRNP particles. Some of these particles are composed of proteins and small nuclear RNAs, and are called small nuclear ribonucleoproteins, or snRNPs (pronounced "snurps"). Various snRNPs assemble into spliceosome complexes at exon-intron boundaries of the pre-mRNA and carry out the splicing reaction.

In some cases, the primary transcript can be spliced in different ways, a process called alternative RNA splicing. For example, an exon that is present in one version of a processed transcript may be spliced out of another version. In this way, the same gene can give rise to different polypeptide chains. Approximately 15% of human genes are processed by alternative splicing. Although alternative splicing is rare in plants, it is involved in the synthesis of rubisco activase, RNA polymerase II, and the gene product of a rice homeobox gene, as well as other proteins .

Before splicing, the pre-mRNA is modified in two important ways. First it is capped by the addition of 7-methylguanylate to the 5' end of the transcript via a 5'- to-5'linkage. The pre-mRNA is capped almost immediately after the initiation of mRNA synthesis. One of the functions of the 5' cap is to protect the growing RNA transcript from degradation by RNases. At a later stage in the synthesis of the primary transcript, the 3' end is cleaved at a specific site, and a poly-A tail, usually consisting of about 100 to 200 adenylic acid residues, is added by the enzyme poly-A polymerase.

The poly-A tail has several functions:

1. It protects against RNases and therefore increases the stability of mRNAmolecules in the cytoplasm,
2. both it and the 5' cap are required for transit through the nuclear pore, and
3. it increases the efficiency of translation on the ribosomes.

The requirement of eukaryotic mRNAs to have both a 5' cap and a poly-A tail ensures that only properly processed transcripts will reach the ribosome and be translated.Each step in eukaryotic gene expression can potentially regulate the amount of gene product in the cell at any given time. Like transcription initiation, splicing may be regulated. Export from the nucleus is also regulated. For example, to exit the nucleus an mRNA must possess a 5' cap and a poly-A tail, and it must be properly spliced. Incompletely processed transcripts remain in the nucleus and are degraded.

The stabilities or turnover rates of mRNA molecules differ from one another, and may vary from tissue to tissue, depending on the physiological conditions. For example, in bean (Vicia faba), fungal infection causes the rapid degradation of the mRNA that encodes the proline-rich protein PvPRP1 of the bean cell wall. Another example of the regulation of gene expression by RNA degradation is the regulation of expression of one of the genes for the small subunit of rubisco in roots of the aquatic duckweed Lemna gibba. Lemna roots are photosynthetic and therefore express genes for the small subunit of rubisco, but the expression of one of the genes (SSU5B) is much lower in roots than in the fronds (leaves). Jane Silverthorne and her colleagues at the University of California, Santa Cruz, showed that the low level of SSU5B in the roots is due to a high rate of turnover of the SSU5B pre-mRNA in the nucleus.

In addition to RNA turnover, the translatability of mRNA molecules is variable. For example, RNAs fold into molecules with varying secondary and tertiary structures that can influence the accessibility of the translation initiation codon (the first AUG sequence) to the ribosome. Another factor that can influence translatability of an mRNA is codon usage. There is redundancy in the triplet codons that specify a given amino acid during translation, and each cell has a characteristic ratio of the different aminoacylated tRNAs available, known as codon bias.

If a message contains a large number of triplet codons that are rare for that cell, the small number of charged tRNAs available for those codons will slow translation. Finally, the cellular location at which translation occurs seems to affect the rate of gene expression. Free polysomes may translate mRNAs at very different rates from those at which polysomes bound to the endoplasmic reticulum do; even within the endoplasmic reticulum, there may be differential translation rates.

The synthesis of most eukaryotic proteins is regulated at the level of transcription. However, transcription in eukaryotes is much more complex than in prokaryotes. First, there are three different RNA polymerases in eukaryotes: I, II, and III. RNA polymerase I is located in the nucleolus and functions in the synthesis of most ribosomal RNAs. RNA polymerase II, located in the nucleoplasm, is responsible for pre-mRNA synthesis. RNA polymerase III, also located in the nucleoplasm, synthesizes small RNAs, such as tRNA and 5S rRNA.

Asecond important difference between transcription in prokaryotes and in eukaryotes is that the RNA polymerases of eukaryotes require additional proteins called general transcription factors to position them at the correct start site. While prokaryotic RNA polymerases also require accessory polypeptides called sigma factors (σ), these polypeptides are considered to be subunits of the RNA polymerase. In contrast, eukaryotic general transcription factors make up a large, multisubunit transcription initiation complex. For example, seven general transcription factors constitute the initiation complex of RNA polymerase II, each of which must be added in a specific order during assembly.

According to one current model, transcription is initiated when the final transcription factor, TFIIH (transcription factor for RNA polymerase II protein H), joins the complex and causes phosphorylation of the RNA polymerase. RNA polymerase II then separates from the initiation complex and proceeds along the antisense strand in the 3'-to-5' direction. While some of the general transcription factors dissociate from the complex at this point, others remain to bind another RNA polymerase molecule and initiate another round of transcription.

Athird difference between transcription in prokaryotes and in eukaryotes is in the complexity of the promoters, the sequences upstream (5') of the initiation site that regulate transcription. We can divide the structure of the eukaryotic promoter into two parts, the core or minimum promoter, consisting of the minimum upstream sequence required for gene expression, and the additional regulatory sequences, which control the activity of the core promoter.

Each of the three RNA polymerases has a different type of promoter. The minimum promoter for genes transcribed by RNA polymerase II typically extends about 100 bp upstream of the transcription initiation site and includes several sequence elements referred to as proximal promoter sequences. About 25 to 35 bp upstream of the transcriptional start site is a short sequence called the TATA box, consisting of the sequence TATAAA(A). The TATA box plays a crucial role in transcription because it serves as the site of assembly of the transcription initiation complex. Approximately 85% of the plant genes sequenced thus far contain TATAboxes.

In addition to the TATA box, the minimum promoters of eukaryotes also contain two additional regulatory sequences: the CAAT box and the GC box. These two sequences are the sites of binding of transcription factors, proteins that enhance the rate of transcription by facilitating the assembly of the initiation complex. The DNA sequences themselves are termed cis-acting sequences, since they are adjacent to the transcription units they are regulating. The transcription factors that bind to the cis-acting sequences are called trans-acting factors, since the genes that encode them are located elsewhere in the genome.

Numerous other cis-acting sequences located farther upstream of the proximal promoter sequences can exert either positive or negative control over eukaryotic promoters. These sequences are termed the distal regulatory sequences and they are usually located within 1000 bp of the transcription initiation site. As with prokaryotes, the positively acting transcription factors that bind to these sites are called activators, while those that inhibit transcription are called repressors.

Cis-acting sequences involved in gene regulation by hormones and other signaling agents are called response elements. In addition to having regulatory sequences within the promoter itself, eukaryotic genes can be regulated by control elements located tens of thousands of base pairs away from the start site. Distantly located positive regulatory sequences are called enhancers. Enhancers may be located either upstream or downstream from the promoter. In plants, many developmentally important plant genes have been shown to be regulated by enhancers.

How do all the DNA-binding proteins on the cis-acting sequences regulate transcription? During formation of the initiation complex, the DNA between the core promoter and the most distally located control elements loops out in such a way as to allow all of the transcription factors bound to that segment of DNA to make physical contact with the initiation complex. Through this physical contact the transcription factor exerts its control, either positive or negative, over transcription. Given the large number of control elements that can modify the activity of a single promoter, the possibilities for differential gene regulation in eukaryotes are nearly infinite.

Transcription Factors

Transcription factors generally have three structural features: a DNA-binding domain, a transcription-activating domain, and a ligand-binding domain. To bind to a specific sequence of DNA, the DNA-binding domain must have extensive interactions with the double helix through the formation of hydrogen, ionic, and hydrophobic bonds. Although the particular combination and spatial distribution of such interactions are unique for each sequence, analyses of many DNA-binding proteins have led to the identification of a small number of highly conserved DNA-binding structural motifs.

Most of the transcription factors characterized thus far in plants belong to the basic zipper (bZIP) class of DNA-binding proteins. DNA-binding proteins containing the zinc finger domain are relatively rare in plants.

The term "homeodomain protein" is derived from a group of Drosophila (fruit fly) genes called selector genes or homeotic genes. Drosophila homeotic genes encode transcription factors that determine which structures develop at specific locations on the fly's body; that is, they act as major developmental switches that activate a large number of genes that constitute the entire genetic program for a particular structure. Mutations in homeotic genes cause homeosis, the transformation of one body part into another. For example, a homeotic mutation in the ANTENNAPEDIA gene causes a leg to form in place of an antenna.

When the sequences of various homeotic genes in Drosophila were compared, the proteins were all found to contain a highly conserved stretch of 60 amino acids called the homeobox. Homologous homeobox sequences have now been identified in developmentally important genes of vertebrates and plants. The KN1 (KNOTTED) gene of maize encodes a homeodomain protein that can affect cell fate during development. Maize plants with the kn1 mutation exhibit abnormal cell divisions in the vascular tissues, giving rise to the "knotted" appearance of the leaf surface.

However, the kn1 mutation is not a homeotic mutation, since it does not involve the substitution of one entire structure for another. Rather, the plant homeodomain protein, KN1, is involved in the regulation of cell division. Thus, not all genes that encode homeodomain proteins are homeotic genes, and vice versa. Four of the floral homeotic genes in plants encode proteins with the DNA-binding helixturn-helix motif called the MADS domain.

Although eukaryotic nuclear genes are not arranged into operons, they are often coordinately regulated in the cell. For example, in yeast, many of the enzymes involved in galactose metabolism and transport are inducible and coregulated, even though the genes are located on different chromosomes. Incubation of wildtype yeast cells in galactose-containing media results in more than a thousandfold increase in the mRNA levels for all of these enzymes.

The six yeast genes that encode the enzymes in the galactose metabolism pathway are under both positive and negative control. Most yeast genes are regulated by a single proximal control element called an upstream activating sequence (UAS). The GAL4 gene encodes a transcription factor that binds to UAS elements located about 200 bp upstream of the transcription start sites of all six genes. The UAS of each of the six genes, while not identical, consists of one or more copies of a similar 17 bp repeated sequence. The GAL4 protein can bind to each of them and activate transcription.

In this way a single transcription factor can control the expression of many genes. Protein-protein interactions can modify the effects of DNA-binding transcription factors. Another gene on a different yeast chromosome, GAL80, encodes a negative transcription regulator that forms a complex with the GAL4 protein when it is bound to the UAS. When the GAL80 protein is complexed with GAL4, transcription is blocked.

In the presence of galactose, however, the metabolite formed by the enzyme that is encoded by the GAL3 gene acts as an inducer by causing the dissociation of GAL80 from GAL4. There are many other examples of coordinate regulation of genes in eukaryotes. In plants, the developmental effects induced by light and hormones , as well as the adaptive responses caused by various types of stress, involve the coordinate regulation of groups of genes that share a common response element upstream of the promoter. In addition, genes that act as major developmental switches, such as the homeotic genes, encode transcription factors that bind to a common regulatory sequence that is present on dozens, or even hundreds, of genes scattered throughout the genome.

An enzyme molecule, once synthesized, has a finite lifetime in the cell, ranging from a few minutes to several hours. Hence, steady-state levels of cellular enzymes are attained as the result of an equilibrium between enzyme synthesis and enzyme degradation, or turnover. Protein turnover plays an important role in development. In etiolated seedlings, for example, the red-light photoreceptor, phytochrome, is regulated by proteolysis.

The phytochrome synthesized in the dark is highly stable and accumulates in the cells to high concentrations. Upon exposure to red light, however, the phytochrome is converted to its active form and simultaneously becomes highly susceptible to degradation by proteases. In animal cells there are two distinct pathways of protein turnover, one in specialized digestive vacuoles called lysosomes and the other in the cytosol. Proteins destined to be digested in lysosomes appear to be specifically targeted to these organelles. Upon entering the lysosomes, the proteins are rapidly degraded by lysosomal proteases. Lysosomes are also capable of engulfing and digesting entire organelles by an autophagic process.

The central vacuole of plant cells is rich in proteases and is the plant equivalent of lysosomes, but as yet there is no clear evidence that plant vacuoles either engulf organelles or participate in the turnover of cytosolic proteins, except during senescence.

The nonlysosomal pathway of protein turnover involves the ATP-dependent formation of a covalent bond to a small, 76-amino-acid polypeptide called ubiquitin. Ubiquitination of an enzyme molecule apparently marks it for destruction by a large ATP-dependent proteolytic complex (26S proteasome) that specifically recognizes the "tagged" molecule. More than 90% of the short-lived proteins in eukaryotic cells are degraded via the ubiquitin pathway . The ubiquitin pathway regulates cytosolic protein turnover in plant cells as well.

Before it can take part in protein tagging, free ubiquitin must be activated. The enzyme E1 catalyzes the ATP-dependent adenylylation of the C terminus of ubiquitin. The adenylylated ubiquitin is then transferred to a second enzyme, called E2. Proteins destined for ubiquitination form complexes with a third protein, E3. Finally, the E2-ubiquitin conjugate is used to transfer ubiquitin to the lysine residues of proteins bound to E3. This process can occur multiple times to form a polymer of ubiquitin. The ubiquitinated protein is then targeted to the proteasome for degradation. The regulation of gene expression by the phytohormone, auxin, may be mediated in part by the activation of the ubiquitin pathway.

Signal Transduction in Prokaryotes

Prokaryotic cells could not have survived billions of years of evolution without an exquisitely developed ability to sense their environment. As we have seen, bacteria respond to the presence of a nutrient by synthesizing the proteins involved in the uptake and metabolism of that nutrient. Bacteria can also respond to nonnutrient signals, both physical and chemical. Motile bacteria can adjust their movements according to the prevailing gradients of light, oxygen, osmolarity, temperature, and toxic chemicals in the medium.

The basic mechanisms that enable bacteria to sense and to respond to their environment are common to all cell sensory systems, and include stimulus detection, signal amplification, and the appropriate output responses. Many bacterial signaling pathways have been shown to consist of modular units called transmitters and receivers. These modules form the basis of the so-called two-component regulatory systems.

Bacteria sense chemicals in the environment by means of a small family of cell surface receptors, each involved in the response to a defined group of chemicals (hereafter referred to as ligands). A protein in the plasma membrane of bacteria binds directly to a ligand, or binds to a soluble protein that has already attached to the ligand, in the periplasmic space between the plasma membrane and the cell wall. Upon binding, the membrane protein undergoes a conformational change that is propagated across the membrane to the cytosolic domain of the receptor protein. This conformational change initiates the signaling pathway that leads to the response.

Abroad spectrum of responses in bacteria, including osmoregulation, chemotaxis, and sporulation, are regulated by two-component systems. Two-component regulatory systems are composed of a sensor protein and a response regulator protein. The function of the sensor is to receive the signal and to pass the signal on to the response regulator, which brings about the cellular response, typically gene expression. Sensor proteins have two domains, an input domain, which receives the environmental signal, and a transmitter domain, which transmits the signal to the response regulator. The response regulator also has two domains, a receiver domain, which receives the signal from the transmitter domain of the sensor protein, and an output domain, such as a DNA-binding domain, which brings about the response.

The signal is passed from transmitter domain to receiver domain via protein phosphorylation. Transmitter domains have the ability to phosphorylate themselves, using ATP, on a specific histidine residue near the amino terminus. For this reason, sensor proteins containing transmitter domains are called autophosphorylating histidine kinases. These proteins normally function as dimers in which the catalytic site of one subunit phosphorylates the acceptor site on the other.

Immediately after the transmitter domain becomes autophosphorylated on a histidine residue, the phosphate is transferred to a specific aspartate residue near the middle of the receiver domain of the response regulator protein. As a result, a specific aspartate residue of the response regulator becomes phosphorylated. Phosphorylation of the aspartate residue causes the response regulator to undergo a conformational change that results in its activation.

An example of a relatively simple bacterial two-component system is the signaling system involved in sensing osmolarity in E. coli. E. coli is a Gram-negative bacterium and thus has two cell membranes, an inner membrane and an outer membrane, separated by a cell wall. The inner membrane is the primary permeability barrier of the cell. The outer membrane contains large pores composed of two types of porin proteins, OmpF and OmpC.

Pores made with OmpF are larger than those made with OmpC. When E. coli is subjected to high osmolarity in the medium, it synthesizes more OmpC than OmpF, resulting in smaller pores on the outer membrane. These smaller pores filter out the solutes from the periplasmic space, shielding the inner membrane from the effects of the high solute concentration in the external medium. When the bacterium is placed in a medium with low osmolarity, more OmpF is synthesized, and the average pore size increases.

Recently, combination sensor-response regulator proteins related to the bacterial two-component systems have been discovered in yeast and in plants. For example, The SLN1 gene of the yeast Saccharomyces cerevisiae encodes a 134-kilodalton protein that has sequence similarities to both the transmitter and the receiver domains of bacteria and appears to function in osmoregulation. There is increasing evidence that several plant signaling systems evolved from bacterial two-component systems. For example, the red/far-red-absorbing pigment, phytochrome, has now been demonstrated in cyanobacteria, and it appears to be related to bacterial sensor proteins. In addition, the genes that encode putative receptors for two plant hormones, cytokinin and ethylene, both contain autophosphorylating histidine kinase domains, as well as contiguous response regulator motifs.

Signal Transduction in Eukaryotes

Many eukaryotic microorganisms use chemical signals in cell-cell communication. For example, in the slime mold Dictyostelium, starvation induces certain cells to secrete cyclic AMP (cAMP). The secreted cAMP diffuses across the substrate and induces nearby cells to aggregate into a sluglike colony. Yeast mating-type factors are another example of chemical communication between the cells of simple microorganisms. Around a billion years ago, however, cell signaling took a great leap in complexity when eukaryotic cells began to associate together as multicellular organisms. After the evolution of multicellularity came a trend toward ever-increasing cell specialization, as well as the development of tissues and organs to perform specific functions.

Coordination of the development and environmental responses of complex multicellular organisms required an array of signaling mechanisms. Two main systems evolved in animals: the nervous system and the endocrine system. Plants, lacking motility, never developed a nervous system, but they did evolve hormones as chemical messengers. As photosynthesizing organisms, plants also evolved mechanisms for adapting their growth and development to the amount and quality of light. However, keep in mind that plant signal transduction pathways may differ in significant ways from those of animals.

Hormones fall into two classes based on their ability to move across the plasma membrane: lipophilic hormones, which diffuse readily across the hydrophobic bilayer of the plasma membrane; and water-soluble hormones, which are unable to enter the cell. Lipophilic hormones bind mainly to receptors in the cytoplasm or nucleus; water-soluble hormones bind to receptors located on the cell surface. In either case, ligand binding alters the receptor, typically by causing a conformational change. Some receptors, such as the steroid hormone receptors , can regulate gene expression directly.

In the vast majority of cases, however, the receptor initiates one or more sequences of biochemical reactions that connect the stimulus to a cellular response. Such a sequence of reactions is called a signal transduction pathway. Typically, the end result of signal transduction pathways is to regulate transcription factors, which in turn regulate gene expression. Signal transduction pathways often involve the generation of second messengers, transient secondary signals inside the cell that greatly amplify the original signal.

For example, a single hormone molecule might lead to the activation of an enzyme that produces hundreds of molecules of a second messenger. Among the most common second messengers are 3',5'-cyclic AMP (cAMP); 3',5'-cyclic GMP (cGMP); nitric oxide (NO); cyclic ADP-ribose (cADPR); 1,2-diacylglycerol (DAG); inositol 1,4,5-trisphosphate (IP_3); and Ca^{2+}. Hormone binding normally causes elevated levels of one or more of these second messengers, resulting in the activation or inactivation of enzymes or regulatory proteins.

Steroid Receptors

The steroid hormones, thyroid hormones, retinoids, and vitamin D all pass freely across the plasma membrane because of their hydrophobic nature and they bind to intracellular receptor proteins. When activated by binding to their ligand, these proteins function as transcription factors. All such steroid receptor proteins have similar DNA-binding domains. Steroid response elements are typically located in enhancer regions of steroid-stimulated genes. Most steroid receptors are localized in the nucleus, where they are anchored to nuclear proteins in an inactive form.

When the receptor binds to the steroid, it is released from the anchor protein and becomes activated as a transcription factor. The activated transcription factor then binds to the enhancer and stimulates transcription. The receptor for thyroid hormone deviates from this pattern in that it is already bound to the DNA but is unable to stimulate transcription in the absence of the hormone. Binding to the hormone converts the receptor to an active transcription factor.

Not all intracellular steroid receptors are localized in the nucleus. The receptor for glucocorticoid hormone (cortisol) differs from the others in that it is located in the cytosol, anchored in an inactive state to a cytosolic protein. Binding of the hormone causes the release of the receptor from its cytosolic anchor, and the receptor hormone complex then migrates into the nucleus, where it binds to the enhancer and stimulates transcription.

Although most studies on animal steroid hormones have focused on their roles in regulating gene expression via receptors that act as transcription factors, increasing evidence suggests that steroids can also interact with proteins on the cell surface. Brassinosteroid has recently been demonstrated to be an authentic steroid hormone in plants, and the gene for a brassinosteroid receptor has recently been cloned and sequenced. It encodes a type of transmembrane receptor called a leucine-rich repeat receptor.

Cell Surface Receptors

All water-soluble mammalian hormones bind to cell surface receptors. Members of the largest class of mammalian cell surface receptors interact with signal-transducing, GTP-binding regulatory proteins called heterotrimeric G proteins. The activated G proteins, in turn, activate an effector enzyme. The activated effector enzyme generates an intracellular second messenger, which stimulates a variety of cellular processes.

Receptors using heterotrimeric G proteins are structurally similar and functionally diverse. Their overall structure is similar to that of bacteriorhodopsin, the purple pigment involved in photosynthesis in bacteria of the genus Halobacterium, and to that of rhodopsin, the visual pigment of the vertebrate eye. The recently characterized olfactory receptors of the vertebrate nose also belong to this group. The receptor proteins consist of seven transmembrane a helices. These receptors are sometimes referred to as seven-spanning, seven-pass, or serpentine receptors.

The G proteins that transduce the signals from the seven-spanning receptors are called heterotrimeric G proteins because they are composed of three different subunits: α, β, and γ (gamma). They are distinct from the monomeric G proteins. Heterotrimeric G proteins cycle between active and inactive forms, thus acting as molecular switches. The β and γ subunits form a tight complex that anchors the trimeric G protein to the membrane on the cytoplasmic side. The G protein becomes activated upon binding to the ligand-activated seven-spanning receptor. In its inactive form, G exists as a trimer with GDP bound to the α subunit. Binding to the receptor-ligand complex induces the α subunit to exchange GDP for GTP. This exchange causes the α subunit to dissociate from β and γ, allowing α to associate instead with an effector enzyme.

The α subunit has a GTPase activity that is activated when it binds to the effector enzyme, in this case adenylyl cyclase (also called adenylate cyclase). GTP is hydrolyzed to GDP, thereby inactivating the α subunit, which in turn inactivates adenylyl cyclase. The α subunit bound to GDP reassociates with the β and γ subunits and can then be reactivated by associating with the hormone-receptor complex.

Level of Cyclic AMP

Cyclic AMP is an important signaling molecule in both prokaryotes and animal cells, and increasing evidence suggests that cAMP plays a similar role in plant cells. In vertebrates, adenylyl cyclase is an integral membrane protein that contains two clusters of six membrane-spanning domains separating two catalytic domains that extend into the cytoplasm. Activation of adenylyl cyclase by heterotrimeric G proteins raises the concentration of cAMP in the cell, which is normally maintained at a low level by the action of cyclic AMP phosphodiesterase, which hydrolyzes cAMP to 5' -AMP.

Nearly all the effects of cAMP in animal cells are mediated by the enzyme protein kinase A (PKA). In unstimulated cells, PKA is in the inactive state because of the presence of a pair of inhibitory subunits. Cyclic AMP binds to these inhibitory subunits, causing them to dissociate from the two catalytic subunits, thereby activating the catalytic subunits. The activated catalytic subunits then are able to phosphorylate specific serine or threonine residues of selected proteins, which may also be protein kinases. An example of an enzyme that is phosphorylated by PKA is glycogen phosphorylase kinase. When phosphorylated by PKA, glycogen phosphorylase kinase phosphorylates (activates) glycogen phosphorylase, the enzyme that breaks down glycogen in muscle cells to glucose-1-phosphate.

In cells in which cAMP regulates gene expression, PKA phosphorylates a transcription factor called CREB (cyclic AMP response element-binding protein). Upon activation by PKA, CREB binds to the cAMP response element (CRE), which is located in the promoter regions of genes that are regulated by cAMP. In addition to activating PKA, cAMP can interact with specific cAMP-gated cation channels. For example, in olfactory receptor neurons, cAMP binds to and opens Na^+ channels on the plasma membrane, resulting in Na^+ influx and membrane depolarization.

Because of the extremely low levels of cyclic AMP that have been detected in plant tissue extracts, the role of cAMP in plant signal transduction has been highly controversial. Nevertheless, various lines of evidence supporting a role of cAMP in plant cells have accumulated. For example, genes that encode homologs of CREB have been identified in plants . Pollen tube growth in lily has been shown to be stimulated by concentrations of cAMP as low as 10 nM .

Li and colleagues showed that cAMP activates K^+ channels in the plasma membrane of fava bean (Vicia faba) mesophyll cells. And Ichikawa and coworkers recently identified possible genes for adenylyl cyclase in tobacco (Nicotiana tabacum) and Arabidopsis. Thus, despite years of doubt, the role of cAMP as a universal signaling agent in living organisms, including plants, seems likely.

Calcium serves as a second messenger for a wide variety of cell signaling events. This role of calcium is well established in animal cells, circumstantial evidence suggests a role for calcium in signal transduction in plants as well. The concentration of free Ca^{2+} in the cytosol normally is maintained at extremely low levels (1×10^{-7} M). Ca^{2+}-ATPases on the plasma membrane and on the endoplasmic reticulum pump calcium ions out of the cell and into the lumen of the ER, respectively. In plant cells, most of the calcium of the cell accumulates in the vacuole. The proton electrochemical gradient across the vacuolar membrane that is generated by tonoplast proton pumps drives calcium uptake via Ca^{2+}-H^+ antiporters.

In animal cells, certain hormones can induce a transient rise in the cytosolic Ca^{2+} concentration to about 5 $\times 10^{-6}$M. This increase may occur even in the absence of extracellular calcium, indicating that the Ca^{2+} is being released from intracellular compartments by the opening of intracellular calcium channels. However, the coupling of hormone binding to the opening of intracellular calcium channels is mediated by yet another second messenger, inositol trisphosphate (IP_3).

Phosphatidylinositol (PI) is a minor phospholipid component of cell membranes. PI can be converted to the polyphosphoinositides PI phosphate (PIP) and PI bisphosphate (PIP_2) by kinases. Although PIP_2 is even less abundant in the membrane than PI is, it plays a central role in signal transduction. In animal cells, binding of a hormone, such as vasopressin, to its receptor leads to the activation of heterotrimeric G proteins. The α subunit then dissociates from G and activates a phosphoinositide-specific phospholipase, phospholipase C (PLC). The activated PLC rapidly hydrolyzes PIP_2, generating inositol trisphosphate (IP_3) and diacylglycerol (DAG) as products. Each of these two molecules plays an important role in cell signaling.

The IP_3 generated by the activated phospholipase C is water soluble and diffuses through the cytosol until it encounters IP_3-binding sites on the ER and (in plants) on the tonoplast. These binding sites are IP_3-gated Ca^{2+} channels that open when they bind IP_3. Since these organelles maintain internal Ca^{2+} concentrations in the millimolar range, calcium diffuses rapidly into the cytosol down a steep concentration gradient. The response is terminated when IP_3 is broken down by specific phosphatases or when the released calcium is pumped out of the cytoplasm by Ca^{2+}-ATPases.

Studies with Ca^{2+}-sensitive fluorescent indicators, such as fura-2 and aequorin, have shown that the calcium signal often originates in a localized region of the cell and propagates as a wave throughout the cytosol. Repeated waves called calcium oscillations can follow the original signal, each lasting from a few seconds to several minutes. The biological significance of calcium oscillation is still unclear, although it has been suggested that it is a mechanism for avoiding the toxicity that might result from a sustained elevation in cytosolic levels of free calcium. Such wavelike oscillations have recently been detected in plant stomatal guard cells.

Cyclic ADP-Ribose (cADPR) acts as a second messenger that can release calcium from intracellular stores, independent of the IP_3 signaling pathway. Like cAMP, cADPR is a cyclic nucleotide, but whereas cAMP brings about its effects by activating protein kinase A, cADPR binds to and activates specific calcium channels, called type-3 ryanodine receptors (ryanodine is a calcium channel blocker). These ryanodine receptor/calcium channels are located on the membranes of calcium-storing organelles, such as sarcoplasmic reticulum of animal cells or the vacuoles of plant cells. By stimulating the release of calcium into the cytosol, cADPR helps to regulate calcium oscillations that bring about physiological effects. Abscisic acid-induced stomatal closure is an example of the roles of cADPR and calcium oscillations in plants.

In IP_3-gated channels, calcium can activate some proteins, such as channels, by binding directly to them. However, most of the effects of calcium result from the binding of calcium to the regulatory protein calmodulinα. Calmodulin is a highly conserved protein that is abundant in all eukaryotic cells, but it appears to be absent from prokaryotic cells. The same calcium-binding site is found in a wide variety of calcium-binding proteins and is called an EF hand. The name is derived from the two α helices, E and F, that are part of the calcium-binding domain of the protein parvalbumin.

Each calmodulin molecule binds four Ca^{2+} ions and changes conformation, enabling it to bind to and activate other proteins. The Ca^{2+}-calmodulin complex can stimulate some enzymes directly, such as the plasma membrane Ca^{2+}-ATPase, which pumps calcium out of the cell. Most of the effects of calcium, however, are brought about by activation of Ca^{2+}-calmodulin-dependent protein kinases (CaM kinases). CaM kinases phosphorylate serine or threonine residues of their target enzymes, causing enzyme activation. Thus, the effect that calcium has on a particular cell depends to a large extent on which CaM kinases are expressed in that cell.

Calcium signaling has been strongly implicated in many developmental processes in plants, ranging from the regulation of development by phytochrome to the regulation of stomatal guard cells by abscisic acid. Thus far, however, there have been few reports of CaM kinase activity in plants. Recently, however, a gene that codes for a CaM kinase has been cloned from lily and shown to be specifically expressed in anthers. The lily CaM kinase is a serine/threonine kinase that phosphorylates various protein substrates in vitro in a Ca^{2+}-calmodulin-dependent manner. The occurrence and regulatory roles of such plant CaM kinases remain to be determined. Plants Contain Calcium-Dependent Protein Kinases

The most abundant calcium-regulated protein kinases in plants appear to be the calcium-dependent protein kinases (CDPKs). CDPKs are strongly activated by calcium, but are insensitive to calmodulin. The proteins are characterized by two domains: a catalytic domain that is similar to those of the animal CaM kinases, and a calmodulin-like domain. The presence of a calmodulinlike domain may explain why the enzyme does not require calmodulin for activity.

CDPKs are widespread in plants and are encoded by multigene families. ACDPK has also been identified in Chara, the giant freshwater green alga thought to be a precursor of land plants. In Chara the enzyme was shown to be associated with the actin microfilaments that line the outer cortex of the cytoplasm along the inner surface of the plasma membrane.

The function of these microfilaments is to drive cytoplasmic streaming around the cell. The rate of cytoplasmic streaming is inhibited by increases in cytosolic calcium, and it has been proposed that CDPKs mediate the effects of calcium by phosphorylating the heavy chain of myosin, a component of the microfilaments. CDPKs may also mediate the effects of calcium in guard cells. Abscisic acid-induced stomatal closure involves calcium as a second messenger . Recent studies using isolated vacuoles from guard cells of Vicia faba (fava bean) suggest that CDPKs can regulate anion channels on the tonoplast. Thus, CDPKs may be a component of the abscisic acid signaling pathway.

Diacylglycerol Activates Protein Kinase C

Cleavage of PIP_2 by phospholipase C produces diacylgycerol (DAG) in addition to IP_3. Whereas IP_3 is hydrophilic and diffuses rapidly into the cytoplasm, DAG is a lipid and remains in the membrane. In animal cells, DAG can associate with and activate the serine/threonine kinase protein kinase C (PKC). The inactive form of PKC is a soluble enzyme that is located in the cytosol. Upon binding to calcium, the soluble, inactive PKC undergoes a conformational change and associates with a PKC receptor protein that transports it to the inner surface of the plasma membrane, where it encounters DAG.

PKCs have been shown to phosphorylate ion channels, transcription factors, and enzymes in animal cells. One of the enzymes phosphorylated by PKC is another protein kinase that regulates cell proliferation and differentiation, MAP kinase kinase kinase. G proteins, phospholipase C, and various protein kinases have been identified in plant membranes. PKC activity has also been detected in plants, and a plant gene encoding the PKC receptor protein that transports the soluble enzyme to the membrane has recently been cloned. However, there is as yet no evidence that activation of PKC by DAG plays a role in plant signal transduction.

In animals, the endocrine system is involved in signaling between hormone-producing cells at one location of the body and hormone-responding cells at another location; in contrast, the autocrine system involves cells sending signals to themselves and their immediate neighbors. One type of autocrine signaling system that plays important roles in pain and inflammatory responses, as well as platelet aggregation and smoothmuscle contraction, is called the eicosanoid pathway.

There are four major classes of eicosanoids: prostaglandins, prostacyclins, thromboxanes, and leukotrienes. All are derived from the breakdown of membrane phospholipids, and in this respect the eicosanoid pathway resembles the IP_3 pathway. There the resemblance ends, however. For whereas the IP_3 pathway begins with the cleavage of IP_3 from PIP_2 by phospholipase C, the eicosanoid pathway is initiated by the cleavage of the 20-carbon fatty acid arachidonic acid from the intact phospholipid by the enzyme phospholipase A_2 (PLA_2). Two oxidative pathways-one cyclooxygenase dependent, the other lipoxygenase dependent-then convert arachidonic acid to the four eicosanoids. Higher plants generally have negligible amounts of arachidonic acid in their membranes, although the level is higher in certain mosses.

In addition to generating arachidonic acid, PLA_2 produces lysophosphatidylcholine (LPC) as a breakdown product of phosphatidylcholine. LPC has detergent properties, and it has been shown to regulate ion channels through its effects on protein kinases. For example, LPC has been shown to modulate the sodium currents in cardiac-muscle cells by signal transduction pathways that involve the activation of both protein kinase C and a tyrosine kinase. Protein kinase C is activated by LPC independently of the phospholipase C pathway.

In recent years plant biologists have become increasingly interested in the eicosanoid pathway because it now appears that an important signaling agent in plant defense responses, jasmonic acid, is produced by a similar pathway. In addition, LPC has been shown to activate plant protein kinases in vitro. LPC is one of many candidates for a second messenger in the rapid responses of plant cells to auxin.

The human eye contains two types of photoreceptor cells: rods and cones. Rods are responsible for monochromatic vision in dim light; cones are involved in color vision in bright light. Signal transduction in response to light has been studied more intensively in rods. The rod is a highly specialized tubular cell that contains an elongated stack of densely packed membrane sacs called discs at the tip, or outer segment, reminiscent of the grana stacks of chloroplasts. The disc membranes of rod cells contain the photosensitive protein pigment rhodopsin, a member of the seven-spanning transmembrane family of receptors.

Rhodopsin consists of the protein opsin covalently bound to the light-absorbing molecule 11-cis-retinal. When 11-cis-retinal absorbs a single photon of light (400 to 600 nm) it immediately isomerizes to all-trans-retinal. This change causes a slower conformational change in the protein, converting it to meta-rhodopsin II, or activated opsin. Activated opsin, in turn, lowers the concentration of the cyclic nucleotide 3'5'-cGMP. Cyclic GMP is synthesized from GTP by the enzyme guanylate cyclase.

In the dark, guanylate cyclase activity results in the buildup of a high concentration of cGMP in the rod cells. Because the plasma membrane contains cGMP-gated Na^+ channels, the high cGMP concentration in the cytosol maintains the Na^+ channels in the open position in the absence of light. When the Na^+ channels are open, Na^+ can enter the cell freely, and this passage of Na^+ tends to depolarize the membrane potential.

When opsin becomes activated by light, however, it binds to the heterotrimeric G protein transducin. This binding causes the α subunit of transducin to exchange GDP for GTP and dissociate from the complex. The α subunit of transducin then activates the enzyme cyclic GMP phosphodiesterase, which breaks down 3'5'-cGMP to 5'-GMP. Light therefore has the effect of decreasing the concentration of cGMP in the rod cell. Alower concentration of cGMP has the effect of closing the cGMP-gated Na^+ channels on the plasma membrane, which are kept open in the dark by a high cGMP concentration. To give some idea of the signal amplification provided, a single photon may cause the closure of hundreds of Na^+ channels, blocking the uptake of about 10 million Na^+ ions.

By preventing the influx of Na^+, which tends to depolarize the membrane, the membrane polarity increases-that is, becomes hyperpolarized. In this way a light signal is converted into an electric signal. Membrane hyperpolarization, in turn, inhibits neurotransmitter release from the synaptic body of the rod cell. Paradoxically, the nervous system detects light as an inhibition rather than a stimulation of neurotransmitter release.

Cyclic GMP, which regulates ion channels and protein kinases in animal cells, appears to be an important regulatory molecule in plant cells as well. Cyclic GMP has been definitively identified in plant extracts by gas chromatography combined with mass spectrometry. Moreover, cGMP has been implicated as a second messenger in the responses of phytochrome and gibberellin.

The level of 3',5'-cyclic GMP in cells is controlled by the balance between the rate of cGMP synthesis by the enzyme, guanylyl (or guanylate) cyclase, and the rate of cGMP degradation by the enzyme cGMP phosphodiesterase. In smooth muscle tissue of animal cells, cGMP levels can be increased via the direct activation of guanylyl cyclase by the signaling intermediate, nitric oxide (NO). NO is synthesized from arginine by the enzyme, NO synthase, in a reaction involving oxygen:

$$\text{Arginine} + O_2 \xrightarrow{\text{NO synthase}} \text{Citrulline} + \text{NO}$$

Once produced in animal endothelial cells, dissolved NO passes rapidly across membranes and acts locally on neighboring smooth muscle cells, with a half-life of 5-10 seconds. Guanylyl cyclase contains a heme group that binds NO tightly, and binding of NO causes a conformational change which activates the enzyme. The NO-induced increase in cGMP causes smooth muscle cells to relax. Nitroglycerine, which can be metabolized to yield NO, has long been administered to heart patients to prevent the coronary artery spasms responsible for variant angina. In plants, NO has recently been implicated as an intermediate in ABA-induced stomatal closure.

Cell Surface Receptors

Some cell surface receptors are enzymes themselves or are directly associated with enzymes. Unlike the sevenspanning receptors, the catalytic receptors, as these enzyme or enzyme-associated receptors are called, are typically attached to the membrane via a single transmembrane helix and do not interact with heterotrimeric G proteins. The six main categories of catalytic receptors in animals include:

1. receptor tyrosine kinases,
2. receptor tyrosine phosphatases,
3. receptor serine/threonine kinases,
4. tyrosine kinase-linked receptors,
5. receptor guanylate cyclases, and
6. cell surface proteases.

Of these, the receptor tyrosine kinases are probably the most abundant in animal cells. Thus far, no receptor tyrosine kinases (RTKs) have been identified in plants. However, plant cells do contain a class of receptors called receptorlike kinases (RLKs) that are structurally similar to the animal RTKs. In addition, some of the components of the RTK signaling pathway of animals have been identified in plants.

After first reviewing the animal RTK pathway, we will examine the RLK receptors of plants.

The receptor tyrosine kinases (RTKs) make up the most important class of enzyme-linked cell surface receptors in animal cells, although so far they have not been found in either plants or fungi. Their ligands are soluble or membrane-bound peptide or protein hormones, including insulin, epidermal growth factor (EGF), platelet-derived growth factor (PDGF), and several other protein growth factors.

Since the transmembrane domain that separates the hormone-binding site on the outer surface of the membrane from the catalytic site on the cytoplasmic surface consists of only a single α helix, the hormone cannot transmit a signal directly to the cytosolic side of the membrane via a conformational change. Rather, binding of the ligand to its receptor induces dimerization of adjacent receptors, which allows the two catalytic domains to come into contact and phosphorylate each other on multiple tyrosine residues (autophosphorylation). Dimerization may be a general mechanism for activating cell surface receptors that contain single transmembrane domains.

Intracellular Signaling Proteins

Once autophosphorylated, the catalytic site of the RTKs binds to a variety of cytosolic signaling proteins. After binding to the RTK, the inactive signaling protein is itself phosphorylated on specific tyrosine residues. Some transcription factors are activated in this way, after which they migrate to the nucleus and stimulate gene expression directly. Other signaling molecules take part in a signaling cascade that ultimately results in the activation of transcription factors. The signaling cascade initiated by RTKs begins with the small, monomeric G protein Ras.

In addition to possessing heterotrimeric G proteins, eukaryotic cells contain small monomeric G proteins that are related to the α subunits of the heterotrimeric G proteins. The three families, Ras, Rab, and Rho/Rac, all belong to the Ras superfamily of monomeric GTPases. Rho and Rac relay signals from surface receptors to the actin cytoskeleton; members of the Rab family of GTPases are involved in regulating intracellular membrane vesicle traffic; the Ras proteins, which are located on the inner surface of the membrane, play a crucial role in initiating the kinase cascade that relays signals from RTKs to the nucleus.

The RAS gene was originally discovered as a viral oncogene (cancer-causing gene) and was later shown to be present as a normal gene in animal cells. Ras is a G protein that cycles between an inactive GDP-binding form and an active GTP-binding form. Ras also possesses GTPase activity that hydrolyzes bound GTP to GDP, thus terminating the response. The RAS oncogene is a mutant form of the protein that is unable to hydrolyze GTP. As a result, the molecular switch remains in the on position, triggering uncontrolled cell division. The study of small GTP-binding proteins in plants is still in its infancy. Thus far, about 30 genes encoding members of monomeric G protein families have been cloned, including homologs of RAB and RHO. Surprisingly, RAS itself has so far not yet been identified in plants.

Ras Recruits Raf to the Plasma Membrane

Binding of the hormone to the RTK induces dimerization followed by autophosphorylation of the catalytic domain. Autophosphorylation of the receptor causes binding to the Grb2 protein, which is tightly associated with another protein, called Sos. As a result, the Grb2-Sos complex attaches to the RTK at the phosphorylation site. The Sos protein then binds to the inactive form of Ras, which is associated with the inner surface of the plasma membrane. Upon binding to Sos, Ras releases GDP and binds GTP instead, which converts Ras to the active form. The activated Ras, in turn, provides a binding site for the soluble serine/threonine kinase Raf. The primary function of the activated Ras is thus to recruit Raf to the plasma membrane. Binding to Ras activates Raf and initiates a chain of phosphorylation reactions called the MAPK cascade.

The MAPK (mitogen-activated protein kinase) cascade owes its name to a series of protein kinases that phosphorylate each other in a specific sequence, much like runners in a relay race passing a baton. The first kinase in the sequence is Raf, referred as MAP kinase kinase kinase (MAPKKK). MAPKKK passes the phosphate baton to MAP kinase kinase (MAPKK), which hands it off to MAP kinase (MAPK). MAPK, the "anchor" of the relay team, enters the nucleus, where it activates still other protein kinases, specific transcription factors, and regulatory proteins.

The transcription factors that are activated by MAPK are called serum response factors (SRFs) because all of the growth factors that bind to RTKs are transported in the serum. Serum response factors bind to specific nucleotide sequences on the genes they regulate called serum response elements (SREs). The entire process from binding of the growth factor to the receptor to transcriptional activation of gene expression can be very rapid, taking place in a few minutes.

Some of the genes that are activated encode other transcription factors that regulate the expression of other genes. Because these genes are important for cell proliferation and growth, many of them are protooncogenes. For example, one of the genes whose expression is stimulated by MAPK is the proto-oncogene FOS. A protooncogene is a normal gene that potentially can cause malignant tumors when mutated. When the Fos protein combines with the phosphorylated Jun protein (one of the nuclear proteins that is phosphorylated by MAPK), it forms a heterodimeric transcription factor called AP- 1, which turns on other genes. Other important protooncogenes that encode nuclear transcription factors include MYC and MYB. Both phytochrome and gibberellin are believed to regulate gene expression via the up-regulation of MYBlike transcription factors.

Plant Receptorlike Kinases Are Structurally Similar to Animal Receptor Tyrosine Kinases

Because of the recent progress in sequencing the genomes of plants such as Arabidopsis and rice, it is possible to use computers to search for DNA nucleotide sequences that correspond to the amino acid sequences of proteins identified in other organisms. Such database searches of plant DNA sequences have successfully identified a large family of receptorlike protein kinases (RLKs) by homology to animal receptor tyrosine kinases. These plant RLKs are structurally similar to the animal RTKs. They have a large extracellular domain, span the membrane only once, and contain a catalytic domain on the cytoplasmic side. Although they resemble the RTKs in their general structure, they differ in catalytic activity. Whereas RTKs of animals are autophosphorylating tyrosine kinases, the plant RLKs are autophosphorylating serine/threonine kinases.

Three types of RLKs have been identified in plants, primarily on the basis of their extracellular domains. The first class is characterized by an extracellular S domain and is called S receptor kinase or SRK. The S domain was first identified in a group of secreted glycoproteins, called S locus glycoproteins (SLGs), which regulate self-incompatibility in Brassica species. Selfincompatibility is characterized by the failure of pollen tubes to grow when placed on pistils from the same plant, and self-incompatibility loci are genes that regulate this phenotype.

The S domain consists of ten cysteines in a particular arrangement with other amino acids. The high degree of homology between the S domains of SRKs and those of SLGs suggests that they are functionally related and are involved in the recognition pathways involved in pollen tube growth. Consistent with this idea, SRK genes are expressed predominantly in pistils. Several other S domain RLKs with highly divergent sequences have been identified in other species, and each of these may play unique roles in plant cell signaling. The leucine-rich repeat (LRR) family of receptors constitute the second group of RLKs. They were first identified as disease resistance genes that may play key roles in the cell surface recognition of ligands produced by pathogens and the subsequent activation of the intracellular defense response.

However, plant LRR receptors have been implicated in normal developmental functions as well. For example, a pollen-specific LRR receptor has been identified in sunflower that may be involved in cell-cell recognition during pollination, and the Arabidopsis ERECTA gene, which regulates the shape and size of organs originating from the shoot apical meristem, encodes an LRR receptor. More recently, the receptor for the plant steroid hormone brassinosteroid has been identified as an LRR receptor .

The LRR receptors are members of a larger family of LRR proteins that includes soluble forms with lower molecular mass that are widespread in plants and animals.

The most conserved element of the LRR domain forms a β sheet with an exposed face that participates in protein-protein interactions.

The small soluble LRR proteins may participate in cell signaling by hydrophobic binding to LRR receptors. For example, in tomato a protein that contains four tandem repeats of a canonical 24-amino-acid leucine-rich repeat motif is up-regulated during virus infection. This protein is apparently secreted into the apoplast along with a protease that digests it to lower molecular weight peptides. These peptides could form part of a signaling pathway by interacting with cell surface LRR receptors.

A third type of RLK that contains an epidermal growth factor-like repeat has been identified in Arabidopsis. Interestingly, the receptor, called PRO25, is localized in the chloroplast and interacts with a lightharvesting chlorophyll a/b-binding protein (LHCP). Little or nothing is known about signaling within plastids, which undoubtedly will be an important area for future research.

8

Interactive Learning Inside the Classroom

Classroom Teaching Methods

There are many classroom activities - apart from lecturing - that can be employed for effective teaching and learning. Some of these are:

— simple demonstrations conducted by the teacher;

— minor experiments (that do not require special equipment) conducted by the students (Needless to say, safety is always the primary concern for the above two activities);

— questions and answers as guided by the teacher;

— class discussions around certain questions or topics (e.g. what are your views on abortion, or euthanasia, or human cloning);

— discussions based on individual input (e.g. "list 3 objectives you want to achieve in attending this course"); discussions after watching videos, listening to recordings, or reading articles together;

— group discussions followed by presentations (and then further discussions);

— presentations of results of either group or individual projects;

— case studies (preferably on real-life examples) using all or some of the above techniques;

— quizzes;

— debates;

— table-top group exercises in problem-solving;

— role-playing exercises;

— videotaping any of the above classroom activities and watching the replays for discussion and/or evaluation.

Asking questions is often the start of a discussion, so let us start with the skill of asking questions.

QUESTIONING SKILLS

Asking the students questions seems to be the simplest task teacher can do. And yet the learning effectiveness of these "questionand-answer sessions" will differ markedly depending on how we have mastered the relevant skills.

Firstly, it is often not necessary to assign a special "Q&A" session in class. Questions can be asked at any time, and in fact, it is good practice to intersperse your lecturing with occasional questions.

In general, questions can be used to:

— focus attention;

— arouse interest;

— enhance inclusion by drawing out the reticent learner;

— obtain student feedback on the progression of the lesson;

— assess the level of understanding;

— assess the ability to apply learned concepts and knowledge;

— stimulate and guide thinking and reflection;

— explore different viewpoints;

— promote discussion and sharing;

— keep the discussion on track;

— summarise progress and consolidate learning.

There are two main types of questions: open and closed. A closed question usually permits only one answer, like "In which year were telecommunications de-regulated by the U.S. government?" On the other hand, an open question has no single, definite answer. An example is "How, in your opinion, should the Internet be regulated?". Both open and closed questions can be put to good use. But generally speaking, open questions lead to more reflexive thinking and hence offer a richer learning experience. Here are a few tips in asking questions:

— in general, do not direct the question to a specific participant;

— direct it to the whole class;

— allow some time for the participants to think the question over;

— do not waste too much time waiting for answers though (30 seconds is about the maximum);

— if nobody responds to the question, choose one participant to give the answer;

— in picking the participant, try to select the more passive and timid participants rather than the more vocal ones;

— if the respondent speaks too softly, ask him/her to speak up so that the whole class can hear;

— repeat the answer for the benefit of the class if necessary;

— ask the respondent to clarify and elaborate if the answer is not clear or is incomplete;

— solicit comments on the given answer so as to involve the whole class and to draw out different opinions;

— avoid asking multiple questions in one go which may create confusion.

Remember: when you are asking questions, you are putting the spotlight on the students instead of yourself. This helps to take pressure off you and let you take stock of the progress of the lesson. Note that due to their cultural upbringing, most adult learners in Hong Kong are not very out-spoken. A lot of encouragement and patience is usually required to bring out active responses from the class. The teaching and learning outcomes, however, are certainly worth the effort.

Facilitating Discussions

Discussion is one of the most powerful tools of teaching and learning. The transition from "lecturing to questioning to discussion" represents roughly the move from the didactic to rhetorical and then to the dialectic mode of teaching and learning. All three modes are important, but for adult learners, it is obvious that the latter two modes carry specil significance.

The best way to start a discussion is by asking a (preferably provocative) question. To conduct a fruitful discussion, the teacher should:

— abstain from imposing his/her opinion or conclusion on the class;

— respect the contributions of all participants by "active listening" (through facial expression and body language), and thanking the respondents ;

— use body language to encourage expression; this includes:

1. nodding;
2. smiling;
3. constant eye contact;
4. leaning forward;
5. raising eyebrows;

— closing eyes momentarily in the way of deep thinking; frowning (encourages clarification).

— use verbal cues to elicit further response; these include:

1. "Aha!"
2. "I see."
3. "Really?"
4. "That's interesting."
5. "Is that the case?"
6. "Go on!"
7. "Do you really think so?"
8. "Tell me more about it." etc.

— encourage the more silent participants to speak up (first by seeking their views directly, and then by body language and verbal cues);

- — prevent one or two participants from dominating the whole discussion by asking for the comments of other participants;
- — play "devil's advocate" from time to time and deliberately raise radical/absurd ideas to stimulate thinking and debate;
- — point out factual errors and faults of reasoning along the way;
- — follow the flow of thinking of the participants, and yet keep the discussion on track by reiterating the main theme when necessary;
- — maintain a balance of views by highlighting opposite viewpoints, especially if the discussion is overwhelmingly slanted in a certain direction; summarise progress from time to time;
- — give a wrap-up at the end of the discussion session.

Problem-Based Learning (PBL)

A major theme running through almost all education theories is the need for integrating theory and practice (or "practicum" in educational jargon). In recent years, the importance of practicum has been elevated to new heights and embodied in the pedagogical movement of problem-based learning (PBL). Carried to the extreme, however, PBL argues for the replacement of ALL didactic learning by problem-oriented modes of learning.

As a teacher, it is up to you to decide to what extent should PBL be adopted in a way that is appropriate to the subject discipline you are teaching. Although some PBL activities can be conducted inside the classroom, a significant proportion will have to be conducted outside, either in mock-up scenarios or in real life situations.

9

Future of Plant Biology

Plant biology has the potential of providing partial solutions to several of the most daunting problems that our species and our planet face in the 21st century. Among these problems will be an increasing shortage of available food, the depletion of global oil reserves, and a mounting scarcity of freshwater. Feeding the growing world population is a major challenge. The world's population currently stands at over 6.3 billion and is increasing by 80 million people per year. Already the global community is failing to supply adequate nutrition and a minimal standard of living to 1 billion of our members, and these problems will only become more acute if, as predicted, the global population swells to 8 to 11 billion people by the year 2050.

Oil, a resource of critical importance to the economic vitality of developed nations, is predicted to become ever more scarce in the 21st century. Available evidence indicates that the world's accessible petroleum reserves may be largely exhausted by 2060. Although several countries, including China and the United States, have adequate coal reserves to support current energy use rates for several hundred years, the utilization of coal, because of mining-associated pollution and acid rain, is even more destructive to the environment than is the production and consumption of oil. It is clear that the world in the not-too-distant future will need to meet its energy demands in a very different manner than it is doing today.

Freshwater is another natural resource that will become increasingly scarce in the 21st century. Because of increased population growth and economic development, global withdrawal rates of surface water are projected to at least double in the next 2 decades. Worldwide, agriculture is the primary consumer of freshwater. About 70% of all water withdrawn each year from rivers, lakes, and aquifers is used to irrigate 17% of the world's cropland. This irrigated land produces approximately 40% of the world's food supply. Water shortages may become even more acute in some areas as a result of global climate change.

How can plant biology provide a partial solution to these daunting problems? One of the few natural resources that is increasing globally is carbon dioxide. Because plants convert carbon dioxide into biomass by the process of photosynthesis, higher carbon dioxide levels increase the potential for biomass production. Plant biomass can, of course, be burned directly and inefficiently for energy as our ancestors did before recorded history.

Using more modern techniques, however, plant biomass can be converted into renewable fuels such as ethanol that are clean burning and whose widespread utilization would not require a complete overhaul of existing technology. Because of population growth, we cannot divert prime agricultural land from the growing of food to the growing of biomass for fuel production. To meet the demands of the future for plants both as food and fuel, it will be necessary to expand agriculture into marginal lands, achieve higher yields per acre, and increase the water use efficiency of crops.

Such attributes in crops, of course, have long been goals of traditional plant breeders, but the progress they have made in achieving them, although commendable, has been slow. Because we are faced with a deadline, it is no longer sufficient merely to experiment with the interactions of a small number of genes and hope for the best: We must gain the ability to engineer the design of crop plants predictably. To do this, it is necessary to gain a comprehensive knowledge of how plants function in a relatively short period of time. We must develop our understanding of how plants function to such an extent that we can precisely predict by modeling how a plant will respond to any given genetic manipulation or environmental perturbation. Fortunately, as we step into the 21st century, the tools for achieving this degree of knowledge are available or within grasp.

Using genomic techniques, we can now identify all the genes in a plant, and have successfully sequenced two plant genomes in their entirety-the model organism Arabidopsis and the crop plant rice (Oryza sativa). Moreover, using microarray and proteomic techniques, we now have the ability to resolve which genes are activated or inactivated during development or in response to an environmental change.

However, identifying all the genes and proteins (system elements) in an organism is comparable with listing all the parts of an airplane. Although such a list provides a catalog of the individual components, by itself it is not sufficient to understand the complexity underlying the engineered object. What we really need to know before we can intelligently engineer plants is how all these system elements interact. Systems biology is a new branch of biology that attempts to discover and understand biological properties that emerge from the interactions of many system elements.

The major reason why systems biology is gaining interest today is that progress in molecular biology, particularly in high-throughput genomics and proteomics, is enabling scientists to collect comprehensive data sets on a wide variety of plant responses. The power of these new tools has led to an explosion of information unparalleled in the history of biology. The implications of these sweeping changes in plant biology were the topic of discussion among a diverse group of scientists who met on January 19, 2003, after the 22nd Riverside Symposium in Plant Biology. The goal of the meeting was to identify some of the needs and opportunities that lie ahead in attaining the comprehensive understanding of plants that is critical if a predictive computer model of a generic plant is to become a reality.

At the very core of systems biology is the goal of being able to model a living organism. Systems biology examines the structure and dynamics of cellular and organismal function, rather than the characteristics of isolated parts of a cell or organism. The major reason systems biology is gaining interest today is that progress in molecular biology, particularly in genomics, proteomics, and high-throughput measurements, is enabling scientists to collect comprehensive data sets on the mechanisms underlying plant growth and plant responses to perturbations.

The new high-throughput tools of genomics have provided biologists with the potential to systematically perturb and monitor biological systems while they are functioning. With the wealth of information provided by these new approaches, plant biological research is becoming more reliant on informational science. This interaction of plant molecular biology with informational sciences will help pinpoint which types of experimental analyses and measurements need to be made. Systems biology requires quantitative data that are high quality and comprehensive. Comprehensiveness in systems biology requires three types of measurements. First, we need to measure the expression levels of a large number of mRNAs, proteins, structural polymers, and metabolites simultaneously. Second, we need to heighten the temporal resolution of such molecular changes to model dynamic changes.

Third, we need to spatially resolve where these changes are occurring in the plant at the level of the cell type. To expedite the collection of comprehensive and accurate data, technical innovations in highthroughput experimental measurement including microscopy and robotics need to be fostered. To design these new high-throughput tools, plant biolo- gists will have to work side by side with engineers who design and operate high-precision and highthroughput measurement systems.

Features of Flowering Plants

Flowering plants (Angiospermae) represent one of the largest groups of primary producers. Their contribution to the production of oxygen as well as that to the nutriment of animals and man is consequently very large. Typically, flowering plants are organized into an underground root and a shoot above ground that consists itself of a stem and leaves. The organs of a plant that serve sexual reproduction are the flowers. Part of the pollinated flower ripens and becomes the fruit. In contrast to many other plant groups, flowering plants are striking, numerous and common. They are the most important group of the so-called primary producers that generate the prerequisite for life on earth: oxygen.

Green plants have the ability to convert solar energy into chemical energy (photosynthesis) producing the oxygen necessary for all other organisms as a by-product. The useable plants among the flowering plants are - directly or indirectly - the basis of human existence; they are, too, an important economical factor. A basic knowledge of flowering plants should therefore be among everybody's general knowledge.

To get an idea of the variety of existing plants and to get to know special species, it is necessary to identify them. The body of vegetation of many-celled algae (and mosses) is called thallus, that of flowering plants, ferns and fern-like plants (pteridophytes) is called cormus. The body of vegetation of a "typical" flowering plant consists of an underground root and a shoot above ground. The shoot is organized into stem and leaves. Each of these basic organs can exist in many variations and these again can be combined in many different ways. The almost unlimited ability of combination is one of the main reasons of the existence of such a high number of species while at the same time, the identification of the relations of the species is aggravated.

If seemingly different organs with different functions can be traced back to the same basic organ, they are called homologous. It is also spoken of homology. Contrasting is analogy where organs with a similar look and function have descended from different organs. Typically, flowering plants are organized into an underground root and a shoot above ground that itself consists of a stem and leaves. The stem is the main supporting axis of a flowering plant. It is made up of nodes, the part where one or more leaves are borne and of the usually longer, in-between lying internodes. Stems are characterized by their type of branching, by their surface and their symmetry. Special cases of stems are those of climbing plants, succulence, runners and rhizomes.

Shoot and root can be clearly distinguished within a seed. After germination, they do develop into the shoot that grows towards the sun and into the root which grows towards the earth's score. The shoot that develops during the first stage of development is called the main- or the primary shoot and depending on the plant, it does bear one, two, or more cotyledons. Growing and sprouted shoots are organized into nodes and the in-between lying internodes. The nodes are the parts where the leaves are inserted. At the tip of a growing shoot sits the terminal bud of the shoot apex that is surrounded by the leaf (or flower) primordias. In the area of the nodes are axillary buds where the axillary shoots insert.

Vegetable shoots are either annual or perennial. The realised alternative depends usually on the species and in some species on the quality of the environment. The shoot of annual species is mostly fleshy and is usually called a stalk while perennial plants lignify and thus form trunks and branches. Some species, like Graminaceae or Poaceae have a hollow stalk that is called a blade of grass. To characterize a shoot, its type of branching and its surface (smooth, hairy, with or without grooves, round or squared) is used, as well as the ratio of heights to diameter.

It can generally be distinguished between monopodial and sympodial branching. Monopodial branching exists, if a continuous main shoot has feeble apical shoots. Sympodial branching is given, if apical shoots of different generations exist at the same time since the apical meristem of each sympodial branch has either died or is differentiated into a flower, a thorn or a tendril and has thus lost its ability to grow. The respective shoot tip is nearer to the ground than that of the next apical shoot. If only one of the apical shoots has the same direction as the main shoot would have had, then a monochasium results which may sometimes be difficult to distinguish from monopodial branching. But if two buds of a sympodial branch sprout at the same time, a more or less fork-shaped pattern, a dichasium, is formed. Hardly ever do several buds put forth at the same time (pleiochasium).

An extreme ratio of heights to diameter is found in climbing plants where the diameter (and the stability) is very small compared to the length so that upright growing is only possible with the support of other plants or growing aids. Succulence is another extreme, that is typical for plants living in arid or saline habitats. Most shoots are of a radial symmetry but with a few species, the apical shoots may be changed into flat, leaf-like phylloclades. Often, especially with wooden plants, the axes are differentiated into long and short shoots. The internodes of the long shoots that cause elongation with trees and shrubs are longer than the short shoots. These again are often specialized apical shoots with shortened internodes. The thorns of white-horn (*Crataegus*), for example, or those of sloe (*Prunus spinosa*) correspond to such short shoots.

Apical shoots may, too, be changed into runners or rhizomes. Runners are horizontally growing shoots with greatly prolonged internodes that are either underground or above ground and are sometimes bearing leaves. The internodes produce sometimes roots at the part that is nearest to the main shoot (shoot-borne roots). Some parts of these runners can switch to an upright growth and thus behave like a normal shoot. They serve to propagate vegetatively (strawberries are a typical example).

Rhizomes are mostly underground and grow in a horizontal (plagiotrop) manner. They are rather enduring shoots whose internodes usually stay short. They serve as survival organs and are often at the same time used for storage; sometimes, they end in specially developed storage tubers like in potatoes. Except for small, scale-like leaves, rhizomes do usually have no leaves. Shoots which happen to come into touch with a moist soil surface may start to develop leaves and flowers .

Roots, the lower, underground part of a plant are characterized by their lack of leaves. They are the structures that function to take up water, nutriments and minerals from the soil. The primary root is the main axis of a root system. Mostly, it bears thinner side-roots. Special types of primary roots are tap roots or turnips. Adventitious roots are roots originating directly from the stem.

The most striking morphological feature of roots is their lack of leaves. Roots are organized into primary roots and side-roots. Among the prominent types of roots are the tap roots where the primary root is dominant while the side-roots are hardly developed at all. The primary root grows deep into the soil. Swollen roots that have developed into storage organs are called turnips. Their formation may involve the hypocotyl. Swollen side-roots can also become storage organs (tubers).

The root-system of many monocots (like, that of the poaceae,for example) is completely formed from adventitious roots. Adventitious roots are roots that originate directly at the shoot. Rhizomes and shoots that touch the soil are able to form adventive roots. This fact is used to propagate plants vegetatively through cuttings (parts with nodes in them). Epiphytes do often develop air roots. They are, just like usual roots able to take up minerals and rain water and sometimes they can even perform photosynthesis. The growing tips of the main root and rootlets absorb water that diffuses in the soil. The decreased water concentration is indicated by dark areas that emerge around the root system. In areas with insufficient water concentration the rootlets cease to grow before they have reached their potential full length.

A leaf is an aerial and lateral outgrowth of the stem of a usually flat and dorsiventral anatomy. It functions mainly to manufacture food by photosynthesis and consists typically of a stalk also called petiole, a flattened blade, the lamina, and the leaf base. Strands of conducting and strengthening tissues, the veins, run through it. Their pattern, also called leaf venation, is a feature of characterization. Leaves may be simple, i.e. undivided or compound (composed of several parts called leaflets). The blade margin and the leaf arrangement at the stem are further features of characterization.

While potentially unlimited growth is a feature of the shoot, that of leaves is usually limited. They are almost always flat and have a dorsiventral anatomy , i.e. their upper and their undersurface are constructed differently and have different functions. This morphological and anatomical peculiarity is strongly connected to the main function of leaves, photosynthesis. With most conifers, the leaves are very thin and often tough (needles).

A typical leaf is organized into blade (lamina), stalk or petiole and leaf base. In some plant species, the leaf base is plainly set off against the petiole while the transition is invisible in others. Sometimes, it is merely indicated by a faint widening. Occasionally, lateral excrescences develop. Most species have clearly recognizable petioles. If they are missing, the leaves are said to be sessile in which case the leaf base may sometimes surround the shoot. The extremes are laminas with fused basal rims evoking the impression of a leave that the shoot grows through (*Claytonia perfoliata*). The basis of the leaf stalk may even grow down on the shoot a little bit further. With many monocots, like Poaceae or Graminaceae, the shoot is completely surrounded by a sheath-forming petiole. The blade is radiated by leaf veins that contain the fibres. It is distinguished between parallel, arched, pinnated or netlike vein structures.

Just as variable as the vein structure is the shape of the leaves. The fundamental difference is that between simple and compound leaves. The compound leaves are built from several small leaves or from pinnations that sit in a regular organisation at the undivided or branched rhachis. Cataphylls are simply organized, scale-like leaves. They can be found at the sprout, at the basis of sprouting shoots or underneath the normal leaves and in wooden plants also as a protection for the buds.

Finally, bracts have to be mentioned that live above the region of the usual leaves, for example at the inflorescence as subtending bracts for the flowers. But they can also have very different functions. Remarkable are the strikingly colored bracts of Bougainvillea spectabilis and Poinsettia pulcherrima (poinsettia) that add strongly to the attractivity of the rather inconspicuous flowers. Another example are the Cuckoo-pint and its relatives where the bract encloses the inflorescence and is at the same time a refined trap for pollinating insects (Arum maculatum).

Some species, especially those that live in water have differently shaped leaves (heterophylly). An example is Ranunculus aquatilis (water crowfoot) which has pinnation-shaped, submerse living leaves and flat swimming leaves. Another feature of recognition is the blade margin that can be shaped very differently. It can be plain, serrated, double serrated, crenated or sinuated. Leaves with deep clefts are called pinnatified, pectinated, palmated or lobed.

Quite a few species have structures called leaf metamorphosis (variations), because they are homologous to leaves. Among these are thorns where the moulding of the blade does not occur and the leaf veins have been strengthened by the deposit of a though material, as well as leaf tendrils that also miss the lamina but have an extremely pliable and tension-proof petiole. There may, too, be succulence of leaves.

Leaves are always organized around the shoot in a regular pattern that can be recognized best when looked at from above. It is obvious in most cases that the leaves are arranged in the way of a screw and that there is always the same angle measurable between subsequent leaves (angle of divergence). In its simplest form, this angle is 180 which means that the leaves are grouped into two opposing rows along the shoot. But other angles do occur, too: 120° (a third of a circle), 144° (five leaves in two circles), or 135° (eight leaves in three circles), etc.. The advantage of a regular arrangement of the leaves is in the optimal yield of light gained.

Whorllike arrangement of the leaves: At each node, two or more leaves insert. The organization of the following node usually places the leaves into the gaps of the preceding one. If two leaves spring from one node, they are without exception opposite. The leaves of the node above (and that beneath) form a right angle with those of the middle node. This is also called a decussate arrangement. Distichous means that all leaves are arranged in a vertical plane

Rosettes are usually sitting near the soil: At the basis of the shoot follows node after node with almost complete reduction of the internodes. Side shoots with greatly prolonged internodes may spring from rosettes. They have one or more flower at their tip, like, for example the primrose. Especially in biennial plants, the main shoot can, too, grow with prolonged internodes and even branch. It is not unusual that the leaves of the rosette and that of the shoot differ in shape.

The organs of a plant serving sexual reproduction are flowers. Their final product is seed. A flower is a rather complex structure formed by the flower axis that is usually transformed into the receptacle and the perianth. The perianth consists of calyx and corolla. The calyx is made up by he sepals, the corolla by the petals, stamens and carpels. If calyx and corolla cannot be distinguished or if the calyx is missing, it is spoken of an incomplete flower or perigon. The androecium is the totality of the male reproductive organs. It comprises the stamens. Each stamen consists of a filament and an anther. The female reproductive organs, the gynoecium, include the carpels.

Carpels are structures that are made up from an ovary and a stigma and that contain one or more ovules. One or more carpels may be combined to a pistil (ovary, style, stigma), the gynoecium as a whole. Taxonomical flower features are the flower symmetry, the way in which the carpels are fused and the resulting position of the ovules, also called placentation, and the position of the ovary. Flowers that contain both androecium and gynoecium are called androgynous or hermaphroditic. If both male and female flowers live on one plant it is called monoecious. Plants with male and female flowers borne on separate plants are termed dioecious.

Flowering plants are structures serving the sexual reproduction: their final product is seed. Flowering plants are thus also called spermatophytes (seed plants). They include two large groups, the gymnosperms and the angiosperms. The gymnosperms are the evolutionary older and more primitive group. They are, in a strictly systematical sense, no class on their own but enclose two real classes, the conifers and the cycadeans that do not have the same ancestors. The angiosperms that are usually seen as the original flowering plants do all belong to just one class. They represent the overwhelming majority of species and what you will learn in the following is principally true for their flowers.

It is taken for granted that everybody has through his own experience gained an impression of the diversity of flower shapes, colors and smells. It will be equally well known that these features developed in an evolutionary process of mutual adjustments of flowers and their individual pollinators (insects: bees, bumble-bees, butterflies, flies, etc.; birds: hummingbirds, etc.). Plants that are pollinated *via* wind have very unobtrusive flowers.

Flowers are short shoots with limited growth. The leaf organs are arranged in several circles (whorls), one above the other at an often strongly compressed flower axis. These structures differ strongly both in their appearance and in their function from normal leaves. Progressing from bottom to top and from the out- to the inside can it be distinguished between the usually unobtrusively colored calyx that consists of sepals, the conspicuously colored corolla that is built of petals, the stamens and finally the carpels.

Calyx and corolla together are the perianth. But if calyx and corolla cannot be distinguished or if the calyx is missing it is spoken of an incomplete flower or perigon. Flowers with a missing perianth are typical for species with wind-mediated pollination. The totality of the stamens, the male reproductive organs, is called androecium that of the female reproductive organs is named gynoecium. The flower axis has hardly any appearance in most angiosperms. It is usually shortened and broadened to the so-called receptacle that is sometimes slightly vaulted or disc-shaped. In gymnosperms, however, as well as in some primitive angiosperms (Magnolia, for example), it has the shape of a cone.

The flowers of angiosperms have originally only had an incomplete perianth that can very likely be traced back to leaflike bracts and occurs in an even more simplified version already in gymnosperms. The majority of angiosperm flowers has a double perianth with a clear separation of function between calyx and corolla. While the corolla has as a rule the function of attracting pollinators (it is, after all, designed mainly on insect aesthetics), the calyx is made to protect the growing bud. It loses its function as soon as the bud flowers; with some species it is even dropped off during flowering, though with most species it just stops growing or shrivels. Only rarely are the sepals reactivated after pollination. If they are, a new growth starts whereby an involucre of the fruit is formed.

All flower structures have originally been organized in a tight screw (*Anemone*). These flowers are strictly spoken asymmetric but are nevertheless grouped together in books on classification with those of a radial symmetry. They are characterized by the arrangement of their flowers in whorls (flowering circles). All structures of one whorl are of the same appearance and every whorl has the same number of structures (three, four and five are very common).

Subsequent whorls are usually organized in a way that brings the structures of one whorl in the gap positions of the preceding (rule of alternation). Such flowers have two or more planes of symmetry; sometimes those with only two planes are called bilateral. Even if the gynoecium shows another number of organs, the flowers are grouped together with those with radial symmetry.

Flowers that have only one plane of symmetry due to either differing shapes of the structures of one whorl or due to incomplete whorls are widespread. They are thought to be of a very high developmental state and are called zygomorph (monosymmetric or dorsiventral). Examples are the pansy (Viola) or the labiates (Lamiaceae). With most flowering plants, the petals are separate from each other (dialypetalae) while they are fused to a tubular corolla with sympetalae. The number of free points shows how many petals are involved.

The petals can often be traced back to reorganized stamens. This interpretation is proven by the fact that links between both categories of structures exist. A classic example is the white waterlily (*Nymphaea alba*, a rather primitive angiosperm) but such metamorphosis can, too, be found in many other species. Cultivators use this feature to select filled flowers. The wild rose (*Rosa canina*), for example, has only five petals and many stamens while most of the cultured varieties are characterized by filled flowers with many petals and a reduced number of fertile stamens.

A normal stamen consists of a pollen-containing, fertile anther (a group of two to four microsporangia) borne at the tip of a blade stalk or filament. The anther has (usually) two theces that are combined *via* the connective. Each theca includes two pollen sacs where the production of the pollen takes place. Sterile stamens are called staminodes. One variation are the nectar-secreting honey leaves that live mostly between perianth and stamens. They can adopt the size and color of petals and belong to the pollinator-attracting apparatus of the plant, like in buttercup (*Ranunculus*, Ranunculaceae).

The central part of a typical angiosperm flower is the gynoecium that is composed of one (simple pistil) or more (compound pistil) carpels. The carpels are, contrary to those of the gymnosperms, fused. Their original structure that of a leaf, is hardly recognizable. The gynoecium contains one or more pistils. A characteristic pistil has, from bottom to top, an enlarged basal ovary that includes the embryo sac, a columnar style and distal stigma, the organ that receives the pollen. Stigmata may be very varied in shape and structure. They are often button-shaped and equipped with papills. It is not rare that they are branched. It is distinguished between dry and moist stigmata. The surface of the dry ones is often studded with hair-shaped papills while moist ones are coated with a sticky film.

The style serves to bring the stigma into a favorable position for pollination. The leafy character of the carpels can easily be seen with a cross-section through the ovary. Both rims of a carpel seem to be rolled in and fused so that a tube-shaped structure is formed. On the basis of the thus built chamber (locule) are the seeds. This protection is missing in gymnosperms. Here the seeds lie openly on the carpels.

The suture that is formed by the fusion of the rims is called the ventral suture in angiosperm carpels while the midrib of the carpel is somewhat misleadingly called the dorsal suture. Normally the gynoecium of angiosperms is composed of several carpels. A remarkable exception is made by the leguminoses where the flower contains just one carpel. Each carpel of a gynoecium may either form a pistil of its own (choricarpy or apocarpy) or several carpels may be fused together to one pistil (coenocarpy).

The way in which carpels are fused together and the resulting position of the ovules within the ovary, the so-called placentation, has been recognized to be an important taxonomical feature for the classification of angiosperms. An ovary that is built from free carpels is called apocarp and is supposed to be the most original form of an angiosperm gynoecium. It is often found in ranunculaceae. Ovaries with fused carpels are derived from it.

In a syncarp ovary, the carpels are fused laterally. Its number of locules fits that of its carpels that are separated from each other by a septum. This can be seen very clearly with the ovary of a tulip. The ovules are inserted at the inner angles of the locules (axial placentation). False septums may have been put in later on which could lead to the misapprehension of a syncarpous ovary at superficial examination. But the unchanged parietal placentation of the ovules enables a definite classification. The syncarpous gynoecium developed from the apocarpous one which again differentiated into the paracarpous and lysicarpous gynoecium. The paracarpous and the lysicarpous types are depicted in two different stages of evolution to elucidate the different ways of development from the basic syncarpous type. The ovules are given in dark brown.

Lysicarpous ovaries display a unified cavity formed through disappearance of the lateral rims. Their ovules are inserted at an axial cone in the centre of the ovary (free central placenta). The position of the ovary in relation to the other structures of a flower is an important taxonomical feature. It has to be distinguished between a hypogynous (the perianth is attached to the receptacle below the pistil), perigynous (perianth and stamens are borne on the rim of a concave structure in the depression of which the pistil is borne) or epigynous ovary (blossom seems to arise upon or above the ovary).

Flowers that contain both an androecium and a gynoecium are called androgynous or hermaphroditic. The flower is male, if just one androecium is present; if only one gynoecium is developed, then it is a female flower. A plant that has both male and female flowers is called monoecious while species where male and female flowers live on different plants, are called dioecious.

In the extreme, the flower is reduced to only one stamen or carpel. An especially interesting case is the spurge (Euphorbia) and some of its closer relatives. With them several extremely reduced flowers are grouped together to a functionally hermaphroditic unity, a cyathium. By integration of a set of bracts that bear great, often yellowish nectaries and some additional colored bracts, the impression of a normal hermaphroditic flower is perfected (example: poinsettia; Poinsettia pulcherrima).

Inflorescences

Inflorescences are arrangements of more than one flower, like bostryx, head, cyme etc. They are modified parts of the shoot with leaves typically reduced to leaflike bracts. Only rarely does the main shoot or a side shoot end with a single, terminally placed flower. More common are flowers that are grouped together to units that are more or less clearly set off from the rest of the plant's body. These units are called inflorescences. An inflorescence is a flowering and thus modified part of the shoot with leaves that are usually reduced to leaflike bracts.

The types of branching occurring in flowering plants can be studied especially well with inflorescences. As has been said when reviewing the different types of branching of the shoot, it is distinguished between monopodial and sympodial inflorescences. Some technical terms to start off:

both determinate and indeterminate inflorescences occur. Indeterminate inflorescences can therefore theoretically continue to elongate and produce new flowers, while determinate inflorescences cannot. Indeterminate types of inflorescences are racemes, corymbs, heads, cones and umbels. They are also called simple inflorescences since their main axis is not branched. Complex types are branched. Among the complex inflorescences are double racemes (where a single flower is replaced by a raceme), double umbels, etc. as well as panicles and thyrsi.

Panicles are typically closed with lateral inflorescences that decrease continuously in branching towards the top of the inflorescence (partial inflorescence). With thyrsi, the single inflorescences are organized sympodially. Since in dicots only the first two leaf organs of a lateral axis can have the function of bractlets, a sympodially organized axis has a maximum of two lateral shoots. This generates a dichasium with an often fork-like appearance. If only one axial product of a bractlet is produced, it is spoken of a monochasium. Depending on whether the branching takes place in an alternating way (left and right) or only at one side, the resulting inflorescence is called a cincinnus (scorpioid cyme) or a bostryx (heliocoid cyme). The corresponding monocotyledon units where usually only one bractlet per lateral axis is developed are called rhipidium (fan-shaped cyme) and drepanium (helicoid cyme).

Fruits and Seeds

Fruits are a uniquely angiosperm feature: part of the pollinated flower ripens and becomes the fruit. Two types of fruits with a generally different mechanism of seed distribution exist: dehiscent and nondehiscent fruits. Dehiscent fruits set the seeds free by opening of the fruit that remains itself with the mother plant. In contrast, nondehiscent fruits and their seeds are a dispersal unit. Dehiscent fruit types are follicles, pulses, pods and capsules. Nondehiscent fruits are berries, drupes and nuts. Seeds are normally surrounded by a tough shell, the testa, that is derived from one or more integuments. It contains the endosperm, a nourishing tissue. Seeds are dispersed either by self-dispersal, also called autochory, or by allochory which means that extern factors are involved. Allochor modes of dispersal are dispersal by wind (anemochorys), water (hydrochory) or by animals (zoochory).

Fructification is a feature of angiosperms during which the seeds are encapsulated by the ovary. Gymnosperms develop seeds that lie naked on the carpels. A fruit is the state that the flower turns to during the ripening of the seeds. Perianth and stamens have usually withered and fallen off. During fructification, the gynoecium is largely rearranged, the ovary extends strongly, the stigma shrivels and the style normally degenerates or falls off but it, too, may develop further, if it serves to enlarge the fruit.

In the simplest case, the seeds are set free from the ovary after ripening by opening of the fruit (dehiscent fruits). But very often, both fruits and seeds form an integrated part of the dispersal unit (nondehiscent fruit). If this happens, the tissue of the ovary is strongly differentiated. The pericarp is the part of a fruit that is formed by the ripening of the ovary wall. It is organized into three layers: the skin (exocarp), the often fleshy middle (mesocarp), and the membranous or stony inner layer (endocarp). These layers may become skin-like and leathery, fleshy or stringy (sclerotic) during fructification.

The fruits produce gadgets for the protection and the dispersal of the seeds. Additionally, other parts of the flower may contribute to the formation of the fruit, like the flower axis (strawberry) or the calyx. Depending on the organization of the gynoecium, single fruits or multiple fruits develop. Single fruits spring either from a monomer (coenocarp) gynoecium or from single carpels of an apocarp gynoecium while multiple fruits develop from flowers with a choricarp gynoecium.

If the fruit opens up to free ripe seeds, it is a dehiscent fruit where the pericarp is always dry. Contrasting are indehiscent fruits where the seed is spread together with the fruit or parts of the fruit.

The Different Dehiscent and Indehiscent Fruit Types

Follicle: It is regarded as the most primitive type of fruit and is common in the ranunculaceen family. The fruit is composed of a single carpel. Opening occurs usually at the ventral suture as with the fruits of larkspur (*Delphinium*). In rare cases, it does take place at the dorsal suture (*Magnolia*, for example).

Pulses: This is the type of fruit that occurs with leguminoses. Contrary to the follicles, both ventral and dorsal suture open at the same time. Both parts of the carpel wind normally up like a screw. The process may occur like an explosion so that the seed is hurled away with full force.

Pods : These are typical for cruciferous plants (Cruciferae, Brassicaceae). A pod stems from a paracarp ovary. It includes only two carpels and is divided by a central septum. When ripening, two flaps fall off while the septum and the placentas (replum) stay. The seeds may stick to them for a while.

Capsules: These are a very widespread type of fruit. They develop from a coenocarp gynoecium, the pericarp is dry. The opening of the fruit can take place in multiple ways by longitudinal tears, pores or by raising of the lid.

Indehiscent fruits do not scatter their seeds. It is distinguished between berries, drupes, and nuts depending on the composition of the pericarp. The pericarp of berries becomes fleshy and juicy in all its parts and is often colored. A berry like, for example, a tomato contains many seeds. The endocarp of drupes differentiates into a stone that encapsulates usually only one seed. The outer layers of the fruit (mesocarp and exocarp) are, just like with berries, fleshy. Well-known examples are cherries, plums, peaches, olives, and walnut.

Berries and drupes have adapted to endozoochory, i.e. they are eaten by animals (birds, mammals) along with the seeds. The seed (sometimes together with the stony endocarp) is excreted without being digested and is thereby scattered. The whole pericarp of nuts becomes hard and develops a thick wall which includes as a rule only one seed (hazelnut, acorn).

The caryopsis of sweet grass belongs to the nuts. Its seed is surrounded by a rather thin shell that is fused with the outer layer of the fruit. Other nut types are the achenes of composite flowers (Compositae, Asteraceae) where the calyx has been rearranged into a pappus (a structure for flying). An especially interesting case is the coconut (Cocos nucifera) where the outer layer is fibrous so that the fruit is able to swim due to the enclosed air.

Multiple fruits develop from flowers with an apocarp (choricarp) gynoecium. The single fruit may have a dry outer layer (single-seeded nuts or follicles with only few seeds) or the outer layer may be fleshy just like that of a drupe. Several fruits are usually combined to a unit by an axial structure that is either a central axial cone (strawberry, blackberry) or an axial cupule (rose hip, apple). With some species, the numerous fruits that develop from the inflorescences stay together as a functional unit (*syconium*).

Fruits with Highly Specialized Devices that Serve their Distribution

— *distribution by wind*: Flat, very light, small and dry pods with a relatively large surface and just one or two seeds per fruit (*Lunaria annua*, Brassicaceae)

— *"Bodenroller"* (winged fruits rolling along the ground): three-dimensionally built, dry and very light fruits that are easily blown away in dry habitats (*Pterodiscus ungamicus*, Pedaliaceae)

— *distribution by wind, burdocks and "Bodenroller" (winged fruits rolling along the ground), a triple strategy*: Flat, dry involucre with a large surface but rather heavy. It can therefore only travel short distances by wind alone. The spiky centre serves epizoochoric distribution by animals; the arrangement of the wing-like gadgets allows an additional drifting at the floor (Pterocarpus angolensis, Fabaceae).

— *trample burs*: lignified fruit shell with spikes and barbs that stick to the softer parts of mammals' hoofs and are dispersed this way (*Harpagophytum procumbens*, Pedaliaceae).

— *distribution by burdocks*: dry fruits with barbs at their surfaces that stick to the fur of mammals. Relatively strong structure of the fruit that falls apart by and by so that the seeds are very effectively lost at different places (*Xanthium riparium*, Compositae)

— *trample bur*: dry and very compactly built fruit with a "drawing pin-principle". This fruit is only dispersed by the hoofs of mammals, it cannot adhere to their fur (*Dicerocaryum senecioides*, Pedaliaceae)

— *and one more trample bur*: this one can also stick to animals' furs. The fruits are, too, able to cling one to another. The respective animal may be hurt by the spikes (*Harpagophytum procumbens*, Pedaliaceae)

Seeds are normally surrounded by a tough shell (*Testa*) that develops from the integument (or several integuments) and that protects a largely developed embryo and its nutriments. The embryo is thus preserved from loss of water and bad weather. The nutriments are in a special nourishing tissue, the endosperm or in the perisperm (developed from tissue of the nucellus as with pepper). They have either to be made useable and to be used during germination or they are already stored in the cotyledons (beans, peas, almonds). Monocotyledons have normally only one cotyledon, dicots have two and gymnosperms several.

With many species, the seeds are unable to germinate immediately after falling off the plant (dormancy). This dormancy can be overcome by a period of cold weather (vernalisation) so that the seeds do not germinate before the beginning of the next period of vegetation. The number of seeds that is produced by a single plant in the course of its life varies enormously. Some species like the coconut palm produce only few but very well provided descendants while others produce up to several million seeds that are inevitably provided rather badly.

Numerous devices support the dispersal of the descendants since only a suitable habitat enables the seed to develop into a viable plant. If the dispersal is achieved only through devices that the plant itself produces, it is spoken of self-dispersal or autochory. If extern factors such as wind, water, animals, etc. are involved, then the mode of dispersal is called allochor. Only rarely the seeds are spread on their own, usually the whole seed-containing fruit is scattered. Among the autochor modes of dispersal is flinging and spurting of seeds.

Dispersal by wind (anemochory) is widespread among plants. The units for dispersal are necessarily either very small and light and / or equipped with specially formed devices for flying or floating. Those devices are, for example, air-filled cavities in the seeds of orchids, seeds that are completely covered with hairs like cotton, pappus-bearing seeds (composite flowers) and units that are equipped with all different kinds of wings.

Dispersal by water (hydrochory) is much less common. Seeds that are spread by water have often an outer layer that cannot be moistened or they are hairy in order to trap air bubbles. Some big fruits that are spread by ocean currents like the coconut are surrounded by a loosely structured, airy layer.

Zoochory, i.e. the dispersal of fruits with the aid of animals has already been met when talking about berries, drupes, and multiple fruits. If seeds are eaten and excreted again, this is called endozoochoric dispersal. Contrasting is epizoochoric dispersal where the seeds or fruits stick to the animal or its fur either by slimy secretings or by variably shaped barbs.

A speciality in the dispersal through animals is that through ants (myrmecochory). Such seeds or fruits bear attachments, the elaiosomes that contain lures and nutriments. Myrmecochory is common with plants that live at the forest soil like violets (*Viola*). The given examples show that zoochory offers a variety of possible mechanisms for the dispersal of seeds. But this variety is far beyond that of the architectural design of flowers. This is due to the fact that special ization and adaptation to seed or fruit dispersing animals is far less advanced than the specialisation of pollination.

GENOMICS AND PROTEOMICS

More has been learned about how plants work in the last decade than in all of preceding history. In no small part, this rapid rate of progress has been due to advances in genetics and genomics. New methods that build on genomics, such as DNA microarrays (DNA chips) have allowed investigators to measure simultaneously which genes are turned on or turned off in a genome in response to an experimental treatment. Thus, many biologists are calling the beginning of the 21st century the "post-genomic era." By this, they are not implying that we should stop sequencing genomes or analyzing the results of such genomic studies but rather that all the major hurdles to obtaining genomic information have been overcome.

The next big challenge is to understand the functions of all gene products. Microarray studies monitor gene expression-which genes are being turned on or off during development or in response to a perturbation. Techniques that profile changes in gene expression permit the analysis of the expression levels of thousands of genes simultaneously. Proteomic methods reveal the proteins translated from the mRNA molecules that are the direct result of gene expression. Twodimensional gels were the first method to allow the identity of proteins in a proteome, but newer methods employing tandem mass spectrometry enable identification of even more proteins. Even with these new techniques, proteomics is a much thornier problem than genomics.

In contrast to DNA and RNA, there are currently no techniques available to amplify proteins of low abundance (the equivalent of PCR for DNA) or to identify them with very high-dynamic resolution. Moreover, all of the cells that compose a plant have the same genome, but each cell type has a different collection of proteins. In addition to these cell-to-cell variations in proteomic expression, we must also consider proteomic variation over time. As a plant cell matures or responds to an environmental perturbation, its proteome and expressed mRNAs are constantly changing.

In proteomics, it is also of interest to determine not just whether a protein is present but how much of the protein is present and how active it is. The activity of many proteins is regulated by interactions with other proteins that form complexes or catalyze structural modifications. Comprehensive proteomics, therefore, requires not only a list of the protein functions but also a detailed understanding of protein-protein interactions within a cell and protein modifications that regulate function, such as phosphorylation, glycosylation, etc.

Methods for the global measurements of various protein modifications, including mass spectrometry and the use of modification-specific antibodies, are only now being developed. In contrast to genomics in which standardized tools and standards for data storage and sharing are available, the current methodology for handling large proteomics data sets is less uniform and organized. Most proteins are enzymes that catalyze specific chemical reactions. Thus, changes in gene expression are typically accompanied by changes in the levels of many cellular chemicals.

The simultaneous measurement of these collective chemical changes is the emerging field of metabolomics. Like proteomic changes, metabolomic changes are highly dynamic and require precise high-throughput measurements with enough spatial and temporal resolution to be useful for modeling purposes. As with proteomics, major advances in analytical chemistry are required to allow us to identify and accurately measure the thousands of metabolites in a plant. Parallel advances in proteomics and metabolomics are expected to add additional layers of resolution to our ability to integrate all aspects of a biological process. Attempts to store and organize proteomic and metabolomic data in an easy-to-access format are still in their infancy. Thus, there is a real need for software developers and data archivists to establish the tools for creating proteomics and metabolomics databases for use by plant biologists.

Cell Biology and Imaging

Improvements in high-throughput optical measurements will be necessary before we can efficiently determine the genomic and proteomic changes with sufficient spatial and temporal resolution to allow accurate simulations of plant responses. Optical methods, in particular, provide the key to understanding how the parts of plants make the whole and to learning how the association of parts-proteins, multiprotein machines, and cells-changes as plants grow and function. Protein interactions can be seen by fluorescence resonance energy transfer, and the movement of proteins within cells can be seen by fluorescent labeling of proteins with extra protein sequences such as green fluorescent protein.

The real-time observation of cell division patterns is possible in living plants with a combination of fluorescent reporter genes, fluorescent dyes, and laser scanning confocal microscopy. Higher resolution methods require fixed or frozen tissue or purified proteins and protein complexes but have the advantage of providing critical detailed information that can be combined with dynamic information from optical methods. The highest resolution methods are those of x-ray crystallography, which with modern robotics and bright-synchrotron x-ray sources can be adapted for high-throughput measurement.

One of the methods now being developed for determining the structures of large protein complexes, at lower resolution, is cryoelectron microscopic tomography. It is not possible to model a eukaryotic cell without knowing where each constituent in the cell is located with respect to the compartments, what the properties of these compartments are, and what defines these properties. Obtaining this information is a major unmet challenge. Conceivably, proteomic approaches combined with innovative methods for subcellular fractionation could provide a catalog of what proteins are located in each compartment.

Information about the properties of each protein could be derived from in vitro studies of each protein or protein complex. However, a similar profile of the metabolite constituents will remain challenging for the foreseeable future. The development of novel methods for visualizing the concentration of specific metabolites in subcellular compartments of living cells provides an example of what may be possible. The challenge now is to implement these and related methods and to develop methods that will allow simultaneous imaging of many constituents in such a way that they can be integrated with parallel information about other biological processes.

Ultimately, it may be impossible to measure the concentration of every constituent in every compartment of every cell. Therefore, we need to develop in vitro or computational models for studying how networks of metabolic pathways perform under the conditions found in subcellular compartments in vivo. It seems likely that by having a small number of "sentinel" metabolites for which the absolute concentrations and fluxes are known, we can model the corresponding concentrations of most other metabolic constituents.

The successful modeling of living organisms is the ultimate goal of systems biology. Clearly, useful modeling will depend on having a large amount of high-quality quantitative information about all aspects of biological processes. Many new types of data have to be systematically determined. For example, it is not currently possible to model flux through a metabolic pathway without knowing the rate constants for the enzymes, how much of the enzymes are present, the subcellular distribution of the enzymes and metabolites, the availability of the inputs, and the disposition of the outputs. Only when we have determined the amounts and locations of each protein and the amounts and locations of each metabolite under a variety of conditions may it prove possible to heuristically derive the necessary quantitative information to support modeling.

Modeling should greatly simplify our attempts to understand plants. For example, genes with similar responses over a range of conditions are often clustered together to form functional groups (networks). Often, these associated genes are under the control of common transcription factors. Recent computer simulations of partial or whole genetic networks have demonstrated the complexity of network behaviors and emergent properties that were not apparent from the examination of a few isolated interactions alone.

Assuming that the challenge of obtaining such information can be met, a substantial challenge remains in developing computer programs that will model biological processes. The ideal program will mimic the performance of a cell or tissue or organism. The modeling of intact higher plants will be especially challenging because of the differential responsiveness of various cell types to a given perturbation. The collection of the comprehensive data needed for modeling might initially be most successful using single-cell microorganisms or higher plant cells grown in defined liquid cultures.

The modeling of Escherichia coli is already under way, and this should facilitate the modeling of cells of more interest to plant biologists. To model plant response accurately, a multitude of software programs of the sorts widely used by engineers (e.g. parameter optimization, flux balance analysis, systems analysis, and computer model simulations, to name a few) need to be adapted for the study of plants. The integration of modeling with experimental work will derive many new insights, with greater complexity, and hopefully greater impact on the global problems we face.

A key benefit of modeling is that we can rapidly do many "virtual experiments" and select those that are most interesting for the real world. The generation of phenotype phase diagrams would enable plant biologists to predict with accuracy which factors are limiting to plant growth under different environmental conditions. If we are to collect data from single cells, and this may be a necessary first step, then there is an urgent need to improve the accuracy and scope of single-cell measurements and even molecular (nanobiological) measurements.

The high quality and comprehensiveness of measurements needed by systems biologists will require further automation and the introduction of inexpensive microfluidic systems for handling and analyzing extremely small sample quantities. The determination of the optimal concentrations of precipitants in protein crystallization experiments provides an example of the use of new technology for an old, difficult, and time-consuming problem. Perhaps the unique ability of microfluidic devices to produce concentration gradients can be coupled with advances in fluorescent substrates or miniaturization of analytical instruments to simplify studies of enzyme reactions.

As we accumulate more and more high-quality data, mathematical modeling of biological processes will become ever more successful; that is, the responses of plants to genetic manipulations and environmental perturbations will become increasingly predictable. This will enable us to engineer plants quickly and with foresight as to the cost benefit of the proposed "reprogramming" of the plant genome.

The amount of biological information that the revolution in genomics, proteomics, and metabolomics is generating is staggering. This has created a new problem: how to store and handle this massive quantity of information, often from databases present on computers around the world and in varied format. Many new types of software need to be developed for archiving and accessing this information efficiently and in a standard method. Because systems biology requires the sharing of data among members of the scientific community, facilities (data warehouses) must be established and maintained.

Traditionally trained biologists, who typically have had little experience manipulating the large data sets of the post-genomic era, have to acquire a working knowledge of data storage and access. Training in the use of such massive data archives must become de rigueur for young biologists. Thus, there is need for training grants to teach biologists-young and old-how to gain competency in data storage, retrieval, and analysis. There is also a need within professional biology for biologists to embrace bioinformatic software developers and data archivists as bona fide members of our community and not as mere adjuncts to it.

The explosive growth of molecular biology in the last decade has helped to break down many artificial barriers that had been erected between different branches of biology. Now, it is necessary that the walls between biology and other scientific disciplines (e.g. mathematics, computer science, and engineering) be breached. Biologists of this new era need to become conversant with software developers, data storage archivists, mathematicians, analytical chemists, and engineers. If we are to achieve the "in silico" plant, the biologists of this new era will need to understand in some depth the models of mathematicians and computer scientists, and biologists will need to supply the accurate measurements of the many parameters that computational scientists will require to make their models robust.

As a consequence, there is a strong need for the development of training programs and the initiation of training grants to foster the intellectual development of both the current and the next generation of scientists in all of the subdisciplines that constitute systems biology. The sociology of science will also need to change. For example, our students need to be trained to thrive in larger and extended research groups, and our universities must acknowledge and reward multidisciplinary collaboration and community service by their faculty. We can learn from successful examples such as high-energy physics and distributed software engineering.

Unfortunately, each of the technical disciplines that systems biology attempts to merge has developed separately, and each has evolved its own technical jargon that seems impenetrable and arcane to the outsider. This barrier to communication must be overcome, and proximity is the best way to do that. This might be achieved through cross-disciplinary research opportunities for graduate students and postdoctoral research associates. Funding special centers devoted to systems biology research and staffed by biologists, computer scientists, mathematicians, and engineers could be another approach to foster the development of systems biology and to achieve the goal of attaining the "in silico plant."

Bibliography

Anderson, E. F., *Plants and people of the Golden Triangle: ethnobotany of the hill tribes of northern Thailand,* Dioscorides Press, Portland, Or., 279p, 1993.

Anderson, E. S., *Plants, man, and life,* University of California Press, Berkeley, CA, 251p, 1967

Balick, M. J. & P. A. Cox, "Plants, people, and culture: the science of ethnobotany", *Scientific American Library series 60,* Scientific American Library, New York, 228p, 1996

Brush, S. B., "Genes in the field: on-farm conservation of crop diversity", *International Plant Genetic Resources Institute,* Rome, 288p, 1999.

Cunningham, A. B., *Applied ethnobotany : people, wild plant use and conservation,* Earthscan, London, 300p, 2001.

Felger, R. S. & M. B. Moser, *People of the desert and sea : ethnobotany of the Seri Indians,* University of Arizona Press, Tucson, Ariz., 435p, 1985.

Heywood, V.H., ed., *Flowering Plants of the World,* New York, NY, Oxford University Press, 1993.

Martin, G. J., *Ethnobotany : a methods manual,* Chapman & Hall, London ; New York, 268p, 1995.

Simpson, B.B. & Conner-Ogorzaly, M., "Economic botany: plants in our world. McGraw-Hill Higher Education, 2000

Tyler, Varro E., *The Honest Herbal: A Sensible Guide to The Use of Herbs and Related Remedies*, New York, Pharmaceutical Products Press, 1993.

Vaughan, J. G. & C. A. Geissler, *The new Oxford book of food plants*, Oxford University Press, Oxford, 239p, 1997.

Index